SCOTLAND:
THE BATTLE FOR INDEPENDENCE

*A History of the
Scottish National Party
1990-2014*

GORDON WILSON

Scots Independent (Newspapers) Ltd.

Published by
Scots Independent (Newspapers) Ltd
35 Cowan Street,
Stirling FK8 1JW
Scotland

www.scotsindependent.org

ISBN: 978-0-9572285-3-5

Printed by Winter and Simpson Print
Tel: (01382) 813813

CONTENTS

DEDICATION AND THANKS

This history of The Scottish National Party follows on Volume 1, SNP: The Turbulent Years 1960 to 1990 and traces the transformation of the SNP under the leaderships of Alex Salmond, John Swinney and Alex Salmond again for a second term. In the first decade, the SNP struggled to assert its identity in an overcrowded Scottish political stage.

Everything changed with establishment of the Scottish Parliament in 1999, particularly with the election of 35 MSPs when it moved from being a campaigning organisation to a full-blown parliamentary party. When the SNP formed its first Government in 2007 and obtained a surprise majority second term in 2011, a referendum on independence became a reality. The book follows the steps in the referendum as the SNP fought a ferocious battle to achieve its goal of Scottish freedom in the face of opposition from the British state through to the outcome in September 18, 2014.

My thanks go to my wife, Edith for her tolerance of the time spent on research and writing and her welcome comments on the draft. As ever, without her support, I would not have started, let alone concluded.

I also wish to place on record my thanks to Maria Castrillo, curator at the National Library of Scotland for access to the older records. Much of the research needed frequent visits to SNP Headquarters where Ian McCann, the Party's Corporate Officer gave patient help – beyond the point of duty – in locating records and in printing out digital minutes, agendas and reports. I am grateful to the Party through its Chief Executive, Peter Murrell for permitting access to more recent records. The election statistics are taken from Wikipedia under their open licence. Special thanks go to Angus Lyon for his comments and proof reading, Colin Wilson who designed the backing and Ian Hamilton at the Scots Independent for taking charge of the business arrangements.

These histories are dedicated to the countless party workers who, often at great personal and financial sacrifice, strove to win independence for their nation.

Chapter 1:

BEGINNINGS

The independence referendum has placed Scotland on the world map. Until recently, Scotland has hardly been noticed save as a geographical area on the northern fringes of the British Isles and known for its scenery and products like whisky or more recently, oil. Little was known of its history or its constitutional status as a partner in the United Kingdom of Great Britain and Northern Ireland. Conversely, Britain is known as England and English people swap between Britain and England without thinking that there is a difference. Only the Scots get uptight when they are described as English or when Britain is referred to as England. To make it even more pointed, the Queen is often referred to as Queen of England and Princes Charles and William as heirs to the English throne.

The referendum has brought Scotland out of the shadows only to disclose an invincible ignorance as the campaign developed. From America to Europe and beyond, their leaders are seemingly unaware that Scotland is a nation. They treat Scotland as a region of the UK rather than as a founding father of that Union whose people still retain full sovereignty even if they have not cared so far to exercise it. It is Scotland's nationhood that explains why Scotland in the 21st century is seeking independence. And this book, dealing as it does with the rise of the Scottish National Party will make no sense unless it is placed in context even by a brief snap-shot. Any more information can be gleaned by international readers from reading one or more of the many books devoted to Scotland's history – which is recommended!

In his book, Scotland – A Concise History B.C. to1990, James Halliday, described how the country developed its character:

> "The land of Scotland has dictated what sort of history its people would have. The Scots have mountains and marshes; long, narrow, steep-sided glens, all too often open to north-west winds; acid soil and a climate which sees the seasons overlapping, the only certainty being that the growing season

1

will be short. Here the Scots have had to do the best that they could with what they had, and all through their history, with hard work and much ingenuity, they have managed to make the land serve its people better than might have been expected."

And after, having described the interaction of proximity to the sea and the impact of the long sea lochs, he continued with one salient factor – the 'elephant in the room'.

"So the nature of the land had largely determined how, and how successfully, the Scots would make their living and organise their activities. But in yet another respect their experiences were dictated by the residence which nature had given them. All through historic times the Scottish people have had to share an island with another people, far stronger than they in all respects – more numerous, more wealthy and usually more advanced technologically, especially in methods of warfare. Consciously and instinctively the Scots have always had to live with this fact and their first and constant political problem has been how they might best co-exist with the English. Different solutions to this problem have been adopted at different times, or have been urged by competing Scottish factions at the same time. In either case the Scots have had to make up their minds whether their interests are best served in collaboration with English objectives and English power, and an acceptance of the fact of English dominance in Britain or whether they should resist absorption, and make the preservation of their national identity a priority."

Scotland took some time to emerge from the dark ages. It had four major kingdoms. The Picts to the north and the Brythonic (Welsh speaking) Celts in the Kingdom that became known as Strathclyde (situated in the west and south west) had faced bloody attempts by the Romans to invade Scotland. 'We have created a desert and called it peace' declared the Roman historian Tacitus in a rather honest summation. The Romans penetrated Scotland to a more substantial degree than is commonly accepted with a series of forts reaching up the east coast as far as Moray and with naval explorations circumnavigating Orkney. But not for long. At first, they stayed behind Hadrian's Wall between Carlisle and Newcastle, advanced to the Forth/Clyde valley and built the Antonine wall before retreating to Hadrian's barrier once more.

After the Romans came the Angles from Bernicia who settled in the Lothians, the Scots from Ireland who founded the Kingdom of Dalriada and then the most fearsome of the invaders, the Vikings who settled Orkney, Shetland, Caithness and the Western Isles. In time these five elements (the Norsemen being the latest) united to form the Kingdom of the Scots or Alba under King Kenneth MacAlpin. Thus, the Scots came largely to occupy settled borders, give or take some fluctuations. In doing this, the Scottish state preceded the creation of a united Anglo-Saxon England.

Needless to say there were continuing problems with England before and after the problem of the Norse had been settled, culminating with an invasion by Edward I of England in 1296, and the resultant wars of independence. Opposition was led firstly by Sir William Wallace and the Earl of Moray and latterly by Robert the Bruce one of the claimants to the Scottish throne. Bruce was crowned king, and won the Battle of Bannockburn in 1314. Yet it was not until 1328 that peace was agreed. During the struggle, Scotland was laid waste and its people cruelly treated.

Out of this destruction emerged a united Scotland, forged by adversity into the first nation in Europe to escape from the hold of feudalism. But the land created stubborn qualities. Even the hero King Robert was given a warning in the Declaration of Arbroath 1320, a petition to the Pope for recognition of Scotland's independence:

> "For so long as a hundred of us remain alive we shall never accept subjection to the domination of the English. For we fight not for glory, or riches or honour, but for freedom alone which no good man will consent to lose save with his life." And then the warning to the King: "if he should abandon our cause....we should make every endeavour to expel him as our enemy and the subverter of his rights and ours, and to choose another for our king."

So for another few hundred years, Scotland continued to exist. The first crack appeared when James VI inherited the English throne in 1603. There was no constitutional impact but with the withdrawal of the royal court to England, power and patronage seeped away. In absence, James governed Scotland more securely through managers than he could have done if resident, writing:

> "This I must say for Scotland, and may truly vaunt it; here I sit
> and govern with my pen. I write and it is done; and by a clerk
> of the council I govern Scotland now which others could not
> do by the sword."

With the arrival of King William and Queen Mary, Scotland's Claim
of Right of 1689 echoed the right of the people to expel a monarch and
choose another. Scotland had escaped from regal control and regained
its independence. But when push came to shove, the monarchs were on
England's side. So that, in 1706, when Queen Anne chose the Scottish
Commissioners to negotiate the terms of a parliamentary union with
England, she selected those favourable to the concept.

In the end, through bribery, coercion, self-interest and the coincident
massing by the English government of an army in the English borders
under General Wade, the Scots Parliament, amidst rioting in the streets
of Edinburgh by the ordinary folk who had no say, passed an Act of Union
(after entering into a Treaty with England) which while protecting the
church, Scots law and other institutions, entailed the ending of Scotland's
parliament. Power moved to London and Scotland had to make do with
minor representation in the Commons and Lords at Westminster in
London. It was not an equal partnership but one of absorption.

The church bells of St Giles cathedral pealed out the tune, "Why should I
be sad on my Wedding Day" when the Union took place in 1707. Chancellor
Seafield remarked cynically, 'That's ane end to ane auld sang'.

And so it appeared. During the next 150 years, Scotland was largely left
alone. There came access to the American colonies and participation in a
burgeoning international empire. North Britain as Scotland often called
herself (England was never South Britain) industrialised. It had world-wide
fame in the late 18th century when the Scottish Enlightenment produced
thinkers, economists and philosophers who shaped modern society.
And yet as the poet Robert Burns and later the novelist Sir Walter Scott
highlighted Scotland's culture, language and history, the spark of Scottish
nationhood re-ignited. Firstly, there was pressure for a Scottish Secretary
or Minister responsible for Scotland's governance within Westminster and
eventually a Secretary of State in the Cabinet was conceded in 1928.

But none of this administrative devolution was enough. On the back of Irish Home Rule, the Liberal Party and the emergent Labour Party had unsuccessfully exerted parliamentary pressure to regain a parliament for Scotland. Indeed if it had not been for the outbreak of the Great War in 1914, a Scottish Home Rule Bill would have followed an Irish Act.

Patience with the failure of the UK parties to deliver a Scottish parliament during the inter-war years ran out. By then nationalist and patriotic feeling, similar in some ways, yet different in character, intensified. It was believed progress would only be achieved when Scots had the opportunity to vote for a Party dedicated to achieving home rule. So the National Party of Scotland was born in 1928. In turn it amalgamated with another group, the Scottish Party, to form the Scottish National Party (SNP) in 1934. The two groups (party was too ambitious a word) were as dissimilar as chalk and cheese. The National Party was nationalist and radical in its outlook. It also had more members. By contrast the Scottish Party was gradualist and to the right of the political spectrum. Its leaders were more prominent socially and publicly soon fronted the new Party.

In fact, the amalgamation created a fault line between nationalists and gradualists. This posed a problem for Party leaders from then on. The new Party was also prone to splits on policy and personality as well as on strategy. After fluctuating success in a minor way before the Second World War and lack of progress during that War, it elected its first MP, Dr. Robert McIntyre in a 1945 by-election in Motherwell constituency. This seat was lost in the ensuing General Election that brought Labour to power. Labour had a manifesto commitment to create a Scottish parliament but this was quickly broken on the excuse that the Westminster Government had to concentrate on post-war economic recovery and social policies.

After a period of division when many members defected to join a campaign for a 'National Covenant' petition calling for a parliament in Scotland – a petition that attracted well over a million signatures and was disregarded by Whitehall - the SNP eventually regrouped. There were some small stirrings expressed in party candidatures, 5 in all at the 1959 General Election. None of the candidates came anywhere near to winning despite some welcome attempts at organisation.

The SNP remained a fringe organisation with some 20 branches and 2,000 members – if that! And then something strange happened. In 1961 in a by-election in Glasgow Bridgeton, following a long campaign over the summer with systematic canvassing by a small group of activists, the

SNP candidate Ian Macdonald obtained a creditable 18.7% of the vote in third place, just behind the Scottish Unionists. While not enough of a break-through to cause a political impact, the result stirred the spirits of SNP members and encouraged them to believe that with organisation and further effort success might be possible.

There was a succeeding by-election in West Lothian in 1962 when the SNP candidate, Billy Wolfe came second with 23.3% - double that of the Scottish Unionists and the Liberal Party. Labour held on to this mining constituency as expected. The media noted the result. The impact on the SNP was massive. Effort swung behind recruitment and during the period of 1963 to 1969, membership doubled year upon year. In 1967, Winnie Ewing won the Hamilton By-election causing world-wide headlines. Since this victory followed one by Plaid Cymru (the Welsh Party) earlier in the year, the political establishment at Westminster panicked. To the horror of his Scottish members, Edward Heath, Conservative Leader of the Opposition in 1969 promised a Scottish Assembly. The Labour Government established a Royal Commission on the Constitution.

Observers have puzzled at the causes of the SNP break-through. It was obviously a protest vote: but why that protest, what was it and why then? There were three reasons, it was thought. Firstly, in the Suez fiasco of 1956 the UK was coerced by an American ultimatum into abandoning an invasion of Egypt to seize control of the Suez Canal. Secondly, this display of weakness was followed by the loss of remaining British colonies, proving that Britain had ceased to be a powerful empire and was in geopolitical decline. British identity weakened. More importantly, the sixties saw the heavy industries of Scotland facing run-down at a time when manufacturing in the midlands and south of England boomed. Unemployment in Scotland rose; emigration soared. Scotland felt neglected by the British government.

The protest vote ebbed in the run up to the 1970 General Election. Hamilton in Scotland's industrial belt was lost, although Donald Stewart won the Western Isles for the SNP. Elsewhere, there were creditable performances in West Lothian, the North East (East Aberdeenshire, Banff and Moray) and Argyll. Elsewhere the SNP vote vanished.

All was not lost. The discovery of oil in the North Sea and a brilliant 'It's Scotland's Oil' campaign run by the Party brought fresh impetus. Good by-election results including the winning of the Glasgow Govan by-election by Margo MacDonald and the publication of the Royal

Commission on the Constitution calling for the creation of an elected Scottish Assembly combined to elect 7 and then 11 SNP MPs in the two General Elections of 1974. The tale that followed – the SNP holding the Labour Government to ransom, the procrastination of the Westminster and Whitehall machines over the legislation, a referendum gerrymandered at the Mother of Parliaments which set an impossible qualifying majority, the fall of the Labour Government, the election of Mrs Thatcher's Conservative Government and the resultant repeal by it of the Scotland Act are part of history. So too is the political crash when the SNP Parliamentary Group was reduced from eleven MPs to a rump of two in 1979!

And then disillusionment and anger within the SNP at the failure and over the rigging of the referendum led to the creation of two internal groups followed by a third and threatened the Party with schism. This was averted only by a decision of the 1982 Conference to abolish all groups. By then severe damage to the Party's membership, morale and credibility had been done. The SNP faced long years within a political wilderness.

Towards the end of the eighties, progress had been made and policies had been modified to bring the SNP into mainstream positions. Jim Sillars (a former Labour MP who had joined the SNP) won a significant by-election in Glasgow Govan (who says lightning does not strike twice?) in 1988, restoring credibility to the SNP. The resultant pressure on the Labour Party in Scotland forced it to turn up the heat on its proposals for devolution, left on the back-burner after 1979.

This was the Party which Alex Salmond inherited in 1990. It still had the structure of a non-governing, non-parliamentary organisation. Topped by an Annual National Conference which was the final determinant of policy, in practice most of the main decisions were taken by a National Council. This was composed of the officebearers and members elected at Conference and delegates from branches, constituencies and affiliated organisations. Like a cut-down Conference it met three to four times a year and held the National Executive Committee and the office bearers to account. The National Executive Committee, meeting monthly, took most of the administrative and strategic decisions with much of the work being done by sub-committees. Additionally, there was a National Assembly tasked with reviewing policy and making recommendations for change. It had no binding policy making powers and its recommendations were forwarded to the National Council or Conference.

The SNP had largely recovered from the internal feuding of the previous decade. Its leaders were broadly working together – though not always! As with all political parties, there were unspoken factions and pressure groups so no leader had complete sway over the Party. The prime task of the National Convener as leader was to manage the Party as much as to give political direction.

A strong campaign against a hated Poll Tax introduced by the Conservative Government helped restore the Party's relevance and credibility. In the elections to the Regional Councils in May 1990 the Party secured 21.8% of the votes compared with 18.2% previously and elected 43 councillors. In the summer, the SNP was polling in the upper twenties. Gil Paterson, Executive Vice Chairman for Administration (with responsibility for fund-raising) was about to launch the Challenge of the Nineties scheme that would professionally revolutionise the SNP's resources and equip it for the larger battles ahead.

Chapter 2:

ASCENT OF ALEX SALMOND

At three thirty in the afternoon of Saturday 22 September 1990, Alex Salmond, MP for Banff and Buchan strode confidently to the rostrum at the Annual Conference of the Scottish National Party to deliver his acceptance speech. He had newly been elected National Convener (leader) of the SNP with a two thirds majority of the votes in a leadership contest between himself and Margaret Ewing MP, leader of the three SNP MPs at Westminster. It was no small triumph for despite the immaculate organisation of his campaign, Margaret Ewing had the support of most of the National Executive, including Salmond's former colleagues on the left of the Party.

He immediately went on the attack in setting out the priorities for the Party under his leadership:

> "We are going to win the battle for the hearts and minds of the Scottish people. The SNP is not interested in running a good second. We are not running for a medal. We are going for gold."

Looking on from the sidelines as an outgoing Chairman and Convener who had served for 11 years, it was a strong beginning. I had first encountered Alex Salmond when he had been a youthful rebel eight years before. Then, at a time of internal feuding following upon the SNP's catastrophic election performance in the 1979 General Election, it was necessary to outlaw the competing groups that were then tearing the SNP apart. Salmond had been a junior member of one such, the 79 Group, who to his consternation found himself temporarily expelled. In 1982, he made an outstanding speech in an appeal for readmission to the Party for himself and others, and after having signed a compulsory undertaking of obedience to Party decisions, came back into the ranks.

From then on, he ascended by rejoining the National Executive Committee, and successively becoming Executive Vice Chairman for Publicity and Senior Vice Chairman (deputy leader). He had been elected

MP for Banff and Buchan in the 1987 General Election and had made a name for himself at Westminster. Now only 36, he was the elected leader of a political party pledged to deliver independence for Scotland. This task was to exercise his considerable talents. And he would need all of them – and a considerable dash of luck - something he would have appreciated since he was a bit of a gambler

Conscious of the need to implement the new Convener's reform strategy, Conference had elected some of the key office bearers from among his associates. These included Alasdair Morgan, as Senior Vice Convener and Mike Russell, his closest aide, as Executive Vice Chairman for Publicity. There would be no trouble from me as the outgoing National Convener. Alex and I had met at his request the morning after Conference when I was asked whether I had any political ambitions. The answer was negative. I needed to concentrate on my legal business and my family. Alex also moved fast to get the powerful National Secretary, John Swinney on board or at least neutralised. Several years before, he had offended Swinney when ousting him from presiding over the launch of a Conference agenda. The two men met and reached an agreement to work together.

All this was necessary since Alex Salmond faced a constant intellectual challenge from Jim Sillars who had many supporters. Now in the House of Commons as an SNP MP, Jim Sillars had been a senior colleague and mentor of Alex in their 79 Group days and afterwards. The close relationship between these two powerful allies had turned sour around 1989. According to Jim Sillars, he did not know why this happened since there was no open declaration of hostility from Alex Salmond – just a drawing away. He suspects that Alex took umbrage when he refused to support a leadership bid by Alex on the basis that the Party was moving forward sweetly with everyone co-operating. Alex Salmond had, he said, denied such a breach. Whatever the reason, they were no longer allies and Jim was definitely not part of the Salmond team. More significantly, Alex Salmond represented the gradualist school within the SNP while Jim Sillars that of the independence wing.

The immediate challenge to the new leadership team lay in by-elections in Paisley North and South Constituencies. The campaigns got off to a bad start with accusations that the new Convener was endeavouring to block the candidacy for Paisley North of Iain Lawson (a former Conservative who had aligned himself with the nationalist left). Lawson shifted to Paisley South while another non-gradualist Roger Mullin, Executive Vice Chairman for Organisation, stood for Paisley North. The campaigns were sound though dogged by bad publicity from within the Party. Both candidates came in second, with swings against Labour.

Paisley North By-election - 29 November 1990

Party	Votes	Percentage
Labour	11,353	44.0%
SNP	7,583	29.4%
Conservative	3,835	14.8%
Liberal Democrat	2,139	8.3%
Green	918	3.6%
Turnout		53.7%

Paisley South By-election - 29 November 1990

Party	Votes	Percentage
Labour	12,485	46.1%
SNP	7,455	27.5%
Conservative	3,627	13.4%
Liberal Democrat	2,660	9.8%
Green	835	3.1%
Turnout		55%

In October, the National Executive looked at a paper from the Convener calling for a multi-option referendum using preferential voting. It was not a new proposal since it had been initiated by constitutional expert, Prof Neil MacCormick in the early seventies and deployed by me in the eighties. Put simply it was a stratagem to widen the Party's political profile and to kick start renewed interest in self-government at a time when it had dropped off the political agenda.

On the face of it this should not have been controversial. The gambit was to get agreement from the other parties to hold a plebiscite under which there would be options for the *status quo* (i.e. Scotland being governed exclusively by and from Westminster), devolution with a provincial assembly or the SNP choice of independence. But to both traditional and left wing nationalists, it was regarded as an attempt by Alex Salmond to involve the SNP in an ongoing debate on devolution (from which the Party had been sidelined as a consequence of its withdrawal from the Labour dominated Constitutional Convention two years before). The NEC and other organs of the Party were to return to the issue over the next few years as there was no consensus within the upper reaches of the Party. (NEC 90/84)

As the proposal would also feature in the early stages of the 2014 referendum as a means of promoting devo-max (the jargon for maximum devolution), it is worthwhile to see what Alex Salmond was putting on the table when the issue re-emerged in August and October 1992, this time after Party approval had been secured as part of a campaign to permit local authorities to take the initiative. The SNP Research Department had issued proposals under the heading 'A Multi-Option Referendum – Let the People Decide', in 1992.

> "In October 1990, the SNP launched our multi-option referendum initiative on Scotland's constitutional future. In the aftermath of the General Election, we re-launched our proposal. All SNP Councillors support and advocate a multi-option referendum in their local authorities.
>
> A multi-option referendum would give Scots a three-way choice between the SNP's Independence in Europe policy, the Convention's devolution scheme and the Tories no-change stance. Preferential voting would ensure that one option secured majority support. Under this system, the ballot papers of the option which commands least support are redistributed among the other two options according to second preference.
>
> The SNP proposal is to establish a committee of Scots of public standing, preferably people not immediately engaged in party politics, which would provide the framework around which the political parties and campaign groups supporting the referendum would organise. This would involve agreement on the terms of the referendum questions, the initial request of the Government to organise such a referendum, and the organisation for the poll – in conjunction with local government – once that request was refused."

It was perfectly obvious that with a Conservative Government in office at Westminster, there was no route available through parliament – even if the Labour opposition had been willing to co-operate. So the paper went on to establish the legalities of a referendum to be carried out at local level. As the concept of referendums was not broadly acceptable in a UK context, the Research Department had a section on the use of them abroad.

Jim Sillars was also taking initiatives. At the National Executive on 10 November 1990, he raised the topic of Party Leadership and The Inter-governmental Conference due to be held in Rome. Here, he argued that the SNP should use the occasion to claim representation for Scotland. The paper was passed to Margaret Ewing as Leader of the Parliamentary Group for consideration. (NEC90/96). There was a further proposal fleshing out the policy of Independence in Europe which, because of its importance, would have to go to National Council and National Conference for decision. (NEC 90/94)

The European issue and the Paisley by-elections created a rift with Jim Fairlie, a member of the NEC and a former senior office bearer over the running of the SNP. Looking back at the event, Jim Fairlie had no doubts what had led to his resignation.

> "I left the SNP on December 3rd 1990, having sent my letter of resignation to HQ a few days previously. National Council met that day and Alex Salmond read out the letter at the meeting. When he was elected Chairman in September, Rob Gibson was elected VC Policy and immediately asked me to prepare a discussion paper on the EU, intending to have it and other papers discussed at a meeting of the National Assembly the week following the National Council. The Paisley by elections were held in November and Salmond instructed that the discussion papers were not to be distributed to branches and CAs because they were too controversial (totally contrary to the party's constitution) which meant that there would be no discussion among party members before Assembly.
>
> I used my column in the SI *(Scots Independent)*, due out the week of the By E *(By-election)*, on the understanding that they would be held over until after the poll on the Thursday of that week. Someone sent a copy to the press and the Glasgow Herald gave it front page coverage. I knew the EU issue would not be discussed as a consequence and, as I had

been deeply unhappy at the Independence in Europe policy for some time and felt strongly that the matter deserved a wider audience than the SNP, I resigned from the party. I was a member of the NEC until the day I resigned from the Party." (Email to author 8.3.13)

At the December meeting, the National Executive accepted proposals from the Convener to appoint two of his aides to oversee the coming General Election campaign. Mike Russell was allocated publicity aspects while Alasdair Morgan was placed in charge of organisation and administration. (NEC 90/96)

But it would not be the SNP if the year did not end on a bout of ill-temper. There had been a long standing fight between the former 79 Group faction, now in majority and the Scots Independent (a newspaper published for and by SNP members but independent of the Party) which they regarded as a faction in its own right during the struggles of the past. This time there was controversy over the by-election coverage. Margaret Ewing, seconded by George Leslie moved that a delegation be sent to remonstrate with the Scots Independent (SI). Mike Russell and Rob Gibson wanted the NEC to appoint the editor. The amended resolution carried by 13 votes to 5 and led to Winnie Ewing and Allan Macartney recording their dissent. (NEC90/110)

As frequently occurred, the affair petered out. The NEC team reported back from their meeting with the Directors of the Scots Independent. They were agreeable to a liaison officer being appointed and would consider appointing an NEC member to the Board. There was no response to the demand that the NEC should have the right to impose an editor of their choosing. Michael Russell expressed his exasperation and the issue blew over.

Conscious of drift in his leadership, Alex Salmond summoned an all-day meeting of the National Executive scheduled for 12 January 1991. This allowed the Committee to put things in place for the General Election preparations which from now on would feature largely. There was also time to consider the issue of financing the Party, advancing the Poll Tax campaign and maintaining momentum in a campaign to save the Scottish steel industry, very much under threat.

But foreign affairs intruded with a dispute over the extent to which

Britain's involvement in the first Gulf war was justified and could be supported by the SNP. Three separate papers were submitted by Alasdair Morgan, Jim Sillars and Allan Macartney. After a lengthy discussion, the meeting was adjourned to permit the framing of a composite resolution which in guarded terms supported the removal of Iraqi forces from Kuwait. Even then there was a series of amendments which were all defeated and the resolution carried by 14 votes to 6. (NEC91/126). As always with the SNP there was reluctance to get involved in any foreign adventures. This time it was accepted that force was to be used in this case as a last resort. Caution proved to be justified as eventually Scottish units of the British Army formed a disproportionate share of 40% of the UK contribution to the international attack force. At the February meeting, a fresh attempt to revive the matter led to a counter-motion moved by Alex Salmond which resulted in a hung vote of 6 – 6 and needed the Convener to use his casting vote to have his own motion carried. (NEC 91/131)

These internal hostilities were irrelevant since the SNP had no power to say Yea or Nay to any military expedition. They were, however, illustrative of general bad feelings and grumbling discontent. This was seen soon after when the Director of Communications, Chris McLean, issued a plea to NEC members to exercise restraint when giving their views to the Press. He warned that this was a distraction which impeded the Press Office from gaining maximum coverage from planned initiatives. Then, Alan McKinney, former Director of Organisation and HQ Chief Executive, resigned as he was 'disillusioned'. (NEC91/159)

Although the Special Conference in March allowed the Party to bury the poll tax campaign (but only after stiff resistance from delegates), there was not much good news around. An opinion poll from Mori put the SNP at only 15%, a steep decrease from the summer and a lesser one from September. A July Gallup Poll registered the SNP at 18% to Labour's 41%, the Tories 26% (and increasing) and the Liberal Democrats trailing at 13%. Then for the beleaguered Convener came the resignation of Mike Russell, his former campaign manager and principal ally. His role as Executive Vice Chairman for Publicity was taken over on an acting basis by one of Alex Salmond's major internal opponents, Alex Neil who would then have a say on the General Election campaign. (NEC91/159)

This was followed by news that his nemesis, Jim Sillars would stand for the Senior Vice-Chairmanship against Alasdair Morgan at the Conference in the autumn. If that were not bad enough there was a drop in membership

(GBC 91/10), combined with the usual cash shortages. Alba Pools which had been a major money spinner for the Party in the sixties and seventies was now running at a loss and was wound-up. A Party shop in Edinburgh was closed. It was too early for the Challenge of the Nineties to have made a significant impact although it was beginning to bring in enough money to modernise HQ equipment, including expensive new computers, as a harbinger of cash to come. (Personalised circular letter from Gil Paterson)

During the course of 1990/91, the normal work of policy formulation continued. The National Assembly on 9 December 1990 considered a detailed paper on the new policy of Independence in Europe prepared by Jim Sillars calling for Scotland to seek membership as a state in Europe. Likewise, George Leslie presented a paper regarding the need for a decentralised, confederal European Community with scope for a referendum. Jim Fairlie had drawn attention to the existing policy set out in a Conference resolution of 1983 as a step beyond which we should not go. Successive meetings of the Assembly looked at papers on the representation of women after independence, electoral reform, housing, the arts, forestry, social policy, the Highlands and Islands and the third world. Conference echoed this diversity with acceptably radical views on renationalisation of electricity, gas and transport and a ban on the sale of council homes.

Criticism of the Convener's leadership as too autocratic and indolent can be dismissed as nit-picking. The allegations were mutually contradictory. If there were reservations, it was with Alex Salmond's dallying with devolution front bodies such as Scotland United (which had Labour activist involvement) as gradualism carried too far. None of this impacted adversely on Alex's leadership ratings with the public. Far from it! On the eve of the Conference, his rating was up 5% at 39% satisfied against 31% dissatisfied (compared with Secretary of State, Ian Lang's 23% against 56%). (Herald 17.9.91). In the run up to the Conference, I announced my intention of running for election as one of the National Council members chosen by Conference (a minor elected post and one of 30). The fact that a former leader was reappearing provoked speculation of a challenge to Alex Salmond's authority. Nothing could have been further from my intentions. Nevertheless, I had already discovered that whenever I wrote an article or made an observation, it was construed as criticism of the leader – very frustrating for me and irritating for him.

Although looking at a substantial article I wrote for the Herald at the time paying tribute for the work he had done, I lectured him on the need for better man-management and improved collective leadership, so in retrospect I was not as diplomatic as I had thought. But that's politics and any one in a top job has to live with criticism, however undeserving it may be. (Herald 17.9.91)

During the year, Alex Neil made a throw away remark at a Press Conference about Scotland being 'free by '93'. It stuck and came back to haunt the SNP leadership at a later time. It was not something endorsed by the leader but one that was difficult to play down in a party which believed in independence as a cardinal virtue

But while the National Convener cannot control everything, and occasionally anything if the Party or fellow office bearers are in a grumpy mood - he has one major advantage - his big speech which is the highlight of the Conference and sets the direction and tone of the coming year. And the speech for 1991 was good. It argued a strategic case that the Party must move away from being a party of protest to one with social democratic credentials becoming the natural party of government, something which he sustained throughout his political career. Alex is a man for surprises and obtained headlines by having Sean Connery, Scotland's James Bond, appear in an SNP party political broadcast. This was good for his ratings and the party's polling performance. It failed to prevent delegates from voting to replace some of his office bearers by others who were supportive of Jim Sillars. Sillars himself was elected Senior Vice Chairman with every intention of using his new position to influence policy and publicity. And everyone, neutrals and committed, expected an explosion which never occurred. Nevertheless, there were tensions.

There was also a further obstacle to overcome – one that had been overhanging the Conference. It was a by-election in Kincardine & Deeside, an area that favoured the Conservatives and where the Liberal Democrats were the principal challengers. The constituency also took in a part of South Aberdeen that was not good territory for the SNP. Nevertheless, the SNP made the best of a bad job. It chose in Allan Macartney, one of its office bearers and an influential academic as its candidate. The result turned out as badly as expected. Consolation came with the result – relief when it was over.

Kincardine and Deeside By-election - 7 November 1991)

Party	Votes	Percentage
Liberal Democrat	20,779	49%
Conservative	12,955	30.6%
SNP	4,705	11.1%
Labour	3,271	7.7%
Scottish Green	683	1.6%
Turnout		67%

Some marginal consolation could be taken from an almost 5% increase in support and pushing Labour into fourth place. Otherwise, the outcome was brutal – a Liberal Democrat gain from the Conservatives and with a huge majority, too.

Despite this set-back, Alex Salmond now sought to increase the pace. Aided by a November poll showing the SNP up to 23%, with 28% of people wanting Independence in Europe, he promoted his scheme to have a multi-option referendum. The Campaign for a Scottish Assembly asked for talks and while this was rejected by the Executive, they resolved to seek the Campaign's views on Alex's referendum proposal. From now on it was a matter of the serious business of preparing for the General Election and the District Elections. As ever the problem for a Westminster election where the issue was the election of UK Government was relevance, credibility and lack of UK media coverage. Out of the blue came a multi-party debate arranged by The Scotsman and held in January 1992 where Alex Salmond convincingly demolished the other Scottish political leaders Donald Dewar (Labour), Ian Lang (Conservative) and Malcolm Bruce (Liberal Democrat). Backed by a supportive audience, Alex Salmond clearly won the day. This debate consolidated the claim that he was the outstanding political debater of the decade.

With the General Election looming, preparations went ahead. Alex Neil prepared a Scottish Budget. The Scottish Sun newspaper switched its support from the Conservatives to the SNP and its policy of an Independent Scotland in Europe in January 1992 (the first time the SNP had received backing from a major newspaper). A week later, an ICM Poll for ITN and the Scotsman put the independence vote at an exceptional – and unbelievable – high of 50%. If there was a split in the views of the SNP leadership as to how the campaign should be planned, it was not obvious. With the SNP party political broadcast featuring the independence of the USA from Britain, it appeared that the 'Scotland Free' claim now held the upper hand in tactical thinking.

In a letter to Alex Salmond dated 2 March, copied to other senior office bearers, I issued some cautionary assessments. I observed that he had diverged from Conference policies of 1983 and 1988 which envisaged that the principle and package of EU membership would be put before the Scottish people for decision after independence. I also said that hitherto the party had never conceded a referendum on the principle of independence from Westminster or that a negotiated settlement be incorporated.

Based on the concept that the mandate would be won in a General Election through holding a majority of seats, I continued:

> "Our policy pledge has always been that we will hold a referendum to approve a draft Constitution. All this is for good reason. In bi-lateral or multi-lateral negotiations with Westminster and the EC (European Community) we cannot dictate the speed of the discussions or whether an acceptable agreement will emerge. If we tie ourselves to a 'package', then the referendum will be delayed. As we know from the Seventies that approach of the English establishment was to spin out the legislative processes in the hope that the pressure would slacken and their counter-propaganda would seep through..... We can however control the timetable for discussions on the Constitution and our own proposals are sufficiently close to those of the Convention on structure and the electoral system, if not on powers, to allow us to reach a working compromise to facilitate the holding of an early referendum within the time span envisaged by the NEC."

I counselled that we should not give support to Labour proposals to avoid being further compromised and not to give Labour's devolution policy a legitimacy which undermined the whole thrust of Independence in Europe.

With a slightly jaundiced view of opinion polls born of hard experience, I questioned one of Alex Salmond's principal colleagues on what was the targeting strategy of the Party. 'What seats are you going for', I asked. Waving his hand expansively he said, 'All of them'. To this day, I am not sure whether he believed it, was being sarcastic about the campaign or was taking the 'mickey'! Certainly, Salmond was initially cautious , before being infected by the excitement mid-way through the campaign. Even up to a week before polling day, the SNP was catching up on Labour and Alex was quoted as 'The Party is surging to victory'.

This success in the opinion polls led to much increased television coverage with some at UK level leading to Prime Minister John Major jumping on to soap boxes in a barnstorming performance, warning that the UK union was in danger of break-up – and winning the election, too.

And then the squeeze came. By polling day on 9 April 1992, there was substantial disappointment. Far from achieving a mandate, the Party emerged with three seats, the 'old faithfuls' of Moray, East Aberdeenshire and Angus. Lost to Labour were Glasgow Govan which had been won by Jim Sillars from Labour in 1988 and Dunfermline West, gained when Dick Douglas defected from Labour over the issue of the Poll Tax. Overall the Party's vote had risen by 7.1% to 21.5%. In terms of a strategic breakthrough in the central belt, there was little progress. The bleak truth was that Labour had won 49 seats, the Conservatives 11 and the Liberal Democrats 9, while the SNP still had three rural constituencies and none in the central belt.

General Election - 9 April 1992

Party	Votes	Percentage	Seats
Labour	1,283,350	39%	49
Conservative	751,950	25.6%	11
Liberal Democrat	383,856	13.1%	9
SNP	629,564	22.1%	3
Turnout			75.5%

I assessed the position in an article published shortly after the general election:

> "The evidence suggests that the Party misinterpreted the mood and psychology of the Scottish people and was insufficiently sensitive to the polling indicators to be able to adapt its strategy and tactics as the election progressed. There was a dangerous degree of optimism which by the time of the March National Council had a suggestion of hysteria ....On the fringes of the campaign I kept expecting the SNP to bring a new direction in the last phase to demonstrate to voters than an SNP vote was essential for Scotland's protection. This did not happen with the end product that our campaign lost relevance and gradually became remote from reality".

Deputy Leader, Jim Sillars, in a memorable diatribe describing Scottish voters as '90-minute patriots' who only supported Scotland at football games, gave up active politics in the SNP to obtain employment. Through his column in The Sun, he was a thorn in the flesh of the Party leadership. With his departure, Alex Salmond had no major personal opposition. The nationalist left remained strong over the next few years and he continued to meet opposition on some of his initiatives. A month after the General Election, the SNP had a consolation prize in the form of the election of 150 District Councillors. The SNP received almost a quarter of the total vote and pushed the Conservatives into third place:

District Council Election - May 1992

Party	Percentage	Councillors
Labour	34%	468
SNP	24.3%	150
Conservative	23.2%	204
Liberal Democrat	9.5%	94
Independent	7.4%	228
Other	1.9%	

Commenting, Alex Salmond said:

> "We have made over thirty net gains, including from Labour in Districts across the Central Belt like West Lothian, Kilmarnock, Falkirk and Renfrew where we not only substantially raised our vote even beyond the General Election level but translated that into some stunning victories. .... and to push for a referendum which will let the people of Scotland, not politicians in England, decide our country's future."

Not letting go of the issue, he defined the ballot as 'multi-option' and promised the SNP would seek this through councillors of other parties organising a people's ballot combined with a challenge to the Labour/ Liberal Democrat leaderships to clarify their stance. (June 1992)

More frankly, the internal Election Review recognised that the Party had been unsuccessful, firstly by failing to defeat the psychology of fear inspired by its opponents and secondly by some of its actions, a coded attack on the informal slogan, 'Scotland Free by '93'. This slogan had become a taunt. At least, as Donald Dewar, Labour Shadow Scottish Secretary teased, it could be recycled every decade. The Review also concluded that there was a need to promote economic arguments in advance of an election. Negative campaigning had a role and in this election had been neglected.

Chapter 3:

BY FITS AND STARTS

The SNP is nothing, if not resilient. Leaving aside the bruises and disappointments of the battle, the Party looked to the future. First into the field was a proposal (NC92/26) by Alex Salmond pushing his idea for a multi-option referendum, this time linked to the General Election outcome where a majority of MPs represented support for a Scottish Assembly or Parliament. The resolution carried by 132 votes to 36 and ran:

> "In the light of the General and District Election results, this Council reaffirms SNP support for a Multi Option Referendum to determine the people's choice for constitutional change in Scotland. This Referendum should involve 3 Options; the status quo, a Scottish Assembly within the UK, and independence in Europe. With the Conservative Government likely to remain opposed to such an initiative Council calls on Scottish Local Authorities and campaign groups to prepare to organise this Referendum with contributions from a public fundraising campaign.
>
> Council commits the Party to co-operate with other groups and individuals who are committed to the holding of a Multi Option Referendum which should be aimed at taking place by June 1993".

Unsurprisingly, the Conservatives were opposed. They had won the Election and there was no way a Conservative Government would bow to any desire for change in Scotland, especially since the Prime Minister had fought the election on a platform of saving the Union. Alex Salmond's initiative provoked a cynical comment that the logic of the referendum on the part of the SNP was the equivalent of saying: vote for us and we'll resign.

Still there was a rare development. The Party had discussions with the Scottish Trade Union Congress (STUC) out of which came a joint declaration in favour of a devolved Parliament, dropping any reference to an Assembly.

The Statement continued:

> "At the General Election 75% of Scots voted for parties committed to constitutional change. With just over 25% of the vote, the present government therefore has no mandate to continue to deny Scots the universally-recognised right of self-determination.
>
> The SNP and STUC have both found this initial discussion useful and productive, and we plan to hold further discussions as part of the process of co-operation which will be essential in order to ensure that the Scottish people are able to determine their own future through a multi-option referendum in the near future."

The declaration was signed by Campbell Christie, General Secretary of the STUC and Alex Salmond MP, National Convener of the SNP. It represented everything that had been sought by the SNP only four years previously when thwarted by the Labour Party.

The advantage of the proposal was that it gave the SNP something to say after an election result which had diminished both its credibility and relevance. It also put the Labour Party on the spot. Labour had swept the field in Scotland yet was in impotent opposition at Westminster. So it was not surprising that at the June meeting of the NEC, party researcher Andrew Wilson produced a campaign plan. More important matters intruded! The SNP had overspent by £25,000! Two senior office bearers, Jim Sillars and Alex Neil announced their intention not to seek re-election although Alex Neil was to remain a member of the NEC.

Looking forward to the next election, the Party's strategy for fighting the European Parliament Elections was set on the following lines:

1.   Independence in Europe

2.   Strengthening credibility

3.   Broadening public support for independence

4.   Achieving detailed targets.

By July, attention had switched to foreign affairs, and particularly the possible outcomes of a referendum in France seeking approval for the

Maastricht Treaty. The European issue was in the forefront since there was due to be European Summit in Edinburgh in December. The Campaign for a Scottish Assembly had expressed interest in the multi-option referendum and the NEC accepted an invitation to meet them. Devolution elsewhere had also caught the eye since Dr. Allan Macartney, Andrew Welsh MP and Winnie Ewing MEP were all to be in Catalonia for a National Day celebration. The SNP NEC was largely of the view that involvement in these issues would up-rate the Party's credibility for the European Elections in the hope that this would fare better for the SNP than the fate of the Independence in Europe message in the British General Election.

Although it was expected that Westminster would scrap the dual local government tiers of Regions and Districts in favour of a single tier which, it was widely reported, would favour Conservative Councils, that was only predicted and not the reality. George Leslie, Executive Vice Chairman for Local Government produced a paper on the implications of the new system (NEC 92/66 10 October 1992). It was expected that the 1994 Regional Elections would take place one month before the European Election and the thinking was that there should be a single strategy for both campaigns. For the local election, it was suggested (Conference Resolution 38) that there should be a Local Income Tax levied by single tier authorities with a Business Tax to be applied by central government to iron out income differentials.

Conference also looked at one controversial internal issue – the status of the Scottish Cabinet set up by Alex Salmond acting as National Convener and Party Leader. This set out a formula for selection of the Cabinet spokespersons and needed an amendment to the party Constitution. The amendment carried the vote by 137 to 106 but failed to achieve the two thirds majority which was needed. From the chair at Conference, Alasdair Morgan attempted to cure the confusion by stating that the Cabinet would be appointed as before (with the NEC approving the Convener's proposals) and that the Conference Procedures Committee would be requested to re-examine the arguments.

Then there was the Party's attitude to The Treaty on European Union, signed at Maastricht on 7 February. This gave rise to continuing grumblings of discontent sufficiently strong to occasion the Research Department to issue an explanatory paper in November. After describing the context and extent of the Treaty, it confirmed the SNP wanted a referendum for its ratification. While criticising Britain's opt out on the Social Chapter, it made clear that SNP MPs unlike Labour MPs who had abstained, had voted for it. The SNP's European credentials cannot be questioned it declared.

> "By confirming that the European Community will be firmly based on its Member States for the foreseeable future, the Maastricht Treaty provides powerful support for the SNP's policy of Independence in Europe. Maastricht leads neither to a European super-state nor to a Europe of the Regions. The SNP supports the development of the EC as a confederal and equal partnership between democratic and European nations, rather than as a centralised, federal European super-state. Under the Maastricht Treaty, the Council of Ministers – comprising the ministerial representatives of Member States – remains the Community's primary decision-making body."

With the Maastricht Treaty now the subject of a Danish Referendum, Alex Neil at the November Executive proposed that the Party look once more at the Maastricht implications through a Working Party consisting of Margaret Ewing, Winifred Ewing, Allan Macartney and Vice Chairman for Policy, Rob Gibson.

I gave support for Maastricht at the time although I should have foreseen that the expansion of the powers of the Community (with its important assumption of the name of the European Union) could be a 'slippery slope' towards federalism. Apart from the strategic demands for securing independence in Europe (that is by playing down the resistance to 'separation' as a barrier to self-government), the ceding of powers clashed both with the need for Scotland to have sovereignty and the Party's long held creed of decentralisation. Other countries had different objectives with the European political elites determined to create a single state to match the strength of the United Sates and the Soviet Union. These salami tactics, especially after the economic difficulties of the depression years following the banking collapse in 2008, have indeed taken Europe a long way to centralisation.

A disappointing year closed with triumph when 25,000 people marched through the streets of Edinburgh with the demand on the occasion of the European Summit that there be a recall of the old Scottish Parliament which had adjourned in 1707 following the Treaty of Union. Not only was there a huge turn-out from a wide representation of Scotland's civic community but the issue related to Scotland's status in Europe and provided a constitutional mechanism for its implementation. The follow-through had no political force and fell by the wayside. Nevertheless, the fact that it occurred was an indication that political Scotland was stirring from a long period of slumber.

Internally, there were major changes in staffing. Chris MacLean, long time Research worker and Director of Communications over a period of 12 years resigned. Lari Don was appointed Press Officer in his place. (NEC93/05) Alex Salmond's Scottish Cabinet engaged in consideration of the Maastricht Treaty, the economy, industry and the environment. There was some cheer from the Treasurer declaring that party income was up only to be dashed by gloom from George Leslie, Local Government Vice Convener over some poor local election results.

And then Maastricht came to a head. At Westminster, John Major's Conservative Government faced internal revolt over the ratification of the Treaty and was looking around for support. After the seventies, it was almost a matter of religious doctrine that the SNP would not support a Conservative Government in any way. But there was also the imperative of the strategic Scotland in Europe policy. When the Government approached the SNP for support, it brought a gift – representation in a new Committee of the Regions with the SNP being conferred a right of nomination of one representative.

In March, the Government reached agreement in the negotiations (led on the part of the SNP by parliamentary leader, Margaret Ewing under which a contentious amendment would be supported by the Liberal Democrats, Plaid Cymru and SNP MPs. Judging that they were on to a good thing on this occasion, breaking the rule of non-support did not bring the expected dividend. Labour MPs, seeing the SNP in the Government voting lobby, rounded on them. Nor was the timing good. Alex Salmond was about to sign a joint declaration for the recall of the Scottish Parliament along with the Leader of the Scottish Liberal Democrats, Jim Wallace at a Press Conference presided over by Campbell Christie and Bill Spiers of the STUC.

Desperate to get out of this 'recall' trap, Labour passed word to the STUC that they would not collaborate in the circumstances. So 'in one leap', Labour was free of its commitments and the SNP was left with a large dollop of egg-on-the-face'. In effect the whole referendum strategy of the SNP collapsed and remained so for a further four years.

With the Party long steeped in anti-Tory sentiment, there were internal repercussions. The three SNP MPs, Margaret Ewing, Alex Salmond and Andrew Welsh came under severe criticism as much for voting with the 'Tories' as its impact on the devolution strategy. Much of the anger came from those who had been publicly hostile to the whole concept of the Referendum.

At a hastily called emergency meeting of the National Executive on 13 March 1993, there was a motion condemning the actions of the MPs by Alex Neil and Kenny Macaskill and another from Rob Gibson seconded by National Treasurer, Tom Chalmers regretting the decision of the MPs and requesting the establishment of procedures under which the Parliamentary Group took emergency decisions. The first resolution faced a paper from the MPs attacking Labour and setting out the case for Scotland in Europe and the consequent decision on the Committee of the Regions. This was presented by Andrew Welsh and seconded by Alex Salmond. Hard words were spoken on both sides. The no confidence motion was defeated by 13 to 8 and the paper from the MPs carried by 13 to 11. Dissents were recorded. (NEC93/26).

The issue was revisited at the National Council meeting on 5 June when the wounds had scarcely healed (NC93/22). A critical counter amendment deflecting the blame for dealing with the Tories by attacking the Secretary for State for reneging on the deal was only carried by 147 votes to 81. Eventually after many procedural votes, the amended resolution passed by a substantial majority.

The run-up to NATO involvement in the Balkans created more dissent. A general motion recognising the integrity of Bosnia Herzegovina proposed by me at the NEC meeting of 8 May provoked an amendment from John Swinney asserting that selective military action might have to be used to implement the diplomatic initiatives and to ensure stability. The amendment carried by 12 votes to 9, with the amended motion being accepted unanimously. (NEC93/46).

And still there remained the problem of how to get independence to the forefront of Scottish politics and to make the SNP the runner to deliver self-government. For example, a System 3 poll in The Herald on 25 May 1993 received front page coverage with claims that the Government was deeply unpopular north of the Border and that there was a threat to the Union. An Attitude Survey showed that more than 80% of Scots were committed to either Home Rule or complete independence, the division being 50% for Home Rule and 31% for independence. Support for independence was down from 35% two years earlier and for Home Rule up 43%. In party terms, the Conservatives crashed from 26% to 16% with that fall in support going equally to Labour and the Liberal Democrats. The SNP was static at 22%.

Leaving 1993, there was a major paper from John Swinney, now Publicity Vice Convener on the strategy for fighting the European Elections in 1994 and from Fiona Hyslop, a paper on the nitty-gritty issues of social policy and the imposition of VAT on fuel bills both received attention. By early 1994, John Swinney returned with a policy that the SNP fight elections as 'The Power for Change'.

The press were unkind as the SNP approached celebrations of its 60th birthday. Scotland on Sunday ran a full article on 20 March 1994. Under the headline, "The party runs out of fizzy stuff", political reporter Kenny Farquharson reviewed the 'diamond jubilee' with a jaundiced eye.

> "Next month the SNP will be 60 years old, and some wringing of hands is going on over whether the party – like a deb of advancing years or an ageing, balding bachelor – should simply pretend the birthday does not exist. .....After decades of roller coaster poll ratings, the current SNP leader of four years' standing, Alex Salmond, is still finding a sufficient number hard to muster and maintain. Today support is 5% lower than the 30.4% it was at its height 20 years ago when the party sent 11 MPs to Westminster. The polls put the SNP a full 22% behind its main rival, Labour".

> Unsurprisingly, all (anonymous activists) share an expectation of encouraging results in the forthcoming Euro and Regional contests in line with current poll showings. But their appraisal of the Party's performance at the next general election is brutally honest; even at this early stage few can honestly express any real hope of it bringing a majority vote for independence.

> .... This, of course, cannot be hinted at in public. More than any other party, the SNPs' success depends on a delicate juggling act with emotions and expectations of the

Scottish people. And the cardinal rule of this game is that the party must be relentlessly upbeat about the future, to the point of near euphoria, always giving the impression that the long awaited break-through is just round the corner."

Kenny Farquharson also records significantly that a clear sighted pragmatism is to be found especially with a growing group of ambitious activists in their 20s and 30s on the left of the Party. **Without embarrassment many of them say their political careers lie not in an independent Scotland but as SNP members of a devolved parliament within the UK.** (Author's emphasis).

1994 was a year of elections. On 5 May, the SNP elected 73 regional councillors with 26.8% of the vote in second place to Labour which had 220 seats on 41.8%. The Conservatives were down to 13.7% and 31 councillors while the Liberal Democrats once more showed their strike power by winning 60 seats on only 12% of the vote. For the SNP, the result was a major improvement on four years before when the Party gained 43 councillors on a vote of 21.8%.

Regional Election - May 1994

Party	Percentage	Councillors
Labour	41.8%	220
SNP	26.8%	73
Conservative	13.7%	31
Liberal Democrat	12%	60
Independent	4.2%	65
Other	1.5%	4

Thus heartened, the SNP surged into the European Parliament election a month later. There the vote rose to 32.6%, greater than the massive vote the SNP had gained in the October 1974 General Election. Until now, the SNP had only one European representative, the formidable Winnie Ewing. Her vote in the Highlands and Islands Constituency rose to a massive 58.4%. More importantly, she was joined by Dr Allan Macartney who ousted Labour to win North East Scotland with 42.8%.

Without a break, the SNP was involved in a by-election in Monklands East, following the death of Labour Leader, John Smith. At first glance, it was not good territory with Labour at 60% of the vote. Kay Ullrich was the SNP Candidate. The election was riddled with claims and counter-claims of sectarianism and was generally unpleasant. Without a miracle, the SNP did well. The Liberal Democrats and the Conservatives were both trounced. A valuable by product was that contact by Alex Salmond was made with the Catholic Church in the person of Tom Winning, Archbishop of Glasgow to make the Archbishop aware that the Party was non-sectarian.

Monklands East By-election - 30 June 1994

Party	Votes	Percentage
Labour	16,950	49.8%
SNP	15,320	44.9%
Liberal Democrat	878	2.6%
Conservative	799	2.3%
Turnout		70%

In a series of heavy weight papers, John Swinney outlined his proposals for the next four years in an update of the Independence Strategy and urged re-adoption of the slogan 'SNP Power for Change'. The Party also approved a re-organisation plan for senior staff in preparation of the appointment of a Chief Executive. This last proposal was controversial and the NEC saw a series of amendments, including provision for public advertising, defeated on recurring majorities around (17-7). The final report was approved by 18 votes to 5. (NEC94/88) It was a surprise to no one when the Convener's principal ally, Michael Russell emerged as the new Chief Executive.

The NEC had also received a request for a meeting from Sinn Fein. Not surprisingly the SNP did not want to be dragged into the turbulences of Northern Ireland politics and replied simply to say that it approved of the peace process.(NEC94/93). In the meantime, the Scottish Cabinet on 15 September fleshed out the programme buttressing the Power for Change campaign. The salient points were:

1.   Challenge over Scotland's Oil

2. Bankrupt Britain dragging Scotland down while oil revenues were propping up the UK

3. Scotland needing economic solutions different from the UK

4. Scotland's budgetary priorities not supported by Labour

5. Other policy differences between the SNP and Labour

There was considerable intellectual input to devising a Scottish Budget intended to underpin the Campaign. Alex Neil was given the task of drawing up a 'Dynamic Budget' to be published a week before the UK Budget, the aim being to establish economic credibility as well as gaining valuable publicity and providing candidates with ammunition.

Concern arose over the finances of the Party. These were showing an improvement but were nowhere near meeting future requirements. The election budget alone stood at a preliminary £46,000 proposed by the General Business Committee. The Challenge of the Nineties was gathering pace and with the increasing professionalisation of the Party, the Cabinet recommended the setting up of a National Convener's Club where for a subscription of £120, members would get privileged access to Alex as National Convener and other privileges. This was the first time access was available on special terms.

After four full years in charge, Alex Salmond's star was rising within the Party. He could not yet get away with everything. There was still dissent from nationalists on the left and occasionally, more traditional supporters of independence who were dubious about readopting devolution. His speech to Conference was significant. Alex's speeches were always lucid but this time he used humour and injected a passion that was well received by delegates.

His position strengthened later in the year when he debated independence versus devolution with Labour's George Robertson. A member of the audience asked them which option they would choose if their preferred choice were not available – independence, devolution or the status quo of government from London. Having laid the ground within the SNP, Salmond was able to opt for devolution as his second choice which he did on the grounds that it was a stepping stone to independence. George Robertson was stumped, turned on the questioner angrily accusing her of being a plant, promptly losing his audience and the debate. All in all, it was a masterly performance appreciated by the Party and more importantly by the media.

1995 brought a number of significant events. The NEC had accepted proposals from the National Convener that an independent Commission be established to examine how Scotland could more easily make a transition to independence and learned in January that the Commission had received acceptances from a distinguished group of academics and a respected journalist.

The same meeting heard also that Alex Salmond had received a letter from the Prime Minister, John Major conceding that Scotland had a right to national self-determination should the Scottish people determine to follow the independence road. With less success, he had written to the Shadow Scottish Secretary to push Labour into a similar commitment.

This allowed him to go to the Council in March 1995 and subsequently to Conference to obtain the consent of the Party to follow a more gradualist route to independence and permit the Party to give positive, instead of reluctant, support to devolution. (NC95/07)

The Conservative Government had passed legislation to reform local government by abolishing the regional and district council structure, replacing it with 29 unitary authorities. The three island authorities Orkney, Shetland and Western Isles were retained. The main casualties were the nine regional councils. Some of the boundaries were dubious and the Conservatives had to face claims that they had been drawn to favour their heartlands. If so they were disappointed as they emerged with no control of councils. Labour swept the field with 20. The SNP won 3 (Angus, Moray & Perth & Kinross). The rest had no overall control or controlled by independents. Although there could be no direct comparison, for the SNP, control of three councils was a very good outcome.

Council Election - May 1995

Party	Votes	Percentage	Councillors
Labour	742,557	45.6%	613
SNP	444,918	26.1%	181
Conservative	196,109	11.5%	82
Liberal Democrat	166,141	9.8%	121
Independent	130,642	7.7%	151
Others	23,781	1.4%	7

The other main electoral event of 1995 was the Perth and Kinross by-election. This was a Conservative seat but in the past the SNP won it 20 years before in October 1974 when Douglas Crawford had been elected. The constituency was much altered by boundary changes. Things started badly for the SNP and unfortunately, involved the Election Committee of which I was Convener. The task of the Committee was to approve a list of candidates from which the Constituency Association would choose. The Committee decided that Roseanna Cunningham should be excluded from the list. A member of the Committee, never identified, leaked the decision to the media leading to a storm of bad publicity.

The Party and the NEC were deeply offended and angry. The end result was that on a motion from the Party Convener at the March NEC, the Committee's recommendation was overruled by 13 votes to 0 and Roseanna's name added to the list of three other names by 18 votes to 0. (NEC95/30).Subsequently as Committee Convener in full penitent mode, I had to apologise to the National Council for the leak. Afterwards, the NEC discharged the Committee and appointed another with changed membership. Being the sole survivor, I was reappointed Convener although somewhat jaundiced with the whole mess.

Not surprisingly, Roseanna Cunningham was selected as the by-election candidate and in a vigorous campaign, overcame a determined challenge by Labour whose candidate Douglas Alexander came second. The Conservatives, having previously held the seat, were pushed into third place. UKIP was sixth, beaten by the Monster Raving Loony Party.

Perth & Kinross By-election - 25 May 1995

Party	Votes	Percentage
SNP	16,931	40.4%
Labour	9,620	22.9%
Conservative	8,990	21.4%
Liberal Democrat	4,952	11.8%
Monster R L	586	1.4%
UKIP	504	1.2%
Turnout		62.1%

By-election victories are rare and Perth & Kinross gave a boost to the SNP. In what I had intended to be a fresh look at the strategy of the Party after the summer euphoria had departed, I was astounded to find that a speech in which I had praised the Party for responding well on the electoral and campaign front, even predicting that we would win more seats at the next election received front page headlines in the Scotsman (11.9.95) 'Wilson Questions party strategy' and then in splash, 'Former SNP Leader Puts Unity at Risk'. And the cause, apart from the proximity of the SNP Conference, always a sensitive time for leaders as the media were desperate for angles and stories, I had dared suggest that it was only when the SNP reached about 43 to 46% that the campaign for a full Scottish Parliament would go critical.

Common sense I would have thought but political parties do not always like the 'unsayable' to be said – publicly at least. The same edition of the Scotsman contained a prophesy from George Robertson of Labour that devolution would kill 'stone dead the rump separatist desire, but that they cannot oppose it because it is so popular'.

The Conference went well and how could it do otherwise on the back of a by-election win. Criticism was expressed that there had been no development of the EU policy in the light of the implications of the Maastricht Treaty creating the single market and its impact on national sovereignty. In the run up to Conference, Gil Paterson, EVC in charge of Fundraising and the author of the Challenge of the Nineties faced misleading criticism about the effectiveness of fund raising operations in America while he was absent abroad. He believed that the leaks came from his rivals and from within the NEC. There was an overdraft around £65,000 despite the growth in fundraising. The Challenge income stood at £108,000 compared with £44,082 in 1991. Total income was £210,624 compared with £91,327. The income of the Party would rise sharply in succeeding years but as ever ability to spend would cut prospects for building reserves. For the time being, there was a financial crisis and the incoming office bearers found themselves under pressure to prepare a financial budget. The year ended with a meeting between the Executive Committees of the SNP and Plaid Cymru over future co-operation especially in relation to General Election campaigns. The SNP could only manage a provisional General Election campaign budget but nevertheless on a vote of 16 votes to 3 took the brave decision to buy phase 1 of a Computerised Electoral Data Base System. The NEC hoped to fund the £15,000 cost by applying to the Trustees of the Fisher Trust. (NEC95/109) The North American project was suspended, prompting expressions of dissent from Gil Paterson and Iain Lawson. A successful St Andrews Day Appeal eased the financial pressures and reduced the overdraft. But soon after, with the appointment of a supervisory committee to look at overseas fundraising, Gil Paterson resigned.

By 1996, the General Election was approaching and Allison Hunter, Director of Organisation was sent to the US to monitor campaigning techniques used during the US Presidential Election. This was something the Party had wanted to do for some time. A Scotsman ICM Poll was not too encouraging. True, the SNP was now in second place with 23%, pushing the Conservatives (18%) into third place and the Liberal Democrats (12%) into fourth. Labour was miles ahead with 45%.

Alex Neil as Vice Convener for Policy produced a Programme for Government. The General Business Committee agreed to accept a substantial donation of £50,000 on condition that £10,000 would be used to finance the Business for Independence Campaign – a lobbying organisation that had been established earlier and designed to woo more progressive members of the business community into giving consideration to independence and support to the Party. Jim Mather was largely responsible for leading the Campaign whose Director was Samantha Barber (GBC 18.6.96).

Dr Allan Macartney's great achievement was the preparation of a major strategic document, The Transition to Independence which was completed in June 1996. The panel was a distinguished one: Dr. Allan Macartney

(Convener), Professor Malcolm Anderson, Neal Ascherson, Mungo Deans (to 31 March 1996), Professor Neil MacCormick, Professor David Murray, Professor Michael Lynch (from March 1995) and Roy MacIver (from January 1996). Of the participants, only Allan Macartney and Prof. Neil MacCormick were members of the Scottish National Party. Based as it was on a working assumption that the mandate could be achieved through electing a majority of MPs at either Westminster or a Scottish parliament it was widely accepted that the issues tackled in the report would be of immense help when the independence was within reach. Time would tell.

By now I was beginning to worry over a growing tendency within the SNP to backpedal on Scottish sovereignty and to pursue the soft options as if that would enable the Scottish people to slide faster down the slippery slope. It seemed to me that some of the leaders and many of the emergent ones in particular would find it too easy to by-pass independence. There were two issues in particular that gave concern. One was devolution on which I was to become increasingly vocal.

The other was the blithe way in which the Independence in Europe message that I had supported when Chairman was being used to smother concerns about the growing assumption of power by organs of the EU as if our campaign for independence was focused solely on our relationships with London. National independence did not form a block to co-operation but was at odds with the transfer of sovereignty. This was particularly true of the successive changeover of Europe from Common Market to Community to Union.

So in conjunction with Alex Neil I successfully proposed an amendment at the April Conference in Dundee calling for a referendum before Scotland opted for the single currency as wanted by the Party hierarchy. I was little pleased when the 'spin-meisters' put it abroad through a statement issued in name of the Parliamentary Leader, Margaret Ewing MP that the referendum did not diminish support for the single currency, driving me to issue a public rebuke by way of a letter to the Herald on 1 May 1996. If party apparatchiks were offended, I was more so.

Not that the Party managers had it all their own way. In a flourish they launched a variation on the Party thistle emblem. The aim was to soften the angular party symbol to make it less threatening. There was no harm in that but the emblem demonstrated had a star at the centre Maoist style. Worse still it looked like the cartoon character Bugs Bunny. It went down with derision or as the Courier and Advertiser put it in a headline (29 April 1996), 'New 'yellow bunny' bugs delegates as a no-go logo'. In a witty article subsequently in the Herald (in May) Alex Salmond tried to garner support. Too late! The Party would not budge and the design was quietly dropped.

While the SNP had its minor embarrassments, greater consternation arose in the Labour Party in Scotland. From London came leaked reports that instead of having a promised manifesto commitment to deliver a Scottish Assembly, Westminster Leaders, notably Tony Blair the Labour Leader, would ditch the agreed proposal in favour of a two pronged pre-legislative referendum with Yes/No questions on whether there should be a Scottish Parliament and if so, whether it should have taxation powers.

So far as the SNP was concerned, there was little surprise. It was well known that the Labour Party when last in Government in the seventies had paid lip-service to devolution and then only because of public support for the SNP. And when in 1979, Labour had a chance to deliver an Assembly by a vote in Parliament, it had flunked it because of internal opposition.

By contrast, for many Labour activists there was dismay and anger. Immediately Shadow Scottish Minister, John McAllion, MP for Dundee East (who had replaced me in 1987) resigned under demands from the Westminster leadership to toe the line. Further anger mounted when Tony Blair in London claimed that the English would be as entitled as the Scots to vote in a referendum 'because the result would have affected the whole of the UK'. It was as clear as ever it could be that the top ranks of the British Labour Party were still centralists and unionist to the core.

Prime Minister, John Major asked whether there would be a threshold – like the 40% rule that had derailed the last Scottish parliament plan in the seventies. Dennis Canavan, MP for Falkirk West spluttered: 'There is no need for a referendum' and warned that watering down the commitment to legislate within a year for the parliament to one of having a referendum would be "met with fierce resistance by the Scottish Labour Party and our supporters. (Press & Journal 27 June 96)

By 28 June (the following day), there was a storm of criticism within the Labour Party and open rebellion from Scottish MPs. Lord Ewing, a former devolution minister in the Scottish Office, resigned as Joint Convener of the Scottish Constitutional Convention after saying on television, 'The whole thing is a disgrace. I'm furious about it.' Campbell Christie, General

Secretary of the Scottish Trade Union Congress (STUC), a prime mover in the Convention was upset by the sudden turn-around.

An emergency Press Conference was held in Glasgow by four Shadow Cabinet MPs from Scotland, George Robertson (Shadow Scottish Secretary, Donald Dewar, Chief Whip, Gordon Brown (Shadow Chancellor) and Robin Cook (Shadow Foreign Secretary) to justify their decision. By all accounts it was an uncomfortable affair. Under the banner 'New Labour for a New Scotland', they reacted under stress. The Herald (28 June 1996) ran an article under two headings, 'The body language does not tell a lie' and 'They should all be included in the Olympic synchronised knuckle clenching team as they brazenly tried to claim that it was a Scottish initiative (despite Wales getting the same brush-off)'. Tony Blair flew into Edinburgh to quell the revolt (but not without being exposed to ridicule). There was a feeling of betrayal amongst Labour Party members in Scotland.   The papers had fun at this sudden and cynical u-turn.

So also did the SNP, the Conservatives and the Liberal Democrats. Within the SNP it cemented deep suspicions about the reliability of Scottish Labour on this issue when the Scottish Branch of the Labour Party had tamely accepted the abandonment of a simple pledge in the manifesto to deliver an Assembly. If this was in opposition, what courage would they show in government?

Recognising the need to obtain a full mandate to buttress wobbly Labour, the SNP fixed an immense target of £500,000 for the Election Fund. This compared with £130,000 for 1992. When the manifesto was drafted, it was based on a concept of liberal civic nationalism and carried the themes of prosperity, social justice, enterprise and compassion. The Conservatives were in a panic as the election approached. Braveheart, the film about the Scottish hero, William Wallace, had been launched on screen. Seemingly there was now much more appreciation in the minds of the electorate of the historical fight for freedom of the Scottish people.

In a desperate gesture, Michael Forsyth MP, the Scottish Secretary fired by Braveheart, or more likely dread, arranged for the repatriation of the Stone of Destiny on which Scottish and British monarchs had been crowned. The Stone, looted by Edward 1 during the Wars of Independence and kept in Westminster Abbey ever since, was ceremoniously escorted over the Border under military escort, taken to Edinburgh and installed in the Castle because Conservative support was ebbing and they had gained the reputation of being anti-Scottish. There was no sign that returning the Stone of Destiny added to Conservative support. Many SNP records relating to the preparations for the General Election are missing but it is undeniable that the Scottish National Party went into the fight better prepared and funded than ever before.

The outcome was a modest improvement in terms of seats won, 6 compared to 3, retention of Perth & Kinross by Roseanna Cunningham and the winning of Tayside North by John Swinney and Dumfries and Galloway by Alasdair Morgan. Alex Salmond (Banff & Buchan), Margaret Ewing (Moray) and Andrew Welsh (Angus) all retained their seats. The SNP share of the vote was 22.1% (marginally up) and the Liberal Democrats emerged with 11 seats on 13%. The main losers were the Conservatives who at 17.5% were whitewashed, losing all 11 of their MPs. Above all, and depressingly for the SNP, Labour had 56 MPs on 45.6% of the vote. Once again there was no breakthrough in central Scotland.

General Election - 1 May 1997

Party	Votes	Percentage	Seats
Labour	1,283,350	45.6%	56
Liberal Democrat	365,362	13%	10
SNP	621,550	22.1%	6
Conservative	493,059	17.5%	0
Others	53,427	0.8%	0

A Party overview put the best face on it. After commenting that the rise in support for Labour in Scotland was proportionately less than in England, it assessed:

"The broad conclusion taken from this result, from the evidence below and from conversations with voters was that the first priority for Scottish electors in May 1997 was to get rid of the Tory government. Electors believed that only a vote for Labour could achieve this result for the UK as a whole, and accordingly voted Labour for that reason. The overwhelming media coverage given to the UK election and to their particular argument seems to have been a persuasive factor, as was the repeated Labour assertion that only they could form a government.

Public reaction to the SNP since Election Day seems to indicate that the SNP has lost no credibility as a result of the high Labour vote, and that our increase in seats has provided a reason to believe that the SNP will remain an effective challenging force in Scottish politics. As the noise from the Labour victory dies down, it is probable that the SNP – with a positive and well presented campaign – can become a principled and much needed opposition to New Labour in Scotland and put together a coherent and consistent campaign designed to increase support at elections for a Scottish Parliament, which are likely to be held within two years."

Another experienced party hand put it more uncharitably – 'no strong message, no reply to the Tories out phenomenon, a poor campaign'!

Chapter 4:

ROAD TO DEVOLUTION

The formation of a Labour Government with a manifesto pledge to hold a two question referendum on the principle of having a Scottish Parliament with financial powers altered the whole scenario. So far, the SNP had made halting progress and the Conservatives had been obliterated. There was a new nationwide consensus that a Scottish Parliament was needed to protect Scotland from the worst excesses of a London Conservative Government. Even Labour, the traditional home UK centralised government had been hauled into support. They were now in Government.

After the record of the UK Labour leadership imposing a referendum as a last desperate attempt to impede progress of a Parliament Bill, the SNP was again suspicious. While Scottish Labour membership was now largely aboard, the power lay in London. No one could be sure where the next blockage would occur. Would there be parliamentary time wasting (despite the pledges) or would there be another 40% barrier? Who could tell? Both had been used successfully in the 1979 devolution referendum.

The SNP was wary. And after the Labour U-turn on the referendum in the previous year, this was more than understandable. It would wait until the Labour position became clear. In July, the NEC had given approval to a National Council proposition that the SNP would not be drawn into declaring its position on Labour's proposals for a referendum on devolution. Yet another post election review took place while the Party awaited events. In this review there was awareness, expressed through Alex Neil that we were still not breaking into Labour heartlands.

Playing for time, Alex Salmond confirmed that no response would be made on the devolution referendum until the White Paper was published by the incoming Labour Government. Under the title, 'Scotland's Parliament', this appeared in late July. With its publication, the NEC resolved to forward a resolution to National Council that the SNP would campaign for a YES/YES vote in the devolution referendum and that while the Party would have its own distinctive campaign to its voters and the many others who backed independence, the NEC should take it as an instruction to work with the campaign group Scotland Forward in order to positively affect the outcome. (NEC97/61)

This decision marked my departure as an influence on the Party. Almost alone, I did not share the belief that devolution would automatically lead to independence. It had always been my view that the SNP should be the path-breaker, 'riding point' as the Americans put it, to advance public opinion by stating the arguments for independence and to consolidate that position when fear of electoral defeat forced the other parties to join a bandwagon that would impel Scotland towards its national freedom. By contrast the new strategy was based on a consensus that the devolved Scottish Parliament would progress gradually by good government until the demand for more powers tipped the balance towards the full status of independence. Both cases were arguable – the difference being that the SNP was locked into the gradualist route.

I did not move against the NEC resolution as that would have been futile but took care to have my dissent recorded. I also made my views known in an article to the Scotsman leading to a phone call from my former protégé, John Swinney in which he expressed regret that my long years of service would now be over. As ever, John made his points gracefully and regretfully but the message was clear. I was in the cold. It was not unexpected. Independent views were frowned upon under the prevailing orthodoxy. Discipline is important but not at the expense of freedom of thought or speech. To retain that freedom, I accepted the price and, faced with the SNP sending me to Coventry, I went the whole hog and booked a holiday in Siberia (a more suitable destination for a nationalist 'revolutionary')!

And so matters progressed. The National Council met urgently in August. The NEC resolution was placed before it in these terms

> "National Council re-iterates standing policy that gives primacy to the independence campaign, but which will not seek to obstruct devolution, In that context National Council resolves that the Scottish National Party will campaign for a "YES/YES" vote in the referendum on September 11th and instructs the NEC to organise and run a distinctive SNP Campaign designed to mobilise the support of more than 620,000 people who voted SNP on 1 May and the many others who back independence. Council further instructs the

NEC to work with 'Scotland Forward' in order to strengthen the positive turnout for the referendum."

Moved by Alex Salmond himself and formally seconded by Alasdair Morgan, the resolution went through with thunderous approval. My contribution was to warn the Party that the way ahead was not as straightforward as appeared and that there could be danger of a rift in years to come if the gradualist strategy did not work out. I was also struck by the ambition of many delegates who wished to have a career in the devolved parliament now that the proposed party list system of proportional representation made this a realistic proposition.

From now on, all the attention was directed to the referendum campaign. With polling day scheduled for 11 September, a balanced team of George Reid, Alex Neil and Kay Ullrich was appointed to the board of Scotland Forward and £25,000 was allocated to the SNP campaign. It was a small sum but the Party had an overdraft that had grown to £147,000. Unlike the previous referendum of 1979, Labour and the Liberal Democrats were on side. The No campaign was correspondingly weak.

This time the Conservatives were isolated and desperately unpopular. Their political credibility had been shot to ribbons with the loss of all their Scottish MPs. Also their negative campaign of fear-mongering and bad news did not strike home. The sight of Donald Dewar, Secretary of State for Scotland, Jim Wallace, leader of the Scottish Liberal Democrats and Alex Salmond for the SNP sharing a united platform told its own story and incidentally, gave Alex Salmond and the SNP improved credibility. Likewise, the SNP persuaded their talisman Scottish film star Sean Connery to appear with the other leaders at a joint devolution event. Sean Connery's reward for his services was to be blocked for a knighthood by Labour!

The one-sided nature of the campaign was manifest in the result:

	% Yes	% No
For a Scottish Parliament	74.3	25.7
For tax varying powers	63.5	36.5

It was a revolution. How else could one describe Scotland expelling all its Conservative MPs and voting decisively for a Scottish Parliament – and with controversial tax raising powers too all in one year!

It also had the effect of giving the SNP an elevated prominence and status as a consequence of its joint identification with Labour during the referendum campaign. The questions were how would that translate into support for the main goal of independence now that a devolved Parliament had been secured and when?

Within the Party, the mood was bullish. It may not have been independence but for most delegates at the Annual Conference after the referendum there was both joy and satisfaction. Unlike, the last referendum in 1979 when a small Yes majority had been disregarded, there was no way the reluctant British Labour Prime Minister, Tony Blair could delay the passing of the Bill in the face of such majorities without causing mayhem within the Scottish Labour Party.

The by-election in Paisley South in November following the death of Labour MP Gordon McMaster produced a douche of cold water. Whatever, the impact of the referendum, the SNP had still to surmount the formidable Labour fortresses in central Scotland, for Westminster at least. In the event, the SNP candidate Ian Blackford achieved a meritorious swing of 11% from Labour while the Labour candidate, Douglas Alexander galloped home with a majority of 2,731.

Paisley South By-election - 6 November 1997

Party	Votes	Percentage
Labour	10,346	44.1%
SNP	7,615	32.5%
Liberal Democrat	2,582	11%
Conservative	1,643	7%
ProLife Alliance	578	2.5%
Scottish Socialist	306	1.3%
Turnout		42.9%

There were three other candidates with no individual vote exceeding 200.

Paisley South was a Westminster by-election where the SNP had again to argue its relevance in the British political system. It was soon apparent that a different pattern would emerge in relation to the Party's results in the forthcoming Scottish Parliament elections – and beyond!

In his book, SNP – The History of the Scottish National Party (2002), Peter Lynch recounted:

> "For example, from March 1998 until March 1999 the SNP found itself in an unprecedented position in opinion polls in Scotland. In February 1998, System 3 placed the SNP on 33% of the vote in its poll for the Scottish Parliament elections, with Labour on 44%. However, after this date, the polls moved strongly in the direction of the Nationalists. For a whole year, the SNP was either neck-and-neck with Labour in opinion polls for the Scottish Parliament or substantially ahead of Labour. In July 1998 System 3 found the SNP had the support of 45% per cent on the first vote for the Scottish Parliament compared to only 37% for Labour. On the second vote, the SNP led by 43% to 32% (Hassan and Lynch 2001 p387). It was only in April 1999 that support for the SNP fell away and Labour's comfortable lead was restored. Meanwhile, a series of new polls on independence, which asked whether people would vote Yes or No at an independence referendum, indicated new levels of support for independence which made it the majority preference in many polls." (Lynch p224)

The new sense of purpose within the SNP did not detract from its ability to play cat and mouse with the leadership – on questions of principle, of course. Conference considered a resolution calling for a referendum to establish the position of the monarch after independence. Alex Salmond advised Conference to support an amendment that the resolution be referred to the National Executive (for a customary decent burial). Conference was having none of it. The amendment was defeated by 177 votes to 166. But the leadership took comfort from a further amendment carried by 208 votes to 153 which deleted a requirement that the Party 'campaign' on the issue.

Two other significant events occurred. After the Scotland Act and the referendum, a number of business people felt the economic powers of the new Scottish Parliament were not enough. Much of the dialogue in the business community at the time had been limited to the status quo and what would happen with the new Parliament. A group of business people, chaired by Dennis McLeod decided to form Business for Scotland to create an environment to broaden the debate and challenge the then thinking around economic and fiscal structures appropriate for the Scottish economy. Other Board members included James Scott, a former senior civil servant, Jim Mather, later an MSP and Government Minister, David McCarthy and Jim Ross

Samantha Barber, an experienced legislative assistant to the SNP in the European Parliament was appointed Chief Executive. She described the aims in an email to the author on 10 September 2013:

> "The purpose was to engage a broad spectrum of business views and through the Business Insider magazine publish inserts which provided a forum for discussion across the business spectrum. Alex Salmond, John Swinney and Jim Mather were regular guests at business lunches and events where the emphasis was very much on the politicians listening to the views within business on the challenges and opportunities for the Scottish economy.

> This was the era of the large set business dinners hosted by each of the three UK political parties charging £2,000 per table. In 1999, Business for Scotland decided to hold a similar event with Alex Salmond speaking as leader of the SNP. Contrary to many predictions there was a turnout of nearly 300 people; companies did buy tables and brought along their guests."

And possibly as part of that campaign, Alex Salmond announced a couple of months later in a speech to the European Movement that the SNP supported an independent Scotland joining the euro (while not mentioning that Conference required a prior referendum).

1998 was a year that saw substantial activity within the Party to prepare for the 1999 Scottish Parliament elections. There was a cascade of applications for approval as Scottish Parliament candidates. Successful members had to be trained in the arts of fighting elections as well as given a sound background knowledge of party policy. The leadership embarked on a round of regional symposia to look at fresh ideas and then to process the policy content through the Party's policy making National Assembly for consideration in the Manifesto. Indeed there was so much material that one wag observed there was enough for three Manifestos. For candidates seeking to be selected for a constituency to be elected 'first past the post', there was the need to go through the time-honoured procedures of selection. Additionally, they and others could be nominated under the party list system of proportional representation and lobby for a high ranking without which, in most circumstances, they would not be elected.

At the same time, the Executive had other worries - money to fight the election. At February 1998, the overdraft had stood at £200,000, giving little scope for mounting a substantial campaign in 1999. Party HQ at North Charlotte Street, Edinburgh which had been on the market for some time stubbornly refused to sell. And Nicola Sturgeon, Executive Vice Convener for Publicity presented a strategy review setting out objectives and tactics such as 'building confidence, maintaining the momentum, stating the case for independence, attacking Labour and probably the most important, presenting the Party as a responsible government.

As the opinion polls showed, the SNP was set fair for the election and even the weak element of election finance was being dealt with by an intensive fundraising campaign which, buoyed by the ratings and the prospect of the SNP being in government, would have a first class chance of raising the money needed. Even before the outcome, the SNP was spending heavily, employing an economist, refurbishing Headquarters, engaging two student assistants or 'gofers' as they were charmingly called, two field assistants and one campaign assistant, and generally putting the national capability on a war footing, including an IT package for telephone canvassing at a cost of £50,000.

Yet, amongst the experienced leadership, there was always a note of caution. Alex Salmond warned that a full onslaught from the Labour Party could be expected and called on people to be calm. (NEC 98/79). The SNP was conscious that this could be a moment of destiny for Scotland. With the novelty of a first Scottish oriented election, there was intense interest amongst the public. Nor was it only in Scotland. Dr Winnie Ewing MEP reported that this interest was widespread in the European Parliament. Also in August, Director of Research, Kevin Pringle informed the NEC that Labour were scrutinising our people rather than our policies so NEC members should be aware of this, and presumably take care over what they said and did.

Executive Vice Convener for Organisation Adam Ingram advised that 27 Constituency Associations had an electoral data base with canvassing results and that there were some 55 call centres in operation. The Director of Organisation reported that membership enquiries were running at 200 a week. Most encouragingly, there were expectations fund-raising would bring in around £450,000 for the election fund.

There were embarrassments, too. The Party failed to make an official return to the Neill Enquiry into Party Funding, leading to bad publicity and a dispute between the National Treasurer, Kenny MacAskill and the Chief Executive, Michael Russell as to who was responsible. This became so vituperative that National Council had to introduce an internal Code of Conduct.

Just as things were looking up, the SNP suffered a major blow in the loss of its Senior Vice Convener and deputy leader, Allan Macartney through a sudden heart attack on 25 August 1998. Allan was a multiple linguist and political scientist. After eight years in Africa as a university lecturer, Allan Macartney had re-entered SNP politics on his return. Along with Professor Neil MacCormick, he represented the academic community within the SNP. Allan had been elected Senior Vice Convener in 1992 and MEP for North East Scotland in 1994. At the time of his death, he was serving as Rector of the University of Aberdeen.

As Senior Vice Convener, he had been instrumental in assembling a group of academics and others who produced a major work, 'Transition to Independence' which was intended to be the handbook to be followed by the SNP in dealing with the political and constitutional problems emerging in an independence referendum. His death at the height of his powers was a real loss to the Party as he was widely respected in Europe, academia and in the field of Scottish politics generally. Witty and amusing, he was good at keeping people on track and was a complementary balance to the Party leader.

John Swinney was elected Senior Vice Convener in Allan's place and in the subsequent European by-election, Ian Hudghton successfully held the North East seat with an increased majority.

North East Scotland European By-election - November 1998

Party	Votes	Percentage
SNP	57,445	48%
Conservative	23,774	19.9%
Labour	22,086	18.5%
Lib/Democrat	11,753	9.8%
Scottish Socialist	2,510	2.1%
Scottish Green	2,067	1.7%
Turnout		20.5%

By now the plans for the first Scottish election were fully in place with John Swinney as Senior Vice Chairman and Alex Neil in the NEC in charge of the Manifesto. The Party was aiming for government, given the good opinion polls both for the Party and independence. To make progress towards independence, George Reid presented a paper on citizenship and Colin Campbell one on defence issues. The year concluded with a public debate between the Secretary of State, Donald Dewar and Alex Salmond for the SNP and the stage was ready for the election. Salmond acquitted himself well without the dominance of earlier performances. Donald Dewar began moving up the popularity rankings as Alex's support declined.

For the first time the SNP introduced a new debating procedure for the Annual Conference. Whereas before, the Conference - whose agenda was controlled by a powerful Standing Orders and Agenda Committee (SOAC) - received and debated resolutions from branches, constituency associations and others, including statements originating from the Party leadership, now debates were structured along themes with public presentation firmly in mind. While new policies were under preparation senior journalist Magnus Linklater (Scotland on Sunday 7 June 98) found the June Conference rather empty of content.

Under the headline, 'Nationalism's heartland is just an ideological wasteland' despite having been assured of the watchwords of 'enterprise, compassion and democracy' by party officials, he commented:

"I searched in vain for evidence of it in Perth. If this is indeed a new model party no one had informed the delegates. One might have thought that after a whole general election campaign, a referendum and now the prospect of a Scottish parliament, the SNP would be bulging with ideas, pamphlets exploring the new philosophy, booklets setting out the way ahead, festschrifts on Europe, leaflets with titles like "Towards a New Scotland", contributions from policy units looking at the prospects for a small country in the global community. There are none." And then prophetically,

"It is, in short, a party without an ideology. Much has been made in recent weeks, about the grim prospects that Labour faces in clawing back its support. I believe it is the SNP that faces the real challenge. Unless it can demonstrate some coherence before next May, some genuine vision and some hard-nosed reality, then its mid-term support will melt away, as it has done so often in the past. Even the good folk of Perth may wonder what it is that they have let themselves in for."

By now the election campaign had effectively moved out of the control of the National Executive Committee as the key players took charge. The background was not encouraging. The Party's standing had declined from the heights of the previous year and momentum had been lost. Of course, Magnus Linklater was correct. On many issues the Party gave a hollow ring. The earlier success of the SNP had rung warning bells with New Labour in London and with the aid of the media in which it had a dominant influence, it launched negative attack after attack on the SNP and separation.

Oddly, the SNP did not respond effectively. It naively thought that it was protected by its high standing in the polls. The only way it could have attempted to sustain its position, admittedly no easy task given its limited media fire-power, was to have embarked on a counter campaign against the Union so that the message of the cost and problems of 'divorce' and 'separation' would have been counter-acted by a message of the benefits of independence.

Instead there was the very strange sight of the SNP putting forward its policies for devolution (Labour's field), as relevant to the powers of the devolved Scottish Parliament while Labour majored negatively on independence (the territory of the SNP!).

Journalists commented then and later that Alex Salmond was not on form, seemingly listless and lacking in dynamism. Some of his associates such as 'John Swinney and Roseanna Cunningham commented that he was tired, off-form or exhausted (Torrance: Salmond: Against the Odds, p184). Whether that came from over-work, a back problem or a virus that was difficult to shake off as variously suggested is immaterial. By now Alex Salmond had become the dominating figure within the SNP and only his decisions counted. I recall being at one of the planning meetings called for a Sunday to set the themes of the campaign. Alex was nearly an hour late. The meeting had reached agreement on most of the policy and campaign issues. When Alex arrived, these proposals were abandoned and he dictated what he thought should take place. And so it was that, ultimately and away from the meeting, out of the 10 listed election priorities of the SNP, independence was relegated to last place.

By March, the writing was on the wall. Labour were stretching ahead There was confusion and a lack of morale amongst SNP supporters. The campaign was increasingly negative and the Party was isolated. So against that background, two risky decisions were made. The first was to present an emergency resolution to the spring pre-election Conference in Aberdeen. Earlier in the UK budget, Gordon Brown as the Chancellor of the Exchequer had offered a 1p reduction in the rate of income tax. The leadership took the gamble to follow a different and controversial path by presenting an emergency resolution moved by Deputy Leader, John Swinney and seconded by Andrew Wilson, the Treasury Spokesman:

> "Conference pledges not to increase the basic rate of income tax in the first four year term of the parliament. The Scottish National Party is committed to ending the crisis in our public services. We reject the cynical penny bribe offered by New Labour and commit ourselves to freeze the basic rate at 23p in the pound, pledging to spend the £690 million revenue that is released on health, education and housing in Scotland."

The resolution was disingenuous. A penny not reduced from a tax bill is a penny increased. Notwithstanding that, with the resolution having the support of the Party generals, no rank and file member would be likely to step out of line in the face of a forthcoming election battle. Only Margo MacDonald with her acute political intuition and long experience was willing to stand up and express reservations. She considered the 'penny' as the equivalent of dumping a mine into the election campaign. And so it proved. Not even a catchy presentation of 'A Penny for Scotland' could save the SNP from a tirade of invective, criticism and insult that was hurled from all quarters, from the left, from business, from the centre and all amplified by coverage from a hostile media.

Unwittingly, the SNP fell into a trap. The Government offered a special party broadcast to the Leaders of Plaid Cymru and the SNP to allow them to make their position known on the NATO bombing of Serbia. The leader of Plaid Cymru made a non-controversial response. Not so Alex Salmond. He accused Prime Minister, Tony Blair and his allies of pursuing a 'policy of dubious legality and unpardonable folly'. He called for a humanitarian aid effort and a full scale economic blockade of Serbia under UN control.

This fired off a full scale onslaught on him masterminded by 10 Downing Street. He was, said Foreign Secretary, Robin Cook, 'the toast of Belgrade'. The ill-judged choice of words proved to be damaging. Alex Salmond was correct. The NATO action was illegal under international law and although the bombing succeeded in ejecting Serb forces from Kosovo, it is an undeniable truth that Serb civilians were then ethnically cleared from Kosovo. Nothing is simple in the Balkans!

In an email to Mike Russell, I expressed reservations; stressing that Salmond's broadcast should have concentrated more on the refugee problem. "By taking a strong line on the penny tax and Kosovo, the Party has taken the initiative and rescued us from a period when we were taking punishment. But be careful of the rest of the Campaign or we could end up with another 1992 when the electorate took fright and left us with an outcome that was less than rosy' (Torrance, Salmond etc, p182). By 22 April, the SNP trailed Labour by 20 points.

In a reaction to the continuing barrage of vicious publicity, the SNP abandoned its scheduled Press Conferences and launched into a barn-storming street campaign, with its own newspaper, led by a rejuvenated Alex Salmond. This culminated in a major rally attended by Sean Connery but even this was eclipsed by publication of the SNP's Economic Policy for Independence where the presentation was messy and less than authoritative.

The SNP always had a safety net – the system of proportional representation under a Party List system which gave electors two votes – one for a constituency MSP and the other for Party representative. Exactly so as it proved. Constituency results were disappointing. Only seven were won, the new one being Inverness, Nairn & Lochaber with Fergus Ewing. Not much better than in 1997. But 28 list seats were won by proportional representation. Although Labour with 56 seats outnumbered the SNP, for the first time the SNP had a powerful parliamentary presence. The SNP would never be the same again.

Scottish Parliament General Election - 6 May 1999

Party	Constituency	%	Seats	Region	%	Seats	Total
Labour	908,392	38.8	53	786,818	33.6	3	56
SNP	672,757	28.7	7	638,644	27.3	28	35
Conservatives	364,225	15.6	0	359,109	15.4	18	18
Lib Democrats	331,279	14.1	12	225,774	12.4	5	17
Scottish Green				4,024	3.6	1	1
Socialist Labour	5,268	0.2	0	55,232	2.4	0	0
Scottish Socialist	23,564	1.0	0	46,635	2	1	1
Independent	18,511	0.8	1	27,700	1.2	0	1
Turnout							59.1%

Immediately after the election, the National Executive reorganised the Party at Headquarters level (NEC99/50). Its decisions were far reaching.

Research, publicity and by implication, political functions hitherto performed at Headquarters were to gravitate to staff at the Parliament working for the MSP Group, leaving administration, finance and organisation at HQ. The transfer recognised that these duties were for parliamentary and not party purposes In so far as HQ represented the membership, it was now effectively headless. It also reduced the authority of the National Executive Committee. The balance had swung. The SNP was now fully a parliamentary party just like the others in the UK.

The influence now enjoyed by the parliamentarians, especially those in the Scottish Parliament, is shown in the list of SNP Shadow Cabinet members (in the following chapter) appointed to oppose the Labour/ Liberal Democrat Coalition Ministers in the Scottish Executive. The portfolios were filled from MSPs, MPs and MEPs. There was no room for non-elected NEC members.

Leading figures were members of both the Scottish Parliament and the NEC. And, of course some of the MSPs were also Members of the Westminster Parliament. Important decisions could still be taken at the NEC and non-MSPs had a say in considering strategy and tactics. Nevertheless, there could be long term consequences from this transfer of political power. In the immediate aftermath of the election, all the MSPs were deemed to be members of the National Council without much reverence for the constitution. There were good political reasons for this integration but it had the effect of potentially diluting the representation of delegates from branches, constituency associations and other affiliated bodies. In all the history of the Party to date, it was the National Council meeting three or four times a year which was the link between the members and the leadership. A wise leadership would be sure to consult it before embarking on controversial matters.

Normally it was the vehicle by which the Party could launch campaigns and approve policy. Occasionally, but no less importantly, it provided a forum for bringing office bearers to account since they, and the NEC, were required to present written reports for approval.

There was a Council election held on the same day as that for the Scottish Parliament and the results were overshadowed by it. A direct comparison with 1995 was not possible since there had been considerable changes in wards. Nevertheless although the SNP saw a rise in the number of councillors and in votes, two of its councils (Moray and Perth and Kinross) passed from SNP control to no overall control. The Labour vote dropped heavily and the Liberal Democrats did well.

Council Election - May 1999

Party	Votes	Percentage	Councillors
Labour	829,921	36.6%	550
SNP	655,299	28,7%	204
Liberal Democrat	289,236	12.7%	156
Conservative	308,170	13.5%	108
Independent	172,297	7.5%	191
Others	30,342	1%	9
Turnout			59.1%

Chapter 5:

THE OFFICIAL OPPOSITION

The SNP now had 35 MSPs, 6 MPs and 2MEPs. By any interpretation it had acquired a huge political presence. But it was not the Government. When the Parliament met for the first time on 12 May 1999, Winnie Ewing MSP acting president by dint of being the mother of the house, declared in stirring words:

"The Scottish Parliament which adjourned
on the 25th day of March in the year 1707
is hereby reconvened."

The Parliament met to choose a First Minister as a preliminary step to forming a working Scottish Executive Ministerial team. Labour were the largest party and having formed a coalition with the Liberal Democrats, were in the driving seat. After a contest between Donald Dewar for Labour and Alex Salmond for the SNP, Dewar emerged an easy winner, leaving the SNP as the official opposition with few of the public funds and other resources open to the main opposition at Westminster.

But also for the first time, the Scottish Cabinet which Salmond had striven against internal opposition to make functional now had a reality as the spokesmen had a direct role in facing the Scottish Ministers in the Parliament so selection was coveted.

Shadow Cabinet 1999

Scottish Parliament Matters

First Minister, Constitution & External Affairs	Alex Salmond MSP
Deputy Leader, & Enterprise & Lifelong Learning	John Swinney MSP
Justice, Equality & land Reform	Roseanna Cunningham MSP

Children & Education	Nicola Sturgeon MSP
Finance	Andrew Wilson MSP
Health & Community Care	Kay Ullrich MSP
Rural Affairs	Alasdair Morgan MSP
Housing & Social Justice	Fiona Hyslop MSP
Local Government	Kenneth Gibson MSP
Transport & the Environment	Kenny MacAskill MSP
Business Manager, Culture, Broadcasting & Gaelic	Michael Russell MSP
Chief Whip	Bruce Crawford MSP

Reserved Matters

Defence	Colin Campbell MSP
Social Security	Alex Neil MSP
Europe	Ian Hudghton MEP

Margaret Ewing MSP was Group Leader. Shona Robison became Group Secretary. George Reid was elected Deputy Presiding Office while Andrew Welsh drew a short straw when he was appointed to the Parliament's Corporate Body overseeing not only the start-up of the Parliament but the erection of the new building. The line up left very many MSPs on the backbenches, not all with political experience. As always with a landslide, some interesting personalities would be thrown into the arena. And there was certainly no political role for Party officebearers who were not a member of any of the three parliaments.

While the Parliament was settling in and would in any event rise for the summer recess some six weeks later, the aftermath of the election campaign and the subsequent reorganisation of functions had to proceed. And more importantly, the SNP faced a European election in June 1999. As one who was fourth on the all-Scotland proportional list and stood no chance of election, I was happy to be a nominal candidate seconded to the former Mid Scotland & Fife Euro Constituency going round on tours in warm

June sunshine with my wife, Edith, in a campaign efficiently organised by my agent, Ruth Marr. No one in the SNP, and I suspect in the other Parties as well, was all that interested. The real contest had been for the Scottish Parliament. Europe is usually low key with poor turn-outs but this one was distinctly more than usually languorous and laid back. The SNP should have won three seats (the two won went to Ian Hudghton, a sitting member who had succeeded Allan Macartney and Prof Neil MacCormick). As for myself, I had the irrelevant satisfaction of being top of the ballot in Mid-Scotland & Fife which was good for the ego if nothing else since I was not elected! Unfortunately, with 27.2% the Party lost on minute calculations within a complex system to Labour 3 seats, (28.7%), another seat to the Conservatives who had 2 (19.8%) and the Liberal Democrats with 1. Under the old constituency system, the SNP would have won 3!

But it also looked as if the SNP might have cracked the problem of winning Westminster by-elections where the batting average was one every ten years. In September 1999, following the elevation of George Robertson Labour MP for Hamilton South to be Secretary General to NATO, the Party with Annabelle Ewing as Candidate came very close to winning – just 556 votes short with a swing of 22%.

Hamilton South By-Election (Westminster)
- 23 September 1999

Party	Votes	Percentage
Labour	7,172	36.9%
SNP	6,616	34%
Scottish Socialist	1,847	9.5%
Conservative	1,406	7.2%
Independent	1,075	5.5%
Liberal Democrat	634	3.3%
ProLife Alliance	257	1.3%
Socialist Labour	238	1.2%
Others (4)	209	
Turnout		41.3%

Of all the problems facing the SNP, the most grievous was finance. The election had overstrained the finances which were rarely far from precarious as a general rule and the debt was over £429,000. This was eventually reduced substantially with the sale of the Party Headquarters at 6 North Charlotte Street, Edinburgh at a price of £260,000 and a major contribution of loans from Party members. Running costs were helped by a move to cheaper, rented accommodation at McDonald Road. Some of the expenditure on the election was controversial and this would lead to an unusual and bitter falling out between the National Treasurer, Ian Blackford and National Convener, Alex Salmond. There was no doubt under the direction of Alex Salmond and Michael Russell there had been a horrendous overspend, particularly on the production of editions of the campaign newspaper estimated at £200,000 by Ian Blackford who claimed that they had panicked as the polls turned nasty. The paper had been a desperate attempt to free the campaign of vicious coverage from the news media that were bitterly hostile.

With the election over, Blackford tried to take control of costs from the Chief Executive. In a messy fight over the Convener's huge taxi costs, the issues moved from the bitterly personal to political as Blackford was deemed by the leadership to be an associate of the fundamentalist grouping involving Alex's opponent, Jim Sillars with the whole feud likely to drag on into the new year (Torrance: Salmond etc, p193)

Before the row Alex Salmond had summed up the outcome of the election and the overall political position at a meeting of the National Council on 19 June 1999 by stating that we should now seek to build on a platform of being the official opposition to secure future successes. The Scottish Parliamentary Group was one of outstanding calibre. We had more than doubled the electoral representation of the Party in all of our 70 years of history in one night.

Despite this, some tension remained and an attempt was made at the December meeting to stipulate that no sitting member of the Scottish Parliament should be eligible for election to Westminster. This was defeated on a motion to remit back by 68 votes to 56, indicative of a rather low voting attendance.(NC99/29).

The Party should have been content. It had emerged as a real political force but the thunderclouds were gathering on a broad front. There was growing frustration with the Scottish Parliament where the SNP, despite its numerical strength, was being brushed aside by the Labour/Liberal Democrat Coalition. The Coalition had used its majority to push through its programme with little or no consultation. Those in civic Scotland who had wanted the parliament to be more consensual than Westminster were disappointed. There was disquiet about the location and design of the new building while the Church of Scotland General Assembly hall serving as a temporary home had inadequate office facilities. More surprisingly, Alex Salmond did not seem to have adapted well to the new procedures quite unlike the formalities of Westminster and was regarded by the media as ineffective - the last thing that party members would have expected. Likewise, the fact that the SNP was locked out of government by a Unionist majority was sowing seeds of doubt amongst the faithful as to whether a devolved parliament could ever deliver independence.

After a joint meeting of the National Executive and the Shadow Cabinet in December, there were rumours that an attempt would be made to alter the strategy of the Party to win independence. The intention was to rely principally on securing a majority in the Scottish Parliament to promote a pre-legislative referendum. There was to be a lessening role for Westminster elections or MPs. It was no surprise when a row broke out in early January 2000. I set the ball rolling with an article in The Sunday Times (9 January 2000) when I questioned the impact a regional Parliament had on the Party's cutting edge. It was, I wrote, no longer radical – and added:

> "In many respects it (the SNP) is undergoing a modernisation process alarmingly similar to that of new Labour. Worse, is it becoming a regional party like the Catalans? There is a very narrow gap in the European context between a post-nationalist party and a regional one." And "The grassroots membership was not happy to see national freedom relegated to 10th place in the Scottish parliament election. Independence will not fall into our hands like a ripe plum. It must be worked for unceasingly and promoted as the solution to economic and social problems controlled from London." I then argued: "If the SNP restricts its mandate to winning power in Holyrood, where does that leave it in the forthcoming Westminster election? It is canvassed at high levels that the SNP should fight for its independence mandate only in Scottish elections and leave the campaign for Westminster to protest issues and the transfer of more

power to Holyrood. This would leave our Westminster candidates politically naked at the hustings and imply that we had written independence out of the script for a major election. I can see the headlines: 'SNP puts independence on the back burner'.

I must have had the gift of prophecy or had induced the outcome for the very next day; the Daily Record (10 September 2000) under the banner headline of 'Salmond Bids to Dump Independence Pledge' launched a critical report with quotes from unnamed sources vehemently attacking the proposal. The ensuing hard-hitting editorial was partly counterbalanced by a more positive critique from the paper's respected senior journalist Tom Brown who was of the view that a halfway house solution with more powers to come could lead to the UK withering on the vine.

Not to be left out, Iain MacWhirter one of the more reflective political journalists, made the provocative response (Herald 12 January 2000) that Home Secretary Jack Straw and I had much in common – potentially leaving him open to a defamatory suit from each of us! The reason? Apparently, we shared a redundant concept of nationalism. His use of phrase was admirable. "But each in their own way is stuck in a time warp."   More interestingly MacWhirter summed up his own opinions:

> "But the idea of establishing a separate Scottish nation state, complete with armed forces, independent currency, a Scottish exchequer, social security systems etc is a non-starter. People do not go in for revolutions these days- and they got a bad name during the last century. Anyway, the days are long gone since nations could exert anything approximating to absolute control over their economic and strategic destinies". He concluded:

> "However there is a real debate going on in the SNP about the nature of independence and nationalism. And it is important for the country to consider what powers the Scottish Parliament needs to reflect the democratic wishes of the new Scotland. Unfortunately this cannot take place openly without it being interpreted as an assault on Alex Salmond's leadership."

The debate should have petered out at this stage despite strong feelings on all sides. Nevertheless, the joint meeting had resolved to take the issue for decision to the March meeting of National Council. The proposal from Party leaders was essentially that election to the Scottish Parliament should be on the basis of devolved policies rather than seeking a direct mandate for independence. That mandate was to be secured by a referendum.

Although lip service was still paid to election of a majority of MPs to Westminster, the emphasis was to concentrate on Edinburgh elections, form a government probably by coalition rather than with a majority (given the system of election by proportional representation), hold a referendum and let the people decide. The opposition perceived this as a step back from concentration on the policy of independence, the imposition of a dual trigger instead of one and/or a tactical blunder to diminish the Westminster route.

As Senior Vice Convener, John Swinney tabled a report to National Council in March 2000 explaining that the Party through the NEC had conducted a review of its political and electoral strategy, enabled by a debate at the 1999 Conference and 11 meetings around the country attended by 600 members. From these had emerged confirmation of the position adopted during three General Elections buttressed by the work of the late Dr. Allan Macartney whose group had published the substantial report Transition to Independence, namely that the mandate for independence would be through a referendum stemming from the Scottish parliament or an election of a majority of SNP MPs at Westminster.

The Resolution (NC00/06) was proposed by John Swinney on behalf of the National Executive Committee and ran:

> "Council asserts that Scotland is in process of becoming an independent country, that our goal of national independence can be reached within a given timescale and that this will be achieved when the people of Scotland vote for independence in a referendum. This referendum, which will be conducted by the Scottish Parliament, will be triggered either by an SNP Administration in the Scottish parliament or the election of a majority of SNP MPs at a Westminster election.
>
> Council calls for the establishment of detailed political, organisational and financial plans and targets at both constituency and national level to ensure we succeed in our

campaign to win Independence as quickly as possible and certainly within the next term of the Scottish Parliament.

Recognising the key place of the Westminster elections in the independence campaign, Council determines that the political strategy for the Westminster elections will be based on the need to –

- Campaign for Scottish Independence on the vision of a prosperous and socially just Scotland that will play a positive role in Europe and the family of nations.

- Seek to expand the powers of the Scottish Parliament in crucial areas such as finance, broadcasting, European and international relations and social security matters.

- Further all Scottish interests through the election of more SNP MPs.

There were two amendments:

The first moved by myself, and opposed by Nicola Sturgeon, allowed the mandate (without a referendum) to be secured if the Party obtained a majority of votes in either a Scottish or Westminster election and the second moved by Calum Miller (and opposed by Stewart Stevenson) called for a general strategy through Westminster or Holyrood providing a mandate to negotiate for independence on an outcome of the Party securing a majority of votes with the agreed settlement being placed before the Scottish people in a referendum for their approval. Both amendments were overwhelmingly defeated.

The atmosphere at National Council was tense – almost brittle. There were strained acknowledgements between the different camps, even involving those who were affable by nature. Everyone knew that this was 'make or break' in the ongoing strategic debate amongst those who were gradualists and saw the Scottish Parliament as the only route towards ultimate self-government and prepared to work within the system and the nationalists who placed securing independence as the prime aim. Others like myself while dubious about the homeopathic dilution of objectives in the long term were willing to keep both options open but with more weight being placed on independence than the benefits of good government.

The debate itself was long and passionate with substantial contributions from the party leadership, including Alex Salmond and my predecessor as Chairman, Billy Wolfe. The main opposition came through a motion to remit back moved by Margo MacDonald rather than through the direct negative although the negative was also moved. The preponderance of speakers in a fair debate lay with the leadership but such was the passion that the outcome always seemed in doubt.

At voting, the motion to remit back secured 149 votes to 112 and the resolution carried by 158 votes to 63. Too little attention has been paid by commentators and academics to this debate and the outcome. It effectively sealed a victory by the gradualists within the Party on a question of strategy which had vexed the SNP from its formation onwards. Whatever the reason, the Scottish National Party had a clear strategy in which the leadership ensconced in the Scottish Parliament held the commanding position. Of course, things are never black and white in politics and Party leaders would continue to make strongly assertive statements in support of independence; and few have doubted that they were sincere in those beliefs - although not all were convinced by its prioritisation in the timetable. It was a debate on essentials and not even my cynical remark that 'referendums were useful things as tactics but let's not put too much faith in them' carried much weight.

Alex Salmond observed later in his address as National Convener that the morning's debate showed how close the Party was to achieving independence. The Party, he said, would work to produce a new statement of policy 'Scotland We Seek' with a great vision and aims for independence, and added:

> "The Party must be aware that Independence will not be judged solely on its merits but also on the perception of the Party in the public's mind."

So having disposed of one thorny problem on strategy, in the afternoon Council moved on to have a wide debate on the controversial issue of whether the MSPs should support the bar on teaching about homosexuality in schools (section 2A) being removed. Although there were many speakers, mostly in favour, the matter proved less contentious and the motion favouring abolition passed by an overwhelming majority.(NC00/09)

But while great matters of state were being decided, there was a bitter row brewing. National Treasurer, Ian Blackford reported that the Party overdraft was £419,672. He presented a financial plan that was agreed unanimously. So far so good, but shortly after at the next meeting of the National Executive, and in the absence of Blackford, Alex Salmond moved a motion of no confidence in him on the twin bases of his competence and destabilisation of the Party. This led in turn to a threat of legal action by Blackford against Salmond for defamation on the grounds that the decision would adversely affect his reputation as an investment banker. Blackford's refusal to resign led to his suspension from membership of the SNP. This dispute was set to rumble on while Alex Salmond had to face up to taking disciplinary action against Margo MacDonald MSP and the resignation of Lloyd Quinlan MSP as a front bench spokesman.

The disciplinary proceedings against Ian Blackford as National Treasurer caused curiosity. There was no constitutional barrier to removal of membership of a national office bearer. There were some parallels in the forties and fifties and the nearest was the expulsion and eventual suspension of members of the National Executive and National Council during the insurrection of the early eighties. It was also out of character for Alex Salmond to take a high profile initiative on suspension. Like most of us Alex could have a rush of blood to the head and lose his temper.

In this case there must have been some calculation since Alex was backed to the hilt by John Swinney. As deputy Leader and involved in all main decisions, John was the Party's planner. As a former National Secretary and Party loyalist, he had been an opponent of Alex Salmond during the latter's socialist phase until Alex repaired the breach on assuming the National Convenership. John Swinney had his own powerbase within the SNP and could never be taken lightly so there must have been political agreement for an action that would attract considerable adverse media attention.

The first by-election in the short lifespan of the Scottish Parliament took place on 16 March 2000 in Ayr Constituency after the resignation of the Labour MSP. It was not a seat Labour would have chosen for an early contest as the majority over the Conservatives one year earlier was a sparse one of 25 votes. Whether the electorate took offence at Labour for an unnecessary election or not, the result thrust them into third place behind the SNP candidate, Jim Mather and also led to the victory of the Conservative candidate, John Scott with a substantial majority of 3,344.

This constituency had been held by the Conservatives at Westminster.

Nevertheless it was a good result for them and a very poor one for Labour. The result also confirmed the developing electoral trend where the SNP could be more popular in Scottish Parliament contests. The SNP share of the vote of 29% was well above that of 19.5% in 1999.

Ayr By-election (Scottish Parliament) - 16 March 2000

Party	Votes	Percentage
Conservative	12,580	39.4%
SNP	9,236	29%
Labour	7,054	22.1%
Scottish Socialist	1,345	4.2%
Liberal Democrat	800	2.5%
Scottish Green	460	1.4%
Others (4)	435	
Turnout		57%

As the year rolled on, problems multiplied. In May, Alex Salmond faced Jim Wallace, the deputy First Minister at Question Time in the absence of Donald Dewar, who was recovering from an operation. It was widely expected that Salmond would 'wipe the floor' with the Liberal Democratic leader. He failed. Indeed, during the remaining eight sessions, Wallace emerged victorious. In the background, the Blackford affair was grinding on and expected to produce acrimony until the Conference in the autumn. There were rumours of a leadership challenge and as Alex Salmond had been in office as leader for 10 years, there was a feeling that he was tired and had grown disinterested. Even so, it was a shock for everyone when he suddenly announced his resignation as SNP National Convener on 17 July 2000.

Naturally, the media and the Party sought further reasons. But the answer is simple. I served as Chairman/National Convener for 11 years; before me Billy Wolfe did 10 and Arthur Donaldson around the same. It is an exhausting role. Everyone comes into office full of enthusiasm and ideas but as the years roll by, ideas dry up and there is a seeping tiredness. It is then time to go. Alex Salmond sensibly took the right option.

In his case, he would not leave the big stage entirely. He was still MP for

Banff and Buchan at Westminster. It would be wrong to write his obituary; he was certainly not politically dead. But the presence of 'a major political beast' in the wings could not but produce problems for his successor. As events proved, he had not fled the scene nor was his contribution ended. For the moment, it is worth recording that he left behind a Party with 35 Members of the Scottish Parliament and forming the official opposition. As a leader he had made himself one of Scotland's main politicians, second only to Donald Dewar. He was also widely recognised within UK politics. His period of office would have been a splendid achievement even if there had not been more to come.

Chapter 6:

SWINNEY TO THE FORE

Contests for election of office bearers including those for the National Convener and Depute National Convener were made by delegates to the Annual Conference. In 2000, this fell in the third week of September. There were two candidates – John Swinney MP, MSP and Alex Neil MSP, both formidable politicians although completely different in character, policies and approach. Alex Neil had been in the Labour Party, an office bearer in the short-lived Scottish Labour Party of his mentor, Jim Sillars. He had joined the SNP in the early 80s and become one of the leading members of the group which pressed for more emphasis on the Party's key policy of independence. Although on the left of the political spectrum, he had not been involved in the 79 Group stramash. He had considerable experience having served on the NEC from 1989, as an Executive Vice Convener for Publicity for three years between 1990 and 1992 and as Treasury Spokesperson from 1991 to 1994. He was a natural politician and was a fine orator in the robust West coast style.

John Swinney had joined the SNP at a young age, become National Secretary in his early twenties, then Executive Vice Chairman for Publicity and latterly Senior Vice Convener. In these roles, he had masterminded many of the Party's campaigns. He had been an invaluable support to me when I was in charge of the Party. In political terms, he was a centrist and a gradualist.

Both candidates addressed Party meetings so often during the run-up to Conference that each declared that he could have delivered the opponent's speech for them – better of course - since neither was overcome with modesty, a character defect rarely to be found or at least admitted to, in a leadership election!

In the immediate run up to the Conference, on 21 September each of the candidates published messages. John Swinney had three elements: advancing independence, initiating open debate and transforming the election fighting capability of the membership. By and large, his main pitch was to emphasise his position as deputy leader, his experience and his willingness to encourage inclusion through open debate.

"I want us to make the case for independence and to win that independence as quickly as possible. The Scottish Parliament is only a start. But it is a good start and we must ensure the powers of our parliament are completed and we grow swiftly and confidently towards independence.

We need to build a convincing vision of an independent Scotland, one where we demonstrate the sort of Scotland we want to create. It must be relevant to each and every person, to each and every family in our country."

Emphasising his service as Senior Vice Convener (deputy leader), he proposed to extend the involvement of Party members in democratic debate as he had done previously by insisting the Party decide the independence strategy. Thirdly, he said his ambitions were electoral:

"I want to transform the SNP into an election-winning force that will unseat Labour. That means making strategic progress at the Westminster elections, establishing a credible alternative platform to win in 2003, reviewing our policy attitudes and developing the strong local campaigning that will defeat Labour in their heartlands.

Many of the innovations that were introduced to our Hamilton South and Ayr by-election campaigns, and the preparations for the Westminster election for which I have been responsible, will be intensified to create this winning campaigning force."

Alex Neil, a list MSP for Central Scotland, had a harder message with a warning to the Party to be careful:

"Scotland will become independent when the idea of Scottish sovereignty gains intellectual ascendancy over Unionism, and is expressed as the majority opinion through the ballot box. The SNP won't achieve this if, as our opponents hope, the party's energy becomes mired in devolution. Never forget, devolution is an invention of Unionists to stop our march to independence.

Devolution is designed to tie down the SNP in the administration of Scotland as a region of the UK. Independence is designed by the SNP to free a sovereign Scotland to use our own resources, fulfil our potential, and be governed as our nation wishes.

In working in our present devolved parliament, I have two aims:

- To stretch the parliament's restricted powers to their limit to improve conditions for people living in Scotland.

- To inform Scots voters of the democratic advance and social fulfilment that can only be achieved by a parliament with full sovereign powers."

And then projecting the issues of fulfilling Scotland's domestic and international potential and changing the country through independence, he closed:

"But of supreme importance is what devolution prevents us from doing for our people – our economy, jobs, education, health service and our senior citizens. Devolution binds us tightly to Westminster control. Scots must set Scotland free – free to create full employment, end poverty, provide for our own folk, care for the sick and create a nation to be proud of."

In a series of leaflets, he emphasised that under his leadership, the first priority of the Party would be independence and in four other pledges, he would maintain the moderate left of centre stance, run an open and democratic style of leadership without fear or favour, rebuild HQ resources for the Party and encourage further membership growth and participation. He asserted that the referendum policy was constructing an unnecessary barrier as winning an election was enough of a mandate to negotiate independence with any referendum to give a verdict on a new Constitution that would be presented for approval following negotiations with Westminster on the share-out of assets and responsibilities.

While the leadership contest was the crucial decision facing Conference, the auguries were good. An ICM Poll put the SNP ahead of Labour in voting intentions for elections to the Scottish Parliament. In the constituency category, the SNP ranked first with 38% compared with Labour 31%, Conservatives at 16% and the Lib Dems at 12%. In the list section, the SNP stood at 36%, Labour at 32%, the Conservatives at 16% and the Lib Dems at 13%. Even in the preferences for Westminster, the SNP ran second to Labour with 27% to 36% respectively.

It came as no surprise when the outgoing leader, Alex Salmond was bullish in his final speech, chronicling the progress made over the last ten years leading to 35 MSPs out of the 129 members of the Scottish Parliament. He then prophesised in these terms:

> "Let us be quite clear. A popular SNP administration will hold a popular vote for freedom. This party will win a referendum on Scottish independence."

And stressing that the SNP was a moderate left of centre party with a radical edge to its social programme and committed to a 'competitive economic policy', he declared:

> "We are ambitious for Scotland. The challenge is to connect all of these social and economic hopes to an independence reality." (BBC News in depth report)

The speech was greeted with a long ovation, halted only by a bomb threat which forced the closure of the hall and a temporary suspension of proceedings. The next day (23 September 2000), saw balloting for the new National Convener to succeed Alex Salmond, made all the more tense by a recount for another office. John Swinney won a resounding victory and at the age of 36 was elected by 547 votes to 268.

In his victory address, he called for Party unity, something that had been somewhat diluted over the last few years, promising to be inclusive by fostering and encouraging democratic debate in the Party about policy, tactics and strategy and insisting that once decisions were taken the Party had to speak with one voice. He ended his oration:

> "This is the hour for a nation to be reborn, this is the hour when Scotland at last and forever can change for good. Let us make our vision real, let us bring independence alive for the people of Scotland, let us persuade and persuade and persuade about the case for independence. Let us make our parliament complete, come with me and let's win our nation's freedom."

In the contest for Senior Vice Convener (deputy leader), Roseanna Cunningham, the shadow Justice Minister defeated Kenneth MacAskill, shadow Transport and Environmental minister by 457 votes to 323. The long running dispute between Alex Salmond and Ian Blackford ended when the latter was defeated for re-election as Treasurer by 632 votes to 143.

For continuity of policy and strategy, John Swinney was probably the best placed to move with the Salmond heritage. For much of the last ten years, he had worked closely with Alex. John shared Alex's view that the best course of events was to enhance the work of the SNP in the Scottish Parliament and build gradually towards a stage when sufficient additional powers were transferred to allow the country to move smoothly towards full autonomy. As a former National Secretary for six years, Vice Convener, Publicity for five and Senior Vice Convener for two, he was fully experienced and equipped. In these posts, he had been the author of most of the major reviews of Party strategy and had the executive ability to implement their recommendations.

In a far ranging report to the NEC after the 1997 election his overview of the situation contained the following assessment:

> "Public reaction to the SNP since election day seems to indicate that the SNP has lost no credibility as a result of the large Labour vote, and that our increase in seats has provided a reason to believe that the SNP will remain an effective challenging force in Scottish politics. As the noise from the Labour victory dies down, it is probable that the SNP – with a positive and well presented campaign – can become a much needed principled opposition to New Labour in Scotland and can put together a coherent and consistent campaign designed to increase support at elections for a Scottish Parliament, which are likely to be held within two years."

In a report of the aims of the leadership candidates in the Sunday Times on 30 July 2000, John Swinney had laid out his independence strategy:

> "If you complete the powers of the Scottish parliament, you have won independence. The biggest mistake the unionists made was to create that institution, because they have just created a symbol of unfinished business. Now, for me once we complete the powers of that parliament – the

word "complete" is a very definite word – we have our independent Scotland. That's what I want to do.

In all of this the decision makers are the people of Scotland. I will always make the case for Scottish independence. I am a democrat. I am happy to put my faith in the hands of first the electorate of the SNP and then the electorate of Scotland. They can have their say

Naturally, if you opt for the status quo, you cannot expect much change in strategy and tactics but with a new broom, there was hope that some important aspects of policy could be reviewed. One of these related to Europe. In the ten years since the SNP had adopted the flagship policy of 'Independence in Europe', Europe had developed whereas European policy of the SNP had lain fallow. In one of a series of articles in The Scotsman debating the future of nationalism, I wrote on 26 July 2000 after pointing out that the Common Market had been replaced by the European Economic Community, the European Community and European Union, each of them embracing greater integration and centralisation

"So where does all this unification and integration leave the SNP and its policy of independence in Europe? Quite frankly, in a stage of intellectual neglect! The party needs a coherent expression of political goals. In recent years too great emphasis has been placed on whether Scotland should join the European Monetary System – something that is theoretical until Scotland becomes independent.

Then the major decision will be: do we swap sterling for the euro and if so, under what conditions and when? I have no great attachment to the British currency, but I agree with Jim Sillars and Malcolm Rifkind (a former Scottish Conservative MP and Foreign Secretary) that a decision to join the euro is premature. We cannot adopt the euro until we know that the exchange rate will be beneficial. Nevertheless, in a recent policy resolution (March 2000), the SNP made the leap of faith to support the euro while protesting that it remains in favour of a confederal Europe.

But that is what the main European states wish to abandon. They intend to create a new Europe with no national veto.

There will be an elected European president with executive powers and an upper house in the federal parliament replacing national representation in the Council of Ministers. Given the salami-like process of the last two decades, where national powers have been sliced away, it is inevitable that this process will continue.

So there is a problem. Within ten years, the concept of 'Independence in Europe' will be meaningless."

The article led to a prompt rejoinder from the author Paul Scott and the topic dropped from public view until the post-2008 Euro-crisis and the controversies of the independence referendum of 2014. I should have known better than waste my time!

The new leader's team selections were announced shortly after his election.

Shadow Cabinet 2000

First Minister	John Swinney
Deputy Leader and Justice	Roseanna Cunningham
Enterprise & Lifelong Learning	Kenny MacAskill
Children & Education	Michael Russell
Social Justice & Housing plus Co-ordination of Policy Programme	Fiona Hyslop
Health & Community Care	Nicola Sturgeon
Rural Affairs	Fergus Ewing
Finance	Andrew Wilson
Local Government	Kenny Gibson
Transport & Environment	Bruce Crawford
Defence	Colin Campbell
Social Security	Christine Grahame
Business Manager	Tricia Marwick

Chief Whip   Kay Ullrich

At HQ level, Peter Murrell took up post as Chief Executive and was instrumental in leading the modernisation of the Party. The sudden death of Labour First Minister, Donald Dewar provoked two by-elections in Glasgow Anniesland in November 2000. They produced intriguing results. In the Westminster By-election against what became a trend of the SNP doing better in Scottish elections than those for Westminster, the SNP candidate, Grant Thoms saw the vote rise by 3.9% whereas for Holyrood candidate Tom Chalmers the gain was 1.8%. Smaller parties such as the Liberal Democrats, the Scottish Greens and especially the Scottish Socialists saw varying but larger shares of votes than usual.

Glasgow Anniesland By-election (Scottish Parliament) - 23 November 2000

Party	Votes	Percentage
Labour	9,838	48.7%
SNP	4,462	22%
Conservative	2,138	10.6%
Scottish Socialist	1,429	7.1%
Liberal Democrat	1,384	6.9%
Scottish Green	662	3.3%
Socialist Labour	298	1.5%
Turnout		38.3%

Glasgow Anniesland By-election (Westminster) - 23 November 2000

Party	Votes	Percentage
Labour	10,359	51.7%
SNP	4,202	21%
Conservative	2,188	10.9%
Liberal Democrat	1,630	8.1%
Scottish Socialist	1,441	7.2%

Independent	212	1.1%
Turnout		38.1%

John Swinney did not have a quiet introduction to his role as Party leader. As the Anniesland campaigns drew to a close, work was already under way for a Westminster by-election in Falkirk West following the resignation of Dennis Canavan who had left the Labour Party to be elected as an independent MSP in the Scottish Parliament. Here the pattern changed and the SNP candidate David Kerr ran Labour close although the Labour candidate Major Eric Joyce won with a majority slashed from 13,783 to 705.

Falkirk West By-election (Westminster) - 21 December 2000

Party	Votes	Percentage
Labour	8,492	43.5%
SNP	7,787	39.9%
Conservative	1,621	8.3%
Scottish Socialist	989	5.1%
Liberal Democrat	615	3.2%
Turnout		36.1%

In a tenure dominated by a succession of elections, John Swinney also had to plan for a General Election likely to occur in 2001. The changes to independence strategy had made the SNP's contests of Westminster elections arguably less relevant to the media and the party membership whose eyes were increasingly focused on Holyrood. In addition, as I and Alex Salmond had both found, it takes time to bed in as a new leader, given that at least one third of delegates had voted for other candidates or different strategies and policies. In John Swinney's case, he had succeeded a high profile predecessor who was an MP at Westminster and had not departed the public stage. Alex Salmond, by dint of a special relationship, also remained the conduit to Sean Connery who was both a major financial benefactor to the party and a substantial political asset.

Likewise, Alex Neil had not gone away and had declared after his defeat his willingness to work for the Party under John's leadership. This led to Swinney appointing him to the chair of the Enterprise and Lifelong

Education Committee of the Parliament. In February 2001, he contributed a thoughtful article in Business in Scotland spelling out why he believed full national status in Europe was vital for Scotland. He argued that decisions taken at Nice for the expansion of the EU and the admission of countries in central and Eastern Europe to membership would have potentially serious consequences for Scotland especially with the advent of qualified majority voting amongst a wide range of key areas of policy. He pointed out that the Scottish Parliament was constrained by constitutional restrictions, direct access to 'the top table' and financial limitations imposed by London. He stressed that it was only with the restoration of national sovereignty that Scotland could have influence on EU decision making in the same manner as Denmark.

In a progress report to National Council (December 2000), John Swinney recorded that the political landscape of Scotland had changed with the death of Donald Dewar and his replacement as First Minister in the Labour/Liberal Democrat Coalition by Henry McLeish. He had stood unsuccessfully for election to this office to underline the lack of democratic authority as well as to expound the arguments for the winning of more powers. In the few short weeks since he had become leader, he had started the process to sharpen policy in seven key areas to create a link between the everyday concerns of the people and the benefits of independence. To achieve this he would spell out the SNP's European stance and the road to independence set against the campaign to win further powers for the Parliament.

A further report to a Special Council (March 2001), the National Convener referred to the success of the Falkirk West by-election and stated that the Party would build upon the high opinion poll rating of 28% for a Westminster election. Additionally he spoke highly of the impact of the shadow ministerial team at Holyrood. We are now, he said, seeing more and more of our key people appearing in the media and strengthening the credibility of the Party.

Although the planning was as meticulous as ever, the 2001 Westminster election did not have a happy outcome. The strategy was advanced in a paving resolution proposed by Stewart Hosie and seconded by Fiona Hyslop to a Special Council and was implemented in an election leaflet with a headline, 'SNP We Stand for Scotland' featuring policies on health, education and crime which were all devolved to the Scottish Parliament and over which Westminster had no control. Even a passage on jobs did not refer to independence as an instrument of delivering economic change. Instead MP candidates pledged themselves to drive Scotland to independence by working to complete the powers of the Scottish Parliament.

They would protect Scotland from the worst failings of Westminster rule through electing more SNP MPs. This would stop the next fuel hike and deliver the best deal for Scotland through increasing the attention London gives to Scotland's needs. There was no mention of 'fiscal autonomy' for the Scottish Parliament that had figured prominently in the months running up to the election. It was an anodyne programme and exemplified the switch from the dual path of Westminster and the Scottish Parliament to a gradualist programme, obtaining independence by completing the powers of Holyrood.

The SNP share of the vote went down by 2.1% to 20.1%. Dumfries & Galloway was lost to the Conservatives. The only party to be pleased were the Liberal Democrats who saw their share of the vote rise by 3.4% to16.3%. The Lib Dems emerged with 10 MPs. Labour lost 2.3% at 43.3% but had 55 seats. Even the Conservatives had little to cheer about, apart from their single new MP as their vote declined by 1.9% to 15.6%. The Scottish Socialists gained 72,516 votes with a substantial increase of 2.8% to 3.1%.

General Election (Westminster) - 7 June 2001

Party	Votes	Percentage	Seats
Labour	1,001,173	43.3%	55
Liberal Democrat	378,034	16.3%	10
SNP	464,314	20.1%	5
Conservative	360,658	15.6%	1
Scottish Socialist	72,516	3.1%	0
Turnout			58.2%

On the same day as the UK election, there were two by elections to the Scottish Parliament. Caused by the resignation of Alex Salmond as an MSP for Banff and Buchan in order to concentrate on Westminster as an MP, the result was straightforward and led to the election of Stewart Stevenson who was a friend and staunch supporter. Given the profile of Alex Salmond, a slight fall of 3% to 49.6% was trifling.

Banff and Buchan By-election (Scottish Parliament)
- 7 June 2001

Party	Votes	Percentage
SNP	15,386	49.6%
Conservative	6,819	22%
Labour	4,897	15.8%
Liberal Democrat	3,231	10.4%
Scottish Socialist	682	2.2%
Turnout		54.7%

In Strathkelvin & Bearsden, caused by the resignation of Labour MSP, Sam Galbraith, the majority of the new Labour MSP, Brian Fitzpatrick was cut sharply by an independent.

Strathkelvin & Bearsden By-election (Scottish Parliament)
- 7 June 2001

Party	Votes	Percentage
Labour	15,401	37%
Save Stobhill Hospital	7,572	18.2%
Liberal Democrat	7,147	17.2%
SNP (Janet Law)	6,457	15.5%
Conservative	5,037	12.1%
Turnout		66.2%

Because of the UK election and the good performance of the independent, this result may not have featured highly in the Party's analysis. In the year there had been two warning signals from the growth of the Scottish Socialist vote and the performance of an independent dedicated to the saving of a local hospital. The electorate had begun to veer away from strict party adherence. Why, no one could be sure but it could be that it was an unexpected outcome of the second vote under the list system. Certainly, the bad publicity coming from overspend on the Scottish Parliament would not have helped the standing of the established parties and it remained to be seen if this was only a wayward by-election phenomenon or something deeper.

On 26 June, there was a reshuffle of members of the shadow cabinet. It was to reflect the parliamentary changes with the SNP now having 42 MSPs, MPs and MEPs.

SHADOW CABINET (Reshuffle)

Leader & Shadow First Minister	John Swinney MSP
Deputy Leader & Justice	Roseanna Cunningham MSP
Leader of Westminster Group	Alex Salmond MP
Parliament Minister & Government Strategy[1]	Fiona Hyslop MSP
Health & Community Care	Nicola Sturgeon MSP
Children & Education	Mike Russell MSP
Economy & Transport[2]	Andrew Wilson MSP
Enterprise & Lifelong Learning	Kenny MacAskill MSP
Finance	Alasdair Morgan MSP
Rural Affairs	Fergus Ewing MSP
Social Justice, Housing & Urban Regeneration	Kenny Gibson MSP

---

[1] Responsible for co-ordinating Parliamentary business in Scotland, Westminster and Europe; policy development; and preparing the SNP Programme for Government.

[2] Responsible for transport; macro-economic issues, including monetary policy; co-ordinating the SNP Economic Team; and developing the economic case for Independence.

Environment	Bruce Crawford MSP
Local Government	Tricia Marwick MSP
Europe	Neil MacCormick MEP
Social Security & Pensions	Annabelle Ewing MP
Defence	Colin Campbell MSP
Foreign Affairs	Angus Robertson MP

Also attending the Cabinet:

Scottish Parliamentary Group Convener	Margaret Ewing MSP
Scottish Parliamentary Group Chief Whip	Kay Ullrich MSP

In his report to National Council on 30 June 2001, John Swinney congratulated party activists on their work. As to the outcome he did not try to hide his disappointment at the loss of Dumfries & Galloway and the slight drop in the overall vote. There were some areas of encouragement. The SNP had held five seats and received healthy swings from Labour in a number of places. The main problem was as always its perceived irrelevance to the formation of a UK government in a contest dominated by UK issues. Battle as the Party did to make its voice heard; it was as often as not drowned out by London based media which suggested that this was a three party election. Despite this, in votes, the SNP had consolidated its position as the second party in Scottish politics.

Chapter 7:

DISAPPOINTMENT, DISRUPTION AND DISLOYALTY

Fresh names began to appear in addition to the MSPs. At the Conference, there were new Vice Conveners - John Brady for Fundraising, Cllr Peter Johnson for Local Government, Anne McNair for Organisation, Fiona Hyslop (an MSP) for Policy, Anne Dana for Publicity and Shirley-Anne Somerville for Youth Affairs. The senior posts of National Secretary and National Treasurer were occupied by Stewart Hosie and Jim Mather respectively. The National Executive was dominated by Alex Salmond MP and 6 MSPs - Nicola Sturgeon, Alex Neil. Kenny MacAskill, Michael Russell, Andrew Wilson and Fergus Ewing all representing the importance of the SNP as a parliamentary party. At HQ, Ian McCann was engaged as Party Clerk, before rising to be Corporate Governance and Compliance manager following on new legislation regulating the functioning of the political parties.

Substantial policy work commenced on an updated Scottish Constitution led by Prof Neil MacCormick MEP, and on Europe and International Affairs with Neil MacCormick and Roseanna Cunningham MSP, the Party's Senior Vice Convener. These latter policies were largely restatements of existing policy.

Under the Europe policy set in the context of the strategic aim of independence within Europe, the SNP reasserted its support for a decentralised Union animated by social and environmental priorities and respect for the principle of 'subsidiarity' (which meant Europe leaving to its members as much decision making as possible). It asserted the right of an independent Scotland and other parts of the UK to continued membership but laid down a proviso that if Scotland were deprived of her rights, the country would follow a different path by applying to join EFTA (the European Free Trade area) and the European Economic Area.

The statement favoured a European Constitution in the shape of a confederal union. It envisaged Scotland being involved in common defence and security relationships (so long as the nation was nuclear free) and welcomed development of a European foreign policy. Subject to fiscal sovereignty (with the Scottish people being consulted in a referendum) it wished Scotland to join the common currency of a Euro Zone. This paper came before the National Council in March 2002 (NC02/09) where, with successful amendments to widen residual sovereignty and to prevent qualified majority voting, it passed unanimously.

In June, the Party considered the principles of international policy which dovetailed with the European policy on membership of the EU and defence policy (relating in particular to the non-nuclear proliferation treaty). It accepted obligations to have the Scottish defence forces involved in a European Rapid Reaction Force for humanitarian and rescue tasks and peace-keeping (even those involving force) – but all subject to expenditure constraints. It opposed NATO as before. It laid out its support for the UN. There were also liberal provisions for international trade, aid and debt relief. It welcomed the opportunities and challenges of globalisation but warned of dangers to underdeveloped countries. The statement passed without problems. (NC02/19).

The updated Scottish Constitution had been delayed because of the Convener's illness and followed upon the strategy set in March 2000. It did not depart much from the preceding version. A Working Party consisting of Gordon Wilson, George Reid and Nicola McEwen was established to examine how the constitutional strategy could be implemented in pursuance of the Party's Constitutional Policy. Neil MacCormick as Convener was strongly of the view that the Parliament could consult on independence since direct enabling legislation could fall foul of the courts as being ultra vires. He preferred a referendum agreed (or forced out of Westminster) by the SNP receiving a mandate in an election. Neil MacCormick articulated the arguments with legal citations. Following general introductory paragraphs 1. and 2., he set out his views:

> 3.   The next opportunity to gain a mandate for a referendum is thus the Scottish election of May 2003, for which the SNP is now preparing.
>
> 4.   It is important that the SNP be ready to carry forward the argument either from the position of the largest party without an overall majority. Or from that of the outright majority party. The latter would give the best possible opportunity, but it will be very difficult to achieve in

practice. The former will force the SNP to be ready with a negotiating stance in relation to the formation of a government in the Scottish Parliament.

5. The Political Parties and Referendums Act, now in force, together with the Scotland Act, impose tight constraints on the ability of the Scottish parliament, acting on its own, to hold a referendum. To fulfil the policy adopted in 2000, it would be essential to frame a referendum bill in terms that would clearly be within the competence of the Scottish Parliament. Alternatively that policy should be reconsidered.

6. One possibility would be to approach the UK government about a referendum to be held. Provided that agreement was reached between the SNP leadership and the UK government on the holding of a referendum and the terms of the question, there would be no problem about the validity of the process. For Westminster can use powers under the Scotland Act to confirm the competency of the legislation involved which would otherwise be open to challenge.

7. It would, however, be unwise to adopt a policy dependent on the reaching of such an agreement.

8. In office, the SNP can frame a referendum that is clearly within the Scottish Parliament's existing powers, hence needs no input from Westminster.

9. Under those powers, Parliament is clearly competent to call on the Executive to embark on negotiations with the UK government for transfer to Scotland of all or any of the powers that are reserved to Westminster in the Scotland Act. It is accordingly competent for Parliament to legislate for a consultative referendum mandating negotiations for the complete transfer to the Scottish Parliament of all the powers currently reserved to Westminster under the Scotland Act 1998.

10. Such an independence referendum would pose a 'Yes/No' choice whether to authorize the Scottish government to

open negotiations for the complete transfer of reserved powers to the Scottish Parliament. A majority vote for independence expressed through such a referendum would possess undeniable political legitimacy.

11. The Executive's right to negotiate with Westminster is the essential basis of an *intra vires* referendum. Parliament can itself hold consultation on the basis of which Parliament can then give instructions to the Executive. A referendum is the most authoritative form of consultation. As this implies, the referendum will be a consultative one. All previous referendums in the UK have been so, including the devolution referendum. Nobody doubts that such referendums, though only consultative, in legal terms, are a powerful source of public legitimacy and indeed political obligation.

12. Achieving independence is a process, not an event. Essentially it would involve transferring powers in as orderly a way as possible, from Westminster to Edinburgh. Apart from the very substantial reservations of powers in the Scotland Act, the Scottish parliament is constituted in a way that corresponds largely with the constitutional principles the SNP has held since at least 1977. These constitutional principles call for a proportionately elected single-chamber Parliament, an executive elected by and answerable to Parliament, a strong committee system, an independent judiciary with a judicial appointments commission, and a charter of rights based on the European Convention of Human Rights. The Scotland Act also provides for a proportionately elected single-chamber Parliament, an executive elected by and answerable to Parliament, a strong committee system, an independent judiciary (though with no judicial appointments commission yet) and observance of the rights laid down in the European Convention. This devolved constitution has been functioning and has proved acceptable, and it will be for the people of Scotland in future to determine by appropriate processes whether any alteration of its

contents or its legislative basis are called for once full powers have been granted.

13. The process of transferring reserved powers is one that can start even before the referendum, as John Swinney has pointed out in recent speeches. On time constraints:

14. The negotiations mandated by the referendum would aim to establish in a short time agreement to start a process with the predetermined purpose of achieving total transference of reserved powers. Once the principle is settled, the practical question of the pace of subsequent stages can safely be left to those who are in office and conducting the negotiations in the political situation and climate prevailing at the time. Initial transfers essential to constitute the reality of independence such as treasury, trade, European and foreign recognition, and aspects of social security, will obviously take priority.

15. This process of transferring powers will inevitably take some time, if only because of the need to develop Scottish institutions (inland revenue, customs and excise, etc.) to transfer reserved powers. According to the Macartney Report the main business of transition to independence could be brought to a conclusion within two years. There is no reason to doubt that this is a reasonable estimate.

16. The SNP's approach should be one that insists on reaching a speedy conclusion on the principle of independence, while being ready to take a flexible view about the phasing of the process of transferring power. (Memo. to Gordon Wilson, George Reid and Nicola McEwan, members of the working party on 21 July 2001 giving draft Input to Constitution Policy).

After the frantic electoral and political activity in his first year and a half in office, John Swinney who had been embattled with criticism from the media and dissidents within the MSP Group since his victory in the election contest was set fair to have a quieter year in 2002. This was just as well since the 2003 Scottish election was looming and likely to bring about internal competition for electable places in list system candidacies. There were now many sitting MSPs whose jobs would be at risk if they did not get a high enough ranking. That controversy was still to come to a head.

In the meantime, the Party launched an Economics of Independence Roadshow under Jim Mather and Andrew Wilson aimed primarily at business which ran during the summer. John Swinney at the autumn Conference developed his thinking on a new approach 'Release Our Potential' designed to show how better off Scotland would be with independence. The policy making initiative continued with the preparation of a detailed policy on oil and gas that was presented to National Council on 30 November. The minute of meeting is missing but it would have undoubtedly passed. In preparation for the Scottish Parliament election a wheen of worthy policies on such topics as local government, flood prevention, culture, hospital hygiene, crime, transport, children, the economy and education were presented to the spring National Council and passed by acclamation.

John Swinney was having a bumpy ride from bad publicity emerging from the competition for high ranking votes under the secondary party list system. The current MSPs were striving to ensure their survival whereas there were new contenders ambitious to be elected to the Parliament at the 2003 election. The infighting was vicious and frequently unfair – a case of survival of the fittest but not necessarily the best.

A case in point was that of Party veteran, Margo MacDonald. In 1999 she had topped the Lothian list. This time she was in an unelectable fifth place. According to Margo's assistant Peter Warren, the battle was not confined to ranking. It extended to elimination. In some Party branches, she was voted last. Under the complex voting system this would give a sufficient adverse loading to ensure she had no chance of re-election. Margo was bitter about it and referred to those who had engineered it as 'snakes'.

She was having none of it and announced she would stand as an independent. No sooner had she held a Press Conference to announce her intention than two letters were received, one removing the whip (and recognition by the SNP) and the other suspending her parliamentary assistant, Peter Warren from membership with a view to his expulsion. The Party was obviously waiting for the announcement and ready to take disciplinary action!

Margo MacDonald was a high profile MSP who also had the knack of getting under the skin of the leadership and was renowned for her independence. But others also faced the lash of poor ranking. Andrew Wilson, George Reid and Michael Russell were in peril of dismissal as a result of low rankings. The system was toxic. John Swinney described it as 'a cauldron of tension'. Another SNP figure called it 'a snake pit.'

The second General Election for the election of the 129 seats in the Scottish Parliament took place on 1 May 2003. On 11 April, John Swinney launched the campaign. The tone of the manifesto was bullish; it offered a programme of change in a challenging world. No one owed us a living, he said. We have to compete in a global world. Yet Scotland had many advantages – a magnificent environment, fabulous natural resources, a worldwide reputation for innovation and integrity and a deeply-ingrained belief in education. Combining a happy mixture of collective values, heritage, individual endeavour, and plain good fortune, Scotland's future was bright. John Swinney declared that under his leadership, he had redefined independence as about economic opportunity and the conferment of normal powers to the Parliament to pursue a green energy strategy, creating employment, stewarding our resources and protecting Scotland from the scourge of nuclear power and nuclear weapons. To obtain independence, with the support of the people, he would hold a referendum.

By all accounts John Swinney performed well in leading the Party in this election campaign. Unfortunately, the Party did not come out of it without harm. The outcome was entirely different from that of 1999. Then the deployment of the second vote mimicked constituency preference. In 2003, the major parties, Labour and SNP lost both votes and seats while the Conservatives and the Liberal Democrats remained static. Labour lost 6 seats while the SNP dropped from 27.3% to 23.8% in the constituency vote and 20.9% on the second list vote compared with 27.4% last time. Allowing for two constituency gains Aberdeen North (Brian Adam) and Dundee East (Shona Robison), the SNP also dropped down 8 seats from 35 to 27. Mike Russell and Andrew Wilson both lost and to the Party leadership's chagrin, Margo MacDonald was elected as an independent with a barrow load of votes. I especially welcomed Shona Robison's victory. It was good to see my old seat return to the fold.

Scottish Parliament General Election - 1 May 2003

Party	Constituency	%	Seats	Region	%	Seats	Total
Labour	659,897	34.6	46	561,379	29.3	4	50
SNP	449,476	23.8	9	399,659	20.9	18	27
Conservative	312,598	16.6	3	296,929	15.5	15	18
Liberal Dem	286,150	15.3	13	225,774	11.8	4	17
Scottish Green				132,138	6.9	7	7
Scottish Socialist	117,709	6.2	0	128,026	6.7	6	6
Socialist Labour				21,657	1.1	0	0
Others	50,820	3.4	2	150,294	7.9	2	4
Turnout							49.4%

But this was not just an inter-party exchange. The big party vote fractured. 2003 saw the emergence of smaller parties and independents. The Scottish Green Party emerged with 7 list seats (6.9% in list alone) and the Scottish Socialist Party 6 list seats and a combined vote of over 6%. There were swings of some 5.5%, from the main parties. There were four other independents. There had been minor clues in earlier by-elections that the support for the major parties was splintering. The reasons? Anybody's guess! But there was fairly widespread disillusionment with the Scottish Parliament. It had not been as different from Westminster as civic opinion had hoped. There was inter-party wrangling. The Coalition had steamrollered legislation in an unsympathetic way and had not been very distinguished. One First Minister, Henry McLeish, more progressive than his predecessor, Donald Dewar and his successor, Jack McConnell, had resigned over a very minor affair affecting Westminster expenses after a witch-hunt. Above all, the new Parliament at Holyrood was subject to delay and galloping over-runs on construction costs. This was probably at the root of the move to independents and small insurgent parties.

The parliamentary complex was not completed by the election. It was a large building designed to house 129 MSPs, 1,000 staff and civil servants as well as journalists. The design by Catalan Architect, Enric Miralles (who died before completion) and the location had been approved before the creation of the Parliament by Donald Dewar, Labour Secretary of State at Westminster as advised by a consultative committee representative of the Scottish Establishment. Both the design and the location were controversial. To this controversy were added delays. Instead of 2001, it was completed only in 2004 and then only after heroic efforts by the Presiding Officer, George Reid. The original unlikely estimate of between £10 million and £40 million rose to a final cost of £414 million – and at the time of the 2003 election, there seemed no end in sight. The problems and resultant disillusionment had nothing to do with the SNP which had tried to have the project scrapped. But in politics, blame settles. The SNP, along, with the Labour Party, had been instrumental in securing the Parliament and in the eyes of sections of the public, were responsible for the mess. Jim Lynch, Editor of the Scots Independent was exasperated years later.

> "So we had a Labour Liberal Coalition, a bit insipid, and a tremendous amount of bad publicity about the cost of building the new Parliament, with the Parliament itself being blamed for the actions of Donald Dewar acting as Secretary of State for Scotland at Westminster. He chose the site, the architect, the design, the builders and the method of payment. Unfortunately he died suddenly, but left the Parliament with the odium and the bill."

Confusion in voting had resulted. There was no settled trend in any one direction other than a wish to dunt the two largest (establishment) parties.

There was another electoral disappointment. Once again the council elections were held on the same day as the big contest. As with the parliamentary election, the SNP and Labour both lost votes and seats with Labour losing more seats numerically than four years earlier although emerging with control of 18 councils. The SNP still held Angus. The vote of the independents and others grew fastest.

Council Election - 1 May 2003

Party	Votes	Percentage	Councillors
Labour	611,843	32.6%	509
SNP	451,660	24.1%	181
Conservative	282,895	15.1%	122
Liberal Democrat	272,057	14.5%	175
Independent	189,749	10.1%	230

| Others | 67,533 | 3.6% | 4 |

From the viewpoint of John Swinney, the disaster lay mainly in the parliamentary sphere. He and Alex Salmond had put all their eggs into the Holyrood basket and received little thanks for their pains. It was also one of a series of indifferent results (and maybe that was one minor reason Alex had bailed out in 2000, anticipating with his political acuity that the coming years would be frustrating). The consequence was a loss of talent at best and at worst some very disappointed former MSPs looking around for someone to blame.

Swinney had to come out fighting, given reports that there might be a 'stalking horse' candidate running against him at the autumn Conference. In a statement released after the election, he made much of the wins first past the post and the loosening of Labour's grip and then:

> "But nothing will fall into our laps. If the results last night tell us anything they tell us this: the SNP is no longer a party of protest but we are not yet viewed as a party of government. Let me make this clear – for the SNP there is no going back. Our future rests – not in attracting votes AGAINST the government – but in attracting votes to BECOME the government. And that means the SNP must behave and act at all times as an alternative government in waiting. To do that – to win the trust of the people – we must develop our arguments and we must transform our party – both inside and outside the Scottish Parliament. The SNP today is better organised, has stronger communication techniques and has a more efficient HQ than at any time in our history. But that is not enough.

> To our members I say: the SNP will always be the party of independence. But if we want to do more than talk about it, if we want to achieve that historic goal, we must change. We have a constitution designed for another political age. We are a national party without a national membership system. And in too many ways we have no effective party structure or party accountability. So the task now is to put the membership into the driving seat, to democratise, to connect much more fully with Scottish civic life, and to ensure that all our parliamentarians are focused on the job in hand."

John Swinney proposed to change the balance of power within the Party from branches, constituency associations and district bodies by handing it to the membership. Although I had a sentimental attachment to the old version of the constitution (much rejigged over the years since I had written it 40 years earlier), it was no longer fit for a political party which had substantial parliamentary representation. Some of the local bodies were democratic but others could be controlled by cliques whose interest was less in expansion than in retaining power. The whole thing had come to a head during the contests for ranking for list seats (and jobs, income and influence in Parliament). The system had turned corrupt. John's solution was dramatic - to reduce internal manipulation by moving to a system dominated by one person one vote.

As in all such changes, there were dangers. In practical terms, power had already passed from Party Headquarters to the leadership in the Scottish Parliament. As described earlier this had happened in a democratic coup in 1999 when the Party accepted transfer of the functions of publicity and research to parliament and thus under control of the Leader and the parliamentary group. The membership, much of it nominal and inactive, would be less aware of the needs in policy and out of loyalty (and ignorance) might side with the leadership when more sophisticated party organs could 'advise, and consent'. Care would have to be taken in the fashioning of the new constitution to retain the necessary checks and balances. Democracy versus bureaucracy can sometimes lead to autocracy.

In the aftermath of the Scottish General Election, John Swinney reallocated the spokespeople in his Shadow Cabinet.

SHADOW CABINET (30 May 2003)

Shadow First Minister & Leader of the Opposition	John Swinney MSP
Deputy Leader & Rural Affairs, Culture & Sport	Roseanna Cunningham MSP
Leader of Westminster Group	Alex Salmond MP
Shadow Minister for Justice (and Europe)	Nicola Sturgeon MSP
Shadow Minister for	

Enterprise & the Economy	Jim Mather MSP
Shadow Minister for Education & Lifelong Learning	Fiona Hyslop MSP
Shadow Minister for Tourism, Transport & Telecoms	Kenny MacAskill MSP
Shadow Minister for Health & Social Justice	Shona Robison MSP
Shadow Minister for Finance & Public Services	Fergus Ewing MSP
Business Manager & Chief Whip	Bruce Crawford MSP
Defence & international Relations	Angus Robertson MP
Social Security	Annabelle Ewing MP
Europe	Neil MacCormick MEP

Also in attendance at Cabinet:

Scottish Parliamentary Group Convener	Alasdair Morgan MSP

There was no respite. SNP members had expected in the first flush of optimism following the creation of the Parliament that it was an instrument that would deliver independence. The harsh reality was that the electoral system had been designed to prevent the SNP from seizing the levers of power. Not only had the party not been rewarded with the votes of the Scottish people to this end but the unionist Labour and Liberal Democrat Parties had formed their second coalition which effectively reduced the SNP to an oppositional role where the coalition under McConnell and Wallace ruled the roost and could and did outvote the SNP at will.

Within the SNP there was despondency and disillusionment. As always the blame was visited on the Leader. John's predecessor, Alex Salmond came out in vocal support of Swinney and their joint policy of a pre-legislative referendum and joined in public controversy with Campbell Martin (a West of Scotland list MSP). The bitter exchange eventually led to Martin's expulsion from the Party. In the meantime, as the Party Conference lay ahead with John Swinney's leadership at stake, the level of acrimony led to a contest for the National Convenership by a stalking horse candidate, Bill Wilson whose bid was dismissed by an overwhelming vote of 577 to 111 in favour of Swinney. The Party had loyally given their embattled leader a vote of confidence.

John Swinney now moved on to fulfil his pledge to reform the Party's structure and write a new Constitution and by 10 January, 2004 he was able to present the draft. The process of consultation had produced 424 responses from the membership. This had been backed up by ten meetings around the country attended by 341 members and as a result he had modified a number of proposals, including diluting the number of parliamentarians on the National Executive.

The principal proposals were:

- The introduction of One Member One Vote for certain Party selection and election processes

- The reduction of the size of the NEC now to be chaired by an appointed Business Convener rather than by the Leader

- The introduction of a new system of nominations for leadership contests

- A code of conduct for members to aid discipline

- A review of the Party's local structures in the light of changing political boundaries

In closing, John Swinney advised that he was absolutely determined that the Party must grasp the thistle of internal reform. For too long it had been trying to work with uncertain and unwieldy internal structures, and it could not delay change any longer, if it was to be placed on a footing to win independence.

The new Constitution, after consultation with NEC members, would be presented to the Spring Conference and be in force for the Annual National

Conference later in the year. The detailed rule book would go through consultation and approval by National Council. The final product threw the old version overboard. In many ways it reflected the move by the SNP from a campaigning Party, always in the British fringe, to one which had a large base load of parliamentarians (42 in all), modern campaigning techniques and outstanding political personalities.

The Party accepted the new, radical constitution. In some ways, the basic structure remained. National Conference composed of delegates and other representatives was the final authority with the National Council reduced to two meetings every year acting in between Conferences (two per year). The President became a fully honorific office-bearer; the terminology of National Convener and Senior Vice Convener changed significantly to Leader and Depute Leader. Although the National Executive Committee still had, at least notional control of the strategic management and political direction of the Party, its place in the Constitution was below that of the Association of Nationalist Councillors! The new Constitution did however reduce the influence of the parliamentarians on National Council to 5 MSPs, 2 MPs and. 1 MEP. The Leader and Depute Leader also did not have to be members of the Scottish Parliament.

Although comprehensively reworked and modernised to reflect the existence of the Scottish Parliament and the needs of the modern age, there was no real change in the constitutional objectives of the Party – that would have cause a real rammy! These were:

"The aims of the Party shall be:

a. Independence for Scotland; that is the restoration of Scottish National sovereignty by restoration of full powers to the Scottish Parliament, so that its authority is limited only by the sovereign power of the Scottish People, to bind it with a written constitution and by such agreements as it may freely enter into with other nations or states or international organisations for the purpose of furthering international co-operation, world peace and the protection of the environment.

b. The furtherance of all Scottish interests."

Nevertheless, during the history of the Scottish National Party, while the leadership notionally abided by both aims, from time to time one could be in the ascendant over the other. Before the emergence of the Scottish Parliament, the balance in the Party could more easily be achieved. With the SNP now the official opposition taking on the coalition on domestic matters within the powers of a devolved parliament, it could be all too easy to skew the direction of the Party over time without it being noticed.

With the Party reeling from the loss of support and MSPs to non-establishment parties, there was concern over the publicity being given to the Greens and the Scottish Socialist Party. There was great worry about the impact of the SSP in West Central Scotland. In a letter to John Swinney on 11 November 2003, Douglas Henderson, the former MP for East Aberdeenshire in the seventies who had returned to active service and was a fourth ranking candidate in the 2004 European Elections nominated by the Glasgow area expressed his concerns:

> "The SSP has clearly made inroads (in) Glasgow and West-Central Scotland. Our members in other parts of the country may not be so aware of the impact they have made: 16% of the list vote in Glasgow, 7% in Central Scotland and 6% in Scotland West. Elsewhere they have averaged 4-5%. Overall they took about 7%, the same as the Greens.

> It is already clear to me from campaigning in Glasgow that the SSP's simplistic message – bit like the tooth-fairy's wish list – has struck a resonance with disillusioned Labour voters who might otherwise have been receptive to our appeal.

> There seem to me to be three alternative strategies for dealing with them:

> 1. Ignore them and hope that their internal contradictions and rivalries will cause them to implode. This was the approach when Sillars launched his Scottish Labour Party. It was justified by events since having attracted the lunatic fringe and provided a home for all the nutcases of the far Left it disintegrated within about a year.

> Sheridan's Party, however, has survived for almost five years and seems to be better organised and structured and I do not know of any evidence which would suggest the early demise of his party.

2. Have a semblance of sympathy and understanding towards them, recognising that we share some views and attitudes in common, but that we naturally disassociate ourselves from their more extreme policies. This seems to me to be our current stance, although we may not have rationalised it as such. I have to question whether this is viable as an ongoing policy.

3. Attack them vigorously on their weakest points and undermine their street cred accordingly. To achieve this I believe we would need an independent costing of their policies and then run the figures through a model of the Scottish economy. My instinct tells me that the cost of their policies would tip many small to medium sized businesses over the edge and create a substantial rise in unemployment. However instinct is not enough and we need a credible measure of cost and effects before we start sounding off.

Whatever the line the Party decides to take I think it should be decided before the New Year. The SSP are buoyed up by their list results last May and generally favourable media coverage since then. Our members seem unsure about how to cope with them and our message is consequently unclear. If nothing is done I fear the SSP's momentum will carry them forward in confident mood to the Euro elections and we have the possibility that they may grab one seat."

In reply John Swinney indicated that while the response should be a mixture of points two and three, he believed we had a duty to explain to the public how weak and ludicrous were their stances on certain issues and that this would be set out in public debate. If there were some common grounds, these should be discussed at the coming National Council which was scheduled to consider the policy for an Independence Convention.

At this meeting there were two challenges to the leadership. There was deep suspicion that the Party was being manipulated. The change in the constitution and the proposed internal reform programme led to a low key debate on a motion to have a special conference. The argument on a motion to remit back was that the exercise was premature.(NC04/11) There was also a resolution (mentioned earlier) from Glasgow Springburn

Branch calling on the SNP to contact other organisations to establish an Independence Convention for Scotland. It was understood this was directed towards contact with the SSP then gathering strength in Glasgow. Aberdeen Central Constituency Association and Edinburgh Newington Branch proposed an amendment to broaden the definition of organisations as follows:

> "including political parties, trade unions, the churches and voluntary groups with a view to setting up a broad based Independence Convention for Scotland. National Council further agrees that, in the interests of building a national consensus for change, all those who want more powers for a Scottish Parliament but who may not yet be persuaded of the case for independence, should be encouraged to participate."

The amendment, moved by Nicola Sturgeon, carried by an overwhelming majority after a lively debate and the amended resolution surmounted the remit back motion and passed. It was apparent that Party leaders wished to defuse the issue of the SSP and to steer the Convention, despite its name to the context of devolution.

The Party continued to focus on the themes of 'We Stand for Scotland' and 'Release Our Potential'. There was a wide ranging narrative encapsulated under the heading 'Building for the Future', although uncomfortably aware of the threat from the Greens and the SSP.

The objectives of the Euro Campaign for 2004 were primarily to see off the Labour Party and increase the number of MEPs to three. Here again there was disappointment. At the previous Conference it had also agreed that the slogan 'Better off with Independence' should appear on all Party literature. The challenge expected from the Greens and Scottish Socialists failed to emerge. Although the Party still had two MEPs – Ian Hudghton and Alyn Smith - it was the biggest loser of the night. The Party vote sank by a quarter from 27.2% to 19.7% a loss of 7.5%. Labour lost 2.3%, the Conservatives 2% (with a vote of 17.8% being perilously close to that of the SNP). The Liberal Democrats gained 3.3% at 13.1%, The Scottish Greens had 6.8% with an extra 1%, and the Scottish Socialists were up 1.2% to 5.2%. The biggest surprise was UKIP which came from nowhere with a gain of 5.4% to attain 6.7%.

European Parliament Election - 2004

Party	Votes	Percentage	Seats
Labour	310,865	26.4%	2
SNP	231,505	19.7%	2
Conservative	209,028	17.8%	2
Liberal Democrat	154,178	13.1%	1
Scottish Green	79,695	6.8%	0
UKIP	78,828	6.7%	0
Scottish Socialist	61,536	5.2%	0
Christian Vote	21,056	1.8%	0
BNP	19,427	1.7%	0
Others (2)	10,879		
Turnout			30.9%

As Leader, John Swinney put as brave a face on it as he could when commenting on the results. He indicated he would press on with the reforms but recognised there was a greater task to get over the SNP's values and policies required to persuade the electorate to support the SNP at the next Scottish Parliament election in 2007. Unfortunately the media had written him off and members had become disillusioned, however much they liked him as a person. It was also evident from off the record statements that candidates would emerge to contest against him

So on 22 June, he bowed to the inevitable and at a press conference announced that after reflection on the results and the implications for the Party, he would not seek re-nomination as leader of the Scottish National Party. In what was a bitter moment, he publicly accepted as a loyal servant of the Party that despite his best efforts over the last four years, many people had not yet a clear understanding of what the SNP stood for – over and above an independent Scotland - nor did they see the Party as a government in waiting. As leader, he had to take responsibility for the fact that we had not made as much progress as he would have liked.

Earlier, he declared:

> "It has become clear to me over the last few days, that the constant and relentless speculation over my position is obscuring – and crucially in my judgement, will continue to obscure – the political objectives of the SNP. I have come to the view that the SNP cannot make the electoral progress I believe is possible, if our vital political message is communicated through an endless debate about my leadership. As someone who has devoted all my adult life to the cause of Scottish Independence, that is something that cannot be allowed to happen."

He closed with an acute observation: 'The post-devolution landscape has proved to be a turbulent time in Scottish politics.' He also might have added - and for the SNP too whose strategy was to build on devolution.

It was a sad moment. John Swinney had been a member of the Party since a teenager. He had become National Secretary when aged 23 and then served as Vice Convener and Senior Vice Convener with distinction. When the Party was inclining too far to the left, he intervened at a critical moment to speak his mind courageously. As candidate, MP and MSP for North Tayside in its various boundary incarnations, he had built up the strongest constituency organisation in the country. He was liked and respected. So how had it all gone wrong? Why had his leadership lasted for only four years?

Yet he had inherited the throne at a time of flux. The SNP had achieved a strategic victory under Alex Salmond with the creation of the Scottish Parliament. And there the excitement ceased. Yes, there was a large new group of MSPs but the campaign in 1999 had been poor and ruinously expensive. The SNP had not achieved its potential and with the Scottish Executive having been taken over and monopolised by the Labour/Liberal Democrat Coalition, the SNP like many an opposition before it, was left high and dry. Other forces were in play.

The Scottish electorate had not seen fit to give the SNP credit for the creation of the Parliament and Labour took advantage of its ascendency. With devolution being so recent the people took breath. The end result was a disinclination to vote SNP. People had got what they had wanted. Or had they? For the first few years, there were scandals over the design of the Parliament building and the costs. The new Parliament had also disappointed people who were looking for something better than Westminster type 'yah-boo' politics. And Holyrood, as the Parliament became known, was not giving them that. There was public realisation that the second list vote gave choices other than votes of the major parties and some of the support for Labour and the SNP had drifted towards the Greens and Scottish Socialist Party. With relatively few 'first past the post' seats, the SNP had suffered worst. And as the succession of disappointing results rolled in, the Leader's prestige and authority suffered.

With Alex Salmond being such a dominating figure, it was not as if John Swinney was able to take over cleanly. Alex was a major political presence with a high profile as an MP at Westminster. Perhaps John Swinney's error, if any, was to try to emulate the macho style of his predecessor.

This was not his way. He might have survived longer under a collective leadership where the responsibilities were spread rather than striving to be a dominant figure. And, of course, he was not lucky. The tide was going out. He had to fight too many elections in too short a time. One or two good results would have transformed morale, and with it his standing and support. It was not to be. It was, however, only a matter of time that the inherent merits of the man became clear when he emerged as an outstanding Finance Minister.

Chapter 8:

RETURN OF THE KING

The election of a new leader and depute leader was like none other that had gone before. The old Constitution had been replaced as had former terms of National Convener and Senior Vice Convener. The important change was that instead of any leadership campaign culminating with voting by delegates attending the National Conference, the franchise now comprised the whole membership under OMOV (one member one vote) with postal ballots and independent verification.

In the first flurry of activity, it appeared that the contest for the prime post of Leader would be fought by Nicola Sturgeon, Roseanna Cunningham and Michael Russell. Alex Salmond, no longer in the Scottish Parliament but a Member of the British Parliament at Westminster, ruled himself out of consideration with a pithy quotation from General Sherman refusing the Republican nomination for the US presidency:

> "If nominated I would decline. If drafted I will defer and if elected I shall resign."

Nicola Sturgeon was Alex's choice. The first indications were that the crown might instead go to Roseanna Cunningham, the former Depute to John Swinney. Roseanna had strong radical leanings and had served well. She had been the winner of a by-election to Westminster and held the Perth seat in the Scottish Parliament. Nicola Sturgeon had made her name in Glasgow, was elected as an MSP from the regional list. She had considerable Party experience having been elected Executive Vice Convener Youth Affairs 1993 to 1997, Vice Convener Publicity in 1997 and been on the NEC during the intervening years.

That contest was not to be. On 15 July, 2004, just as the campaigns were beginning to roll, there came a sudden announcement from Alex Salmond. He had decided to come back after all and had persuaded Nicola Sturgeon to withdraw and to stand instead for the Depute Leadership in a joint team. As Jim Lynch described it: 'Alex Salmond entering the contest certainly put the cat amongst the pigeons'.

It was obvious that Alex Salmond was in an expansive and optimistic mood, believing that he had the capacity to take the SNP to victory. Nobody knows, except Alex, who is notoriously reticent about his intentions until he announces them, whether this was a planned intervention or one brought about by the struggling campaign of his protégée. It could be either but it did represent a major gamble on his part. The Party had poor morale and had suffered from an indifferent set of elections.

He was also no longer a member of the Scottish Parliament and would need to delegate important parliamentary exchanges to his deputy. Above all he would need to seek re-election to the Scottish Parliament at the next election in 2007 and as he had already boldly juggled between Westminster and Holyrood that could not be taken for granted.

Because the voters were scattered throughout the country the leadership campaigns were by necessity prolonged and expensive, with campaign glossy leaflets in circulation. In the case of Alex Salmond, with great confidence, if not chutzpah, he declared that he was not just campaigning to be SNP leader. He was launching his candidacy to be First Minister of Scotland – a target, given the SNP's limited performance in both previous Holyrood elections, which in the eyes of both observers seemed out of reach of most mortals. But then, Alex Salmond was never short of bravery, even to the point of recklessness. He had a bravura personality which transcended that of most politicians. Combined with political astuteness on tactical matters this had taken him successfully over past hurdles. To declare his aim to be First Minister was still a big task.

Nevertheless, he had yet to secure the minor task of being elected Party Leader and in a well run campaign based on a joint ticket with Nicola Sturgeon, he surged forward. Typically, his campaign leaflet was bold on promises. 'Let's get winning again' was his slogan, going on to say:

> "To win independence, we must start winning as a Party. My goal is to win seats at the Westminster election and win government in 2007. I said when I announced my candidacy that I was not just campaigning to be SNP Leader and meant it. I am campaigning to be Scotland's next First Minister.
>
> I am standing as part of a team with Nicola Sturgeon because I know that together we can win. Between us we can reach out to all of Scotland north and south, male and female, young and well .... the slightly more experienced. We offer a ticket for success and I hope you will join us on the journey to freedom"

And when it came to the ethos and policy of the Party under his future leadership, he made it clear that the SNP had to rediscover its heart and soul as well as deploy the brain. Under his leadership, the Party would be social democratic with the common weal being the guiding principle. And although Scotland was a country rich in human resources, no one owed it a living. It should foster a spirit of enterprise and banish forever the politics and economics of dependency. While asserting that Scotland was a great country, it could be so much more with independence. His aim was to make our fellow Scots seek independence in their hearts, their heads and their souls.

By contrast, Roseanna Cunningham declared that the Scottish Parliament was now to the focus of Scottish politics, delicately making the point that Alex Salmond was away in Westminster and that Michael Russell was neither an MP nor an MSP. She conceded that the Party had been through difficult times. There was no room for short term fixes. The Party had to look to the reality of modern Scotland where voter disillusion and cynicism, particularly with the perceived failure of the Parliament, were rife. She wanted a new image and style, and believed that a united party could defeat the Labour First Minister, Jack McConnell in the 2007 election.

On the policy front, she called on the SNP not to be afraid of its radical roots. It should campaign on the removal of nuclear weapons, keeping Scotland out of illegal wars, pursuing the goal of affordable housing and economic growth, democratising the health service and providing a real choice in social matters such as schools, family support and child birth. She was determined to campaign on issues where independence could make a difference.

The third candidate was Mike Russell, a battle hardened former MSP and Party Chief Executive. An ally and supporter of Alex Salmond, he found himself pitched against his former friend and 'boss'. He began with the disadvantage of not having a seat at Holyrood or Westminster in which to focus his leadership. Astutely, he decided to base his campaign on the need for change calling for the release of new ideas and policies and stressed his experience and abilities in communication. He placed his main task in people management to make the Party united and to harness the skills and energies of members more effectively.

He laid out five steps to Independence – new thinking on issues of fairness and equality, renewal of the Party through redefining its mission, marrying public services to enterprise and opportunity, seeking fiscal autonomy through taxation powers and re-engaging the people of Scotland with their democratic institutions and (a dangerous one this for any party leader) allowing MSPs greater latitude in voting through less use of the whipping system.

This then was the line up for the leadership. Almost as important was the election for Depute Leader. Again there were three candidates – Nicola Sturgeon, Fergus Ewing and Christine Grahame, all MSPs.

Nicola Sturgeon's name has occurred frequently. The youngest of the three at 34, she had been around in the SNP for a long time having been a member of Glasgow University Scottish Nationalist Association while studying law. Her career path was through the Youth Movement and Publicity as a Vice Chairman for each successively. In Glasgow Shettleston Constituency in 1992, she was the youngest parliamentary candidate in Scotland. Certainly, her youth did not faze her. Articulate to the point of aggression in debate, she had gained a reputation as 'a nippy sweetie' in her early days but with the passage of years had mellowed – somewhat - as anyone debating against her would find! There was little surprise that she had been adopted as running mate by Alex Salmond. They thought alike and she had increasing support in her own right because of her performance in the Scottish Parliament.

In her literature she explained, as she needed to, that she had stood down from the leadership contest as it was in the best interests of the SNP, especially since she and Alex had the united goal of putting the passion back into independence. Her principal task would be to steer the Party's policy development and to lead the SNP Group of MSPs at Holyrood. Her main policy aim would be to make Scotland a better place to live in. Above all, she would be working in joint harness with Alex Salmond in building a team.

In other circumstances, Fergus Ewing would have been a serious candidate. Another lawyer, he had won his spurs by winning Inverness, Nairn & Lochaber in 1999 and held on to the seat when it became Inverness and Nairn with an increased majority in the days when winning a constituency seat was a solid achievement. His campaign was firmly directed towards the issue of independence and how we were to get it. He promised a policy review of defence, Europe, taxation and energy. He emphasised his record in standing up for 'the under-dog' and undertook to make the quango state accountable, to tackle bureaucracy and to cut wasteful expenditure.

Christine Grahame, yet another lawyer, was the third candidate for the deputy leadership. A genuine character, she relished being the 'wild card' entry to the competition and ran a freebooting campaign with panache. Representing the Borders region, she stood as an anti-establishment candidate and sought to represent the grass roots members within the Party and to make MSPs and MPs more accountable to the membership. On policy issues she focused on the elimination of poverty – especially for the young and pensioners. She saw Scotland taking an international position as a free and non-aligned nation in the UN working for peace and justice in the world. Above all, she would seek to build a coalition with others having a common cause for independence.

After an intensive campaign with many meetings throughout the country, the final votes were clear cut. Alex Salmond emerged the winner with almost 76% in a ballot of 60% of the participating membership. Nicola Sturgeon emerged with 54% to become Depute Leader. Of the unsuccessful leadership candidates Roseanna Cunningham secured 15% and Mike Russell 10% (all rounded up). For the deputy leadership candidates Fergus Ewing won 25% and Christine Grahame 22%

There was a new sense of hope and determination in the SNP with the election of fresh leadership. Nicola Sturgeon got to work on the promised policy review while Alex Salmond used the freedom of being a Westminster MP to tour the country and to kindle fresh life. Because of the reverses, the Party organisation had shrunk and a recruitment campaign followed. Despite the troubles, membership had risen, then fallen slightly at the changeover before climbing to 10,995 in 2005. By 2006, it had risen to 12,571. The Party needed to address a large funding deficit and build up the election funds for the 2005 Westminster Election.

Shadow Cabinet 2004/05

The reconstituted shadow cabinet was:

Leader & Westminster Group Leader	Alex Salmond MP
Depute Leader & Group Leader	Nicola Sturgeon MSP
Environment, Rural Affairs & Fisheries	Richard Lochhead MSP

Justice	Kenny MacAskill MSP
Enterprise & the Economy	Jim Mather MSP
Education & lifelong Learning	Fiona Hyslop MSP
Tourism Transport & Telecoms	Fergus Ewing MSP
Health & Community Care	Shona Robison MSP
Finance	Alasdair Morgan MSP
Social Justice	Christine Grahame MSP
Culture & Sport	Michael Matheson MSP
Business Manager & Scottish Chief Whip	Tricia Marwick MSP
Work & pensions	Mike Weir MP
Europe	Ian Hudghton MEP
Local Government	Cllr David Alexander

The policy review commenced immediately and 'Green Papers' appeared on the agenda of National Council in December 2004. There were three papers presented: 'Revitalising Local Democracy' from Fiona Hyslop and Shona Robison, 'A New Economic Policy' from Richard Lochhead and Jim Mather and 'Active Citizenship' from Kenny MacAskill. A fair number of speakers gave their views as part of a process of consultation.

It was the new Treasurer Colin Beattie who sounded financial warnings. The Party had a total indebtedness of £850,000 and a bank overdraft of £390,000. There were the Westminster elections ahead with a target of £200,000 for the election fund towards which only £35,000 had been collected. These numbers were of an entirely different magnitude to the worrying sums of the nineties which now appeared trifling! The Treasurer emphasised that the Party's traditional income streams failed to meet the needs of running what was now a complex, and sophisticated political entity, which required to fund and support political activity across a wide spectrum of Scottish politics. He hoped to fund the election through a forthcoming campaign under the label of 'Alex's Army'. Meantime the experiment of a team where the 'boss' was absent from the main political cockpit seemed to work with Nicola having the incisiveness to attack what had become a tired and discredited coalition administration of the Labour and Liberal Democrat parties. Alex Salmond added to his profile in the autumn when he led an attempt to have Prime Minister Tony Blair impeached for the illegal Iraqi war.

2005 was a General Election year and although the Westminster Elections had joined the Euro Contests as 'also rans' to the Scottish Parliament where all the political action and publicity were centred, they were still important from the viewpoint of credibility. A special conference was convened for the spring to lay down the organisational platform and policy manifesto for the election.

The campaign concentrated on domestic issues spotlighted in a detailed and ambitious manifesto featuring the economy, pensions, the council tax, disbanding of the Scottish regiments and nuclear weapons. There was once more reliance on the message of holding the balance of power in a hung parliament.

Surprisingly, Alex Salmond according to accounts was not in his best form. The results led to gains in two constituencies, my old stamping ground of Dundee East where to my joy, Stewart Hosie was successful and the Western Isles (under its Gaelic name of Na h-Eileanan an Iar) last held by Donald Stewart in 1987 and now regained by Angus MacNeill from Labour like Dundee East. The number of Scottish seats had been reduced from 72 to 59 with substantial Boundary Commission changes. Comparisons were not possible but Labour emerged with 41 MPs, the Liberal Democrats with 11, the SNP with 6 and the Conservatives back again with 1 (Dumfriesshire, Clydesdale and Teviotdale). In terms of votes, the SNP did less well with a fall of 2.4% to 17.4%, marginally ahead of the Conservatives (15.8%) and third after the Liberal Democrats who had 22.6%. Labour was well ahead with 39.5% although they had sustained a loss of 4.5%. Of the minor parties, the Scottish Socialists secured 1.9% while losing ground and the Scottish Greens who had 1.1%.

General Election (Westminster) - 5 May 2005

Party	Votes	Percentage	Seats
Labour	922,402	39.5%	41
Liberal Democrat	528,076	22.6%	11
SNP	412,267	17.7%	6
Conservative	369,388	15.8%	1
Scottish Socialist	43,514	1.9%	0
Scottish Green	25,760	1.1%	0
Turnout			60.6%

In the aftermath of the Westminster election, there were few tensions. The winning of two seats was more than adequate consolation for the general fall off in the SNP's vote and in any event, Westminster was no longer of dominant interest. So instead of having critical post mortem examinations, the Party began its preparations for the 2007 Scottish General election. There was one curious debate involving Westminster. At the June National Council, the Party considered a resolution from Glasgow proposed by MSP Sandra White that no member of the Scottish National Party should take a seat in the Upper House of the United Kingdom Government, except by direct election. There was an amendment to the effect that the SNP should contest such elections with the rider that no successful candidate should take up a seat until the Party was satisfied that the Upper House (political speak for the House of Lords) was reformed and truly democratic. The amendment was defeated overwhelmingly and a motion to remit back carried. This non-decision made no difference. Unlike its sister party Plaid Cymru, the SNP has never appointed anyone to the Lords and has managed well enough without 'Lairds and Barons'!

Cllr Willie Sawyers, organisation convener, presented a paper on preparations for the 2007 local government elections which would be held for the first time under the Single Transferable Vote system. The new electoral system had the power to transform local government and end Labour hegemony in the central belt.

Before that the Party had to face two by-elections on 29 September. To its anger they were to be held on the same day. But as the Presiding Officer, George Reid (an SNP MSP before elevation to the chair) had made the decision, any complaints had to be restrained amid silent gnashing of teeth.

Glasgow Cathcart By-election (Scottish Parliament)
- 29 September 2005

Party	Votes	Percentage
Labour	5,811	37.7%
SNP	3,406	22.1%
Conservative	2,306	15%
Liberal Democrat	1,557	10.1%
Independent	856	5.6%
Scottish Socialist	819	5.3%
Scottish Green	548	3.6%
Others (2)	102	
Turnout		45%

It was a Labour hold despite the former Labour MSP having just been jailed for fire raising but the SNP candidate Maire Whitehead gained a creditable increase of 5.8%, mainly at the expense of the independent who had been a prominent Labour Councillor and Scottish Socialists, indicating that the former mood swing to non-establishment parties and independents had abated. The Conservative and particularly the Liberal Democrat tallies were also up.

Livingston By-election (Westminster) - 29 September 2005

Party	Votes	Percentage
Labour	12,319	41.8%
SNP	9,639	32.7%
Liberal Democrat	4,362	14.8%
Conservative	1,993	6.8%
Scottish Green	529	1.8%
Scottish Socialist	407	1.4%
Others (4)	228	
Turnout		58.1%

This was another Labour hold, this time following the death of their leading MP, Robin Cook. Given the need to fight on both fronts, the SNP had put most of its national effort into this constituency, with their candidate, Angela Constance adding 11% to the SNP vote, mainly at the expense of Labour and the Conservatives.

There was also a readjustment of parliamentary spokesmen for 2005/06.

Shadow Cabinet

Leader & Westminster Group Leader	Alex Salmond MP
Depute Leader & Group Leader	Nicola Sturgeon MSP
Party Business Manager	Bruce Crawford MSP
Scottish Group Manager & Chief Whip	Alasdair Morgan MSP
Party President	Ian Hudghton MEP
Environment, Rural Affairs, Energy and Fisheries	Richard Lochhead MSP
Justice	Kenny MacAskill MSP
Enterprise	Jim Mather MSP
Economy	Stewart Hosie MP
Education & Lifelong Learning	Fiona Hyslop MSP
Tourism, Transport & Telecoms	Fergus Ewing MSP
Health & Community Care	Shona Robison MSP
Finance & Public Services	John Swinney MSP
Social Justice	Christine Graham MSP

Culture & Sport	Michael Matheson MSP
Housing	Tricia Marwick MSP
Defence & international Relations	Angus Robertson MP
Work & Pensions	Mike Weir MP
Europe	Alyn Smith MEP

The year closed with a meeting of National Council on 3 December 2005. It concentrated largely on business matters with Nicola Sturgeon reporting on progress on reformulating policy through National Assemblies and a spring Conference.

There was a debate on the European Constitution which followed on the mothballing of the proposals after adverse referenda in France and the Netherlands. This requested the Shadow Cabinet to set up a Working Party to reappraise the stance of the SNP and called for the strengthening of rules on subsidiarity, ending the EU's exclusive jurisdiction of marine biological resources and campaigning for support to terminate the Common Fisheries Policy. Amended by proposals for the Council of Ministers to meet in public and for a period of reflection, the resolution was carried overwhelmingly. Further resolutions on pensions and asylum seekers were debated and went through by acclaim. There was a debate on nuclear power. It called on the Scottish Executive to use planning powers to block new nuclear build in Scotland. This generated a motion to remit back. Council would have nothing of it and the remit back failed by an overwhelming majority, allowing the resolution to pass.

The main issue confronting the Party in 2006 was the organisation of the coming Scottish Parliament election the coming year. In preparation some of the SNP's younger leaders and staffers had met in Speyside in June 2005. Comprising Angus Robertson, Peter Murrell, Stephen Noon, Alasdair Allan, Angus MacNeill and Kevin Pringle, they had looked afresh at the priorities of communications, governance, message, organisation and resources. In other words, the intent was to prepare for Government. (Torrance, Salmond Against the Odds p. 238) Party HQ also had the services of Gordon Guthrie, an IT expert who had devised a more advanced version of Activate, the information system used to identify supporters. A lot of myth has grown out of Activate as if it were a magic weapon. It was not.

It could not work without intelligence gathering from canvasses by Party members. With that information, it was indeed a valuable tool which the SNP used comprehensively.

A taste of the battle on the referendum that lay ahead was given in an article in the Herald by their Scottish Political Editor, Douglas Fraser. He publicised newly released 1970s government records. In the article, Douglas Fraser recounted the dirty tricks of Government officials to do down the SNP whose MPs were then holding the balance of power at Westminster:

> "Whitehall officials broke the rules in the 1970s by knowingly providing party political ammunition for Labour against the SNP, it was revealed yesterday. The documents uncovered under the freedom of information law have ratcheted up the row over the Civil Service undermining the SNP during its heyday at the time. They show Scottish Labour headquarters had Whitehall officials do its research, despite officials having firm rules that they should serve ministers but never do party work.

> Asked to provide 'return ammunition' against the SNP with a promise it would be treated confidentially, energy department officials, with Scottish Office support, duly supplied a file of notes of use to the Labour party. The energy department's director of information said undermining the SNP and its claims about North Sea oil belonging to Scotland was 'part of my standard sales patter'. This was Bernard Ingham, a civil servant before he took on an overtly political role as Margaret Thatcher's spokesman.

> The revelations followed the release of a secret memo by a senior Scottish Office economist Gavin McCrone and circulated to ministers in 1975, warning them the SNP case for funding an independent Scotland with oil revenues was much stronger than the government admitted. Gavin said the only flaw in the SNP case was that it had under-estimated the potential wealth.

> The investigations have also shown Labour Ministers in the 1970s successfully leaned on BBC executives to block the

broadcast of documentaries believed to be too friendly to the nationalist case when Labour faced difficult local elections."

The British civil service was not neutral when it came to defending the interests of the British state against the tiresome democracy of Scotland. Exhaustive preparations for battle were needed if the SNP were to advance to its constitutional objective against the efforts of the Whitehall campaigning machine. The school of hard knocks had a further disappointment in store for the SNP activists as well as the leadership. Grand ambitions looked to be misplaced. It was all the more difficult as the SNP was widely expected to make progress, if not win the forthcoming Dunfermline & West Fife By-election. Early canvassing seemed to bear out this optimism.

The election came about due to the early death of sitting Labour MP Rachel Squire. After the Livingston by-election it was felt the SNP had a chance, aided by ructions in the Labour & Conservative ranks over candidate choice. The Liberal Democrats nationally were at low ebb and virtually nobody talked up their chances. Despite all this, the Liberal Democrats stormed past Labour to win the constituency with the SNP candidate, Douglas Chapman relegated to third place.

Dunfermline & West Fife By-election (Westminster)
- 9 February 2006

Party	Votes	Percentage
Liberal Democrat	12,391	35.8%
Labour	10,591	30.6%
SNP	7,261	21%
Conservative	2,702	7.8%
Scottish Socialist	537	1.6%
Scottish Christian	411	1.2%
Abolish Forth Bridge Tolls	374	1.1%
Others (2)	311	
Turnout		47.9%

There is no record of any discussion of this result at the National Council meeting several weeks later. Instead, a recent victor in a local government election in Milton addressed the meeting and Organisation Convener, Willie Sawyers called for continued campaigning for the Scottish election in 14 months time. A wide range of policies on rendition flights, nuclear power, Scottish Water and climate chaos went through on the nod. Interestingly, a trace of vested interest emerged with debates on the rule of 85 (varying pensions for public sector workers) where the resolution was amended before passing unanimously and severance pay for councillors (arising for those who were retiring before the new electoral system came into effect).

There was a vigorous debate on this resolution which failed when remitted back by a substantial majority. Towards the end of the session, when obviously the audience had diminished, a resolution welcoming the take-over of The Scotsman by a Scottish company met a mixed reception when it carried by 30 for to 24 votes against. (NC06/09) As experience proved, ownership by a Scottish company did little to dispel a unionist ethos.

The SNP also sustained a severe personal loss in late March with the death of Margaret Ewing, MSP for Moray. As Margaret Bain, she had won the difficult seat of Dunbartonshire East by a miniscule majority in October 1974. Despite indifferent health, Margaret had distinguished herself in the cockpit of Westminster when the SNP had held the balance of power during the seventies. She had been re-elected as MP for Moray in 1987 and subsequently as an MSP. She had served in various Party offices over the years (including being a candidate for the leadership) and as Westminster Parliamentary Leader. She was loved as well as admired and her premature death came as a shock.

The by-election was held in late April. At first sight, given the run of results, there was speculation in the media that Moray might prove difficult. This did not deter the SNP candidate, Richard Lochhead from resigning his list seat in order to seek full constituency status. The constituency was held by the SNP in style with an increased majority and an extra 4% of the vote at the expense of Labour. The Conservatives had a small increase and were obviously losers to the Liberal Democrat candidate who saw her share of the vote soar by 7.2%.

Moray By-election (Scottish Parliament) - 27 April 2006

Party	Votes	Percentage
SNP	12,653	46.1%
Conservative	6,268	22.9%
Liberal Democrat	5,315	19.4%
Labour	2,696	9.8%
NHSFirst Party	493	1.8%
Turnout		45.7%

The result was a timely boost to SNP fortunes that had been flagging. It also led to the introduction of Maureen Watt as the replacement list member for the North East. Maureen took the oath in English and Doric. A happy by-product of the result was it discomfited the other Parties as much as it enhanced SNP morale. It was just as well as the June National Council showed branches were being merged and derecognised, usually a sign of retreat rather than advance. Despite this retrenchment and the number of by-elections involving considerable expense to central funds, the National Treasurer, Colin Beattie was still sanguine. This was surprising. Although income had increased from £908,200 in 2003, to £1,305,775 in 2004, £1,118,148 in 2005, £1,836,405 in 2006 and £2,562,970 in 2007 (election year), the corresponding net liabilities were, £906,404, £649,093, £796,475, £344,224 and £564,814. (an Electoral Commission Scotland summary). Apart from fundraising and appeals, much of the commercial debt with the Bank was reduced through internal loans from members. After a busy spell in office, Alasdair Allan, the National Secretary resigned to be a candidate for the Western Isles the following year.

Yet another loss was sustained when Douglas Henderson died. Douglas had been MP for East Aberdeenshire from 1974 to 79. As a politically astute Chief Whip with a subtle mind he had engaged in complex and taut negotiations with the Labour Government dependent on the votes of the SNP MPs. He had served as deputy leader of the Party for several years later on. After a long period of illness, he had returned to fight elections in Dumfries & Galloway for Westminster and Glasgow for the European Parliament. At the time of his death, he was a list candidate for the 2007 election with a reasonable ranking that could make him an MSP when his experience would have been invaluable.

The remainder of the year saw massive steps - forward with large donations from Tom Farmer (£100,000) and Brian Soutar (£500,000) and a great surge of other donations to the election fund. New techniques such as a pod-cast of an address by Alex Salmond were brought into play. The Party was all too well aware that the Scottish election was due to take place close to the 300th anniversary of the Treaty of Union when the old Scottish Parliament had been adjourned to be replaced by the Union Parliament in London.

The SNP was certainly ready for the contest as never before. Since 2003, the membership had grown almost a third to 12,571. In the 2006/07 period, its income was £1,836, 405, 57% of which came from donations. The election appeal itself raised £672,014. There had been prior discussions with civil servant, so for the first time the SNP looked like an alternative government. Endorsements came from major figures like George Matthewson, former Chair of RBS. Alex Salmond was marketed as a likely government leader and indeed, the regional list ballot papers of Scottish parliamentary candidates were to refer to 'Alex Salmond for First Minister' rather than to the Scottish National Party. The Party was committed to an independence referendum as a way of seeking support from those in the electorate who thought independence went too far but, nevertheless were desperate to be rid of the increasingly unpopular Labour/Liberal coalition! People wanted change and the sole credible route lay in transferring support to the SNP. Ahead in the opinion polls as the SNP was, the voters could be sure that this time a vote for the SNP would not be wasted.

The manifesto was built around Alex Salmond and what his government could offer Scotland. Other than the pledge of a referendum on independence by 2010, it had little else that might conceivably scare the horses. It featured campaigning aspects like smaller class sizes, lifting the burden of graduate debt, retention of local hospitals (facing a purge under Labour), more police on the beat, abolishing the council tax, introducing a local income tax, cutting rates for small businesses, a White Paper on Independence and working with Westminster. It ran to great detail as a costed policy for government. It was backed up by a charter of what Alex's government would tackle in the first 100 days.

What was different was the tone. The usual rhetoric of a more successful Scotland was there. But it seized upon a widespread feeling that the Liberal/Labour Coalition had become tired and complacent with no ambition. It was as the literature said 'Time for a Change, a Time for Fresh

Thinking, a Time to move Forward and a Time for the SNP. The message? This was a political Party brim full of determination and confidence. It was ready for government. The Manifesto was of superb quality. No expense in design and layout had been spared. The Campaign had associated leaflets and broadcasts that took up and expanded the theme. SNP TV went on line. Scottish stars like Sean Connery, Martin Compston and Sandi Thom gave interviews

The opinion polls still held up and as they did, elements of the Scottish press became more favourable. The new team under Campaign Director, Angus Robertson was delivering on its vision.

The night was a long one. While the first election results indicated that the SNP was doing well, there were protracted delays at the counts. Some were due to bad weather. Most however came from confusion of voters over the second regional list ballots, through poor guidance explaining the regional list ballot paper. More problems arose from the local government votes under a new system of proportional representation, all exacerbated by the failure of digital scanning machines.

So it was not until the afternoon of 4th May that it became apparent that it was touch and go between Labour and the SNP. Indeed, it seemed that Labour might win by one MSP. At the count in Inverness, one SNP candidate, David Thompson thought the initial results were wrong and entered a challenge. Jim Lynch describes the position graphically:

> "On the day after the election, where the voting using a new system put in by the coalition was a shambles (step forward Douglas Alexander and Iain Gray joint planners), SNP and Labour were neck and neck with the Highland Regional Vote still to come in. Up in Inverness the returning officer called the candidates together to tell them the results of the 7 seats; he made it Labour 4, Conservatives 2 and Green 1. The SNP's David Thompson had been watching the results all night long and spotted that something was wrong. He challenged the figures. The Returning Officer (allegedly) said "I suppose you want to see the calculations?" David said "Yes, please" – his Election Agent, Angus Walker, backing him up. The Returning Officer went off and half an hour later reappeared with profuse apologies. The correct figures were 3 Labour, 2 SNP and 2 Conservatives. And that was enough to give the SNP 47 seats to 46 Labour, and the first SNP

Government ever. As one of my close friends the late Chris Grahame sometimes reminded me 'Don't forget – a handful of determined men can change the course of history.' David Thompson is in that handful."

The Scottish election was a near run thing between SNP and Labour. In the final tally, the SNP emerged with 47 seats to Labour's 46 – thanks to David Thompson that final gain from Labour on the list vote tipped the balance, leaving the SNP as the largest party even though it had no overall majority. In terms of votes, it was also a narrow squeak with the SNP securing 664,227 votes to 648,374 for Labour. The division of the list vote was similarly narrow – SNP, 633,401 to Labour, 595,415. In terms of gains, the SNP had won 20 with 32.9% and 31% of the respective votes. It had lost none while Labour lost 4. In the overall make-up of the Parliament the Conservatives won 17 seats, losing 1 and the Liberal Democrats 16 seats, also losing 1 - Gordon Constituency - to Alex Salmond. The election was a reversal of the defection of list voters to the Greens and Scottish Socialists in the 2003 election when voting patterns fractured. The Greens now stood at 2, down 5 while the Scottish Socialists lost all 6 of their MSPs. The Scottish Senior Citizens Party and independent, Dr Jean Turner both lost. The indomitable Margo MacDonald glided through to become the sole independent MSP.

Scottish Parliament General Election - 3 May 2007

Party	Constituency	%	Seats	Region	%	Seats	Total
SNP	664,227	32.9	21	633,401	31	26	47
Labour	648,374	32.2	37	595,415	29.2	9	46
Conservative	334,743	16.6	4	284,005	13.9	13	17
Liberal Dems	326,232	16.2	11	230,671	11.3	5	16
Scottish Green	2,971	0.2	0	82,584	2	2	2
Independents	25,047	1.2	0	21,320	1	1	1
Scottish Snr Citizens	1,702	0.1	0	38,743	1.9	0	0
Solidarity				31,066	1.5	0	0
Scottish Christian	4,586	0.2	0	26,575	1.3	0	0
BNP				24,616	1.2	0	0
Turnout	51.7%			52.4%			

The newspaper headlines blared out the victory of the SNP. SNP members exulted in a dream far beyond their imagination and expectations. But it was not as easy as that. Jim Lynch's joy was premature. The SNP was in minority and needed to forge a coalition or otherwise persuade the Parliament to back it coming into office. The SNP had hoped that the Liberal Democrats would agree to a coalition. Unfortunately, they were embittered with the loss of Gordon to Alex Salmond. There was also the not inconsiderable matter of the pledge by the SNP to hold an independence referendum by 2010. The Liberal Democrats (especially the Liberals before them) had always been supporters of Home Rule, preferably on a federal basis within the United Kingdom (an aim blighted by lack of interest on the part of the English people who not unnaturally did not want to see their nation balkanised to placate the Celtic fringe!). Yet despite this historical loyalty, they were if anything more Unionist that the Labour and Conservative Parties. And while there was no comparison with the vicious war between the SNP and Labour, the Liberals saw the SNP as a block to their further progress in Scotland.

The Scottish Parliament being relatively new had not yet formulated constitutional precedents and traditions; yet one rule accepted was that the largest party had the right to attempt to form a government if it did not possess an outright majority. On this basis, the SNP approached the Liberal Democrats to see if they would enter into negotiations with a view to hammering out a programme for government. The Liberal Democrats met in caucus when a significant majority was opposed. Instead of turning down the proposal flat they announced there would be no talks unless the SNP renounced the independence referendum. Alex Salmond refused to abandon it but promised he would attempt to find creative solutions even to the extent of consulting his Party, if only they could meet. The outcome was negative. The Liberal Democrats refused to budge but at least offered a concession that the SNP could form a minority government. The Greens likewise refused to hitch their wagon of 1 to a coalition administration.

After all the comings and goings, a minority government it was to be. SNP members gave a collective sigh of relief although they realised as did the other parties and the media that its longevity was precarious. So on 16 May 2007 by a majority of 49 votes to 46 (Labour voting against), Alex Salmond was elected to office as First Minister.

Chapter 9:

IN GOVERNMENT

In his acceptance speech, Alex Salmond set out his objectives:

"We should remember the Parliament was created by the people of Scotland by referendum. It is bigger than any of its members or any party. I believe Scotland is ready for change and ready for reform. We are only a small nation, but we have a big future. We also face some big challenges.

Earlier on it was said that Scotland is a divided nation. Given the closeness of the election result, I understand why people might feel that way. However, it is not the case; we are not divided. Certainly the gap between rich and poor is far too great; we need to grow the economy faster; we need to heal the scars of the past; we need to be greener; and we need to be smarter still – but we are not divided. We have a sense of ourselves, a sense of community, and above all, a sense of the commonweal of Scotland.

In some ways, we are not even a divided Parliament. Of course, those in this part of the chamber seek independence and equality for Scotland. I am told that not everyone in the chamber agrees with that policy, although some members do. However, there is a broad consensus for the Parliament to assume greater responsibility for the governance of Scotland, as well as an understanding that we are engaged in a process of self-government and an awareness of the distance we have already travelled.

In 1961, Bashir Ahmad came to Glasgow to drive buses. The very idea of a Scottish Parliament was unimaginable. In 1961, the idea of a Scots Asian sitting in a Scots Parliament was doubly unimaginable, but Bashir is here and we are here. That part of the community of Scotland is now woven into the Parliament's tartan and we are much stronger as a result.

We are therefore diverse, not divided.

The nature and composition of the Scottish Parliament in its third session makes it imperative for this Government to rely on the strength of argument in the Parliament rather than the argument of parliamentary strength. Despite all the challenges that will mean, I welcome the chance to develop a new and fundamentally more reflective model of democracy in Scotland.

The days since the election have been dominated by questions about the structure of the Government. Will there be a coalition or will there be a minority Government? I say to the whole Parliament that the structure of Government matters less to people whom we represent than what we achieve on their behalf.

All of us in the Parliament have a responsibility to conduct ourselves in a way that respects the Parliament that the people have chosen to elect. That will take patience, maturity and leadership on all sides of the chamber. My pledge to the Parliament today is that any Scottish Government that is led by me will respect and include the Parliament in the governance of Scotland in the next four years.

In this century, there are limits to what Governments can achieve, but one thing that any Government I lead will never lack is ambition for Scotland. Today, I commit myself to leadership wholly and exclusively in the Scottish national interest. We will appeal for support across the chamber policy by policy. That is the Parliament that the people of Scotland have elected and that is the Government that I will be proud to lead."

The next day, his list of Ministers was ratified by the Scottish Parliament.

SNP Scottish Cabinet 2007

First Minister   Alex Salmond

Deputy First Minister &
Cabinet Secretary
Health & Wellbeing   Nicola Sturgeon

Cabinet Secretaries

Finance & Sustainable Growth	John Swinney
Education & Lifelong Learning	Fiona Hyslop
Justice	Kenny MacAskill
Rural Affairs & the Environment	Richard Lochhead

Junior Ministers

Parliamentary Business	Bruce Crawford
Europe, External Affairs & Culture	Linda Fabiani
Enterprise, Energy & Tourism	Jim Mather
Transport, Infrastructure & Climate Change	Stewart Stevenson
Schools & Skills	Maureen Watt
Children & Early Years	Adam Ingram
Public Health	Shona Robison
Communities & Sport	Stewart Maxwell
Community Safety	Fergus Ewing
Environment	Michael Russell

These are the bare facts. The formation of a government had been the longstanding dream of Party members. Many lifelong supporters had died without seeing the day, yet it was their sustained work for Scotland and faith in the ability of the Party that helped achieve it. Amidst disappointments and disasters leavened only by the odd success, this was clearly against reason. But they kept the faith and for those veterans, the reward had come. Jim Lynch's account tells it all:

> "I had taken over as the Editor of the Scots Independent in late 2005, but between one thing and the other, well it was only for 3 months, I hadn't got around to going in to the parliament, which was now at Holyrood. My wife and I went there as guests of Christine Grahame MSP to see Alex Salmond elected First Minister – a joyous occasion. My wife was sitting next to an elderly gentleman, and when he told me his name I said "You were involved in Robert McIntyre's Motherwell victory in 1945." He nearly fell off his seat because he did not think anyone would know him. I thought it was wonderful; someone who worked to get our very first Member of Parliament elected, sitting there to see an SNP First Minister take office, 62 years later. Like many, he never thought he would see that day."

The victory had a profound impact on the Scottish National Party in many other ways. It reinforced centralising trends apparent since the creation of the Parliament eight years before. Nor could it be disputed that the transfer of power from a decentralised party (at times controlled by branches run by small cliques) to a parliamentary leadership backed up by a well resourced headquarters had not borne fruit. In the early days of the Scottish Parliament, there was discord within the SNP group where individuals who opposed the leadership or had little experience of Party or group discipline did not hesitate to make their views known – and sometimes on a discordant basis. This led in time to resignations from the SNP Group.

This was a burden to the leaders who tried to instil the need for discipline if ever the SNP was to make progress against the ruling Labour/ Liberal Democratic administration of the first two terms. In the second session of Parliament, the grim reaper of the electorate had removed some of the opposition although it also cut down a number of MSPs with leadership potential.

The forming of the first SNP Government had a number of consequences. For the first time, a large number of MSPs and the Party membership had a lot to lose. The survival of the Government hung on a thin thread. It was in minority. It could be brought down at any time on legislative policy or governmental decisions. The need to pass a budget was the obvious danger. While Governments defeated on minor matters can always back track and make concessions, a budgetary defeat would spell the end. So obviously, MSPs had to be reined back and this could be done with the consent of Party which would no longer tolerate aberrant behaviour if it were to put at risk this precarious first minority government formed by the SNP. External pressure was not necessary. The strongest form of discipline is self-discipline and this was employed firstly by the MSPs themselves who adopted a self-denying ordinance to toe the line, mute criticism and give unswerving support to SNP Ministers – much to the disgruntlement of the media lobby whose supply of off-the-record or even open criticism of the Government dried up.

And down the line it went. The National Executive Committee had long been neutered. It could discuss political issues or ask for consultation and there it stopped. National Council was still an important instrument, however it too gave due deference to Ministerial policy. As for the National Conference, its agenda was controlled by the Standing Orders and Agenda Committee (SOAC) able to filter out controversy. Conference – and there were two a year – existed as a showpiece of the Party with the great advantage of a credible parade of Cabinet Secretaries with announcements of 'sweetmeats' for good causes. And the reason for this new unnatural loyalty from those who held strongly diverse opinions? Very simple! Success! Success on a scale never seen before, cemented by trust in those who had delivered it. Yet, it must be wondered whether this iron discipline over the longer term might not stifle new talent and new ideas.

Alex Salmond deserved full credit. He had not taken the easy path of being elected from the party list. He had gambled on winning the Gordon Constituency from the Liberals. No doubt his phenomenal organisation in Banff and Buchan had done its homework. After all parts of Gordon had once been in Banff and Buchan. Nevertheless, other politicians have gambled and crashed disastrously. With all his chopping and changing between Holyrood and Westminster, the electorate might have become stroppy. He took the risk and won. Also, by consenting to the presentation of the campaign on the personal theme of 'Alex Salmond for First Minister' he had laid his personal reputation on the line. The SNP knew this and appreciated it. So for someone described many years ago in his 'revolutionary' years as 'the young Robespierre', he had travelled a long way. Far now from being a 'Robespierre', he could fairly be described as 'a Scottish First Consul' as well as First Minister.

Despite their new eminence, Ministers realised that at heart the SNP consisted of its members and that their support depended on the leaders' ability to deliver success. The 2007 victory gave immense power to the leadership and at this stage at least it was important that the membership know the basics of the strategy for the advancement of the Party and independence. At the June National Council, Depute Leader Nicola Sturgeon (she it was who now delivered written reports in place of the Leader whose contribution was made orally) said that the government would proceed on the basis of competitiveness, consensus and vision. They would concentrate on the economy and the green revolution. She also warned that their ability to deliver rested on some thin parliamentary arithmetic. At the triumphant Conference in October, Alex Salmond moved a resolution, seconded by Nicola welcoming the publication of a White Paper on Independence and a National Conversation with the Scottish people. It also highlighted the area where Scotland could do better – the economy, employment and external relations.

The composition of the Cabinet was known. But where did real power lie? The Cabinet was largely composed of senior SNP politicians who were in Alex's camp and not likely to kick over the traces. Obviously, Alex Salmond and Nicola Sturgeon were a formidable team. Slightly further away from the centre of power was John Swinney, the former SNP leader. As Finance Secretary, he had the most important executive position in the Cabinet and as time progressed, he would be part of the Salmond, Sturgeon, Swinney triumvirate that ruled the Government and Party. A word must also be put in for Bruce Crawford, the Business Manager who was crucial in making the Government 'tick' by liaising with the other Parties to obtain a majority for Government policies. His advice on feasibility would be taken seriously. However, when it came down to decision making, it was Alex Salmond who decided!

The team of Ministers, whatever their provenance, proved to be able and most remained in post for many years. There were some changes and also readjustments of responsibilities. Alex Neil came in from the cold with appointment in 2009 as Minister for Communities. Amongst the Cabinet Secretaries, 2009 saw Michael Russell taking over from Fiona Hyslop in Education & Lifelong Learning. Fiona Hyslop moved to Minister for Culture & External Affairs, an amalgam of posts formerly held by Michael Russell and Linda Fabiani. Linda left the Government as did Maureen Watt as Minister for Schools & Skills, duties transferred to incoming Minister

Keith Brown. Shona Robison added Sport to her portfolio while Stewart Maxwell left office. In 2010, Stewart Stevenson resigned as Minister for Transport, Infrastructure & Climate Change and was replaced by Keith Brown in Transport & Infrastructure while Roseanna Cunningham took over Environment & Climate Change in a new department. In coming years, the ability of the Cabinet Secretaries and junior Ministers would firmly establish the reputation of the Scottish Government.

While all this was taking place on the Holyrood stage, the Party enjoyed a further triumph at local governmental level. This election had been held on the same day as that of the Scottish General Election. Because of the counting problems over the second list vote and the success of the SNP in the main election, the counting of the local government votes was severely delayed. In addition to the problems with the list vote, there were delays associated with the complexity of the new electoral system. As part of the price of coalition with the Liberal Democrats, and to the horror of their councillors in local power bases, the Labour Party had agreed to move to the Single Transferable Vote. This was a true system of proportional representation for Scotland's thirty two Councils. Using larger electoral areas, it replaced the former system of 'first past the post'. The end result was disastrous for Labour and beneficial for the other Parties, mainly the SNP as it gave them substantial membership in all councils and potentially a share of power in local coalitions. Labour kept control of North Lanarkshire and Glasgow but not in other strongholds where they had ruled without challenge for generations.

Council Election - May 2007

Party	First Pref. Votes	%	Gain/ Loss	Councillors	Gain/ Loss
Labour	590,085	28.1%	-4.5%	348	-161
SNP	585,885	27.9%	+3.8%	363	+182
Conservative	327,591	15.6%	+0.05%	143	+21
Lib Democrat	266,693	12.7%	-1.8%	166	-9
Independent	228,894	10.9%	+0.8%	192	-38
Others	102,897	4.9%	+1.3%	10	+6

In terms of control of Councils, the SNP had none; Labour had two; and others three. As most Councils had no overall control, the SNP and Labour respectively went into coalition or minority in 11, the Conservatives 11, the Liberal Democrats 8 and Others 9.

The huge number of gains for the SNP added honey to the victory in the election for the Scottish parliament and assured that the Party would have ground level activists in large numbers.

Naturally, no one could be sure of the impact of these major advances on the internal structures of the Party. In June, the National Secretary was asked by 'arch-proceduralist', Gerry Fisher whether National Council Reports would be altered to take into account the relationship between the Party and Ministers and was told that National Council must be maintained as at present and care would be needed to ensure the approachability of Ministers to the National Executive Committee.

Of course, being in Government was a new experience and Jim Lynch was taken aback early on:

> "They (the Liberal Democrats) probably imagined that an SNP minority government would stagger and fall over in months – if not weeks. As it happened, the SNP government lasted 4 years. The main problem each year was the Budget; the SNP needed support from one other party to get its budget through, so a lot of wheeling and dealing was necessary. When the Party produced its first draft budget in 2007 I, for one, was livid. We had 1000 police in our manifesto, and the Finance Secretary, John Swinney, put 500 police in the budget. I was not pleased, to say the least of it, at this flaunting of a manifesto promise. However, at dealing time, the Tories said they would support the budget but needed a few sweeties for that support. John scratched his head, hummed and hawed a bit, then opened his desk drawer: "Would you be interested in 500 police?" he asked. Game set and match! Worth noting that John Swinney got every budget through. It fell one year, as the Greens took the huff, at insulation as I remember, and Labour kept up its posturing. Local government in Scotland went mad as that was their funds being cut off, the telephone wires were red hot, and the Budget was reinstated and passed in days! The line at the time was 'The first time a Government defeat brought down the Opposition!' "

This study is primarily about the Party and the impact on it of a large parliamentary group in the Scottish Parliament and the campaign for the achievement of independence. The inside story of that Government and the inter-relationship of Ministers with the SNP Parliamentary Group is one for those involved to relate. This Government team was settled with little turnover. As time would pass, we would also be interested to see who would emerge from the ranks of junior ministers and the parliamentary group with the ambition to become future leaders of the Party.

Also extremely important is how the actions and performance of the Government would advance the Party's main objective of independence. Reminding ourselves that a principal leg of SNP strategy was to build up confidence in the Parliament to demonstrate that Scotland was able to manage all its own affairs, it was then vital for SNP Ministers to show confidence and sensitivity. One of the reasons for the change in Government was public disillusionment with Holyrood prior to the 2003 Election and subsequent dissatisfaction with the uninspiring performance of the Labour/Liberal Democrat administration.

The SNP Government, of course, did not have a majority. On the face of it this was a supreme disadvantage. It could not easily implement policies in the Manifesto. So much was this a problem that many commentators and opposition politicians did not expect the minority Government to survive for long with the expectation that when Alex Salmond's Government fell, the Labour/Liberal Democrat coalition would resurface – and given the SNP's pledge on an independence referendum, either the SNP or the Liberal Democrats would have had to swallow a considerable amount of humble pie for there to emerge an SNP/Liberal Democrat administration. Not impossible in the practical politics of keeping and winning power but mightily uncomfortable all the same!

However, being in a minority proved advantageous for winning support for the Government amongst the Scottish public. Scotland was slightly nervous at having put a 'rookie' party into a position of governance. Most legislation in any parliamentary democracy is non-controversial and all-party support is readily available. But when you come to Manifesto commitments or matters of crisis or controversy, it is different. Given that most of the opposition would be happy to sink a minority government, goodwill can be scarce. That is where Ministers needed to be flexible, to make concessions, to give in gracefully on what they thought relatively unimportant in order to get a Bill through the House. That is not always easy when Manifesto commitments have to be compromised.

So, in this situation the crucially important member of the Government is the Business Manager whose skills at persuasion, coercion and downright parliamentary bribery can make the difference between success and failure. The first holder of this job was Bruce Crawford who as a former civil servant had experience of the processes of government although hardly in a post of this sensitivity. Not surprisingly, he headed the list of Junior Ministers.

Right from the outset, Alex Salmond strove to give an impression of change at high tempo. During the first 100 days, the Government made a series of announcements implementing by executive act many of the achievable cardinal points of policy that did not require controversial legislation. In some cases, the opposition were dared to oppose popular innovations for which a political price would be paid. He also set the foundations for a future Scotland when he established a Council of Economic Advisers under the Chairmanship of Crawford Beveridge, an international businessman who had served as Chief Executive of Scottish Enterprise. The Council had a distinguished panel of members. In 2012, it spawned The Fiscal Commission Working Group with a smaller membership. Its task was to oversee the work of the Scottish Government in designing a macro-economic model for an independent Scotland and to support the engagement of key institutions to help the Scottish Government with its proposals.

The first crunch of minority Government occurred on 27 June when a parliamentary vote to give £500 million funding to an Edinburgh tram project was forced through against the wishes of the Government. This made a serious hole in the budget under preparation by the Finance Secretary, John Swinney. Reluctantly forced to back the 'trams' when defeated in a parliamentary vote, John Swinney capped any future government investment and made it clear that the trams were now the sole responsibility of Edinburgh Council – very wise precaution given the future fiasco!

When the SNP was elected to be the statutory Scottish Executive – the change of name to 'Government' occurring immediately after the SNP came to power, there appeared to be no clouds in the financial sky. The Government had been given a share of funding under the Barnett Formula which followed expenditure of the UK Departments. This expenditure was financed by UK government borrowing and as with all UK expenditure had been steadily increasing. In the summer, however, queues formed outside Branches of Northern Rock where customers demanded their money back in a 'bank run'. Over the next year major Banks domestically and internationally including HBOS (the bank that owned Bank of Scotland following a takeover by Halifax) and RBS (which had recklessly taken over a Dutch/Belgian Bank, ABN AMRO, infested with debt) collapsed like skittles. This ushered in an era of austerity with cuts in public spending. A depression is not the best time to be in government!

In particular, the restraints in income made it successively more difficult for John Swinney to frame and balance a budget that would prove acceptable to the opposition parties. It was his patient skill that managed to devise concessions acceptable to most of the minority parties. Labour was the exception. As Jim Lynch indicated, on the one occasion in 2008/09 the budget was defeated despite the Finance Secretary revising the figures to give Labour most of what they had demanded, they still voted it down. Alex Salmond threatened to call a general election. It was not this threat that caused a climb down. Horrified Labour Councils panicked when they realised that a defeat on the budget would turn off their local funding. Representations were made to Labour MSPs causing Scottish Labour to pull back their opposition.

Some policies caused the administration considerable difficulty. The Labour/Liberal Democrat Coalition like the Labour Government in the UK had embarked on a large number of ruinously expensive Public Finance Initiative (PFI) schemes whereby capital investments like schools and hospitals were built on cash provided by private sector consortia on terms which were punitively expensive. The SNP had quite rightly proposed to end these expensive 'hire purchase' schemes. It had proposed that funding be done through a Scottish Futures Trust where money would be borrowed more cheaply. More easily said than done to construct an entirely new system of public sector finance when the Scottish Parliament had no borrowing powers and the Treasury could be relied on to object to Scottish borrowing (however indirectly) at a time when the UK Government was in crisis mode over UK borrowing! It was done but several years of experimentation and some concessions to private investment were necessary.

In a depression, capital projects are needed to replace private investment so this whole matter was important. In the shallow world of parliamentary bickering, another promise to abolish the unpopular Council Tax and replace it with a Local Income Tax proved impossible. The SNP could not command a parliamentary majority. The Treasury was obstructive when it came to vital changes to tax collection through the UK wide agency of HMRC. In the short run, the Scottish Government froze the Council Tax and compensated the local authorities for the loss of revenue. Intended as a stop gap measure, the freeze proved very popular and was continued on a running basis.

Yet, if the prime purpose of having an SNP government is to prepare the ground for full self-government, the SNP had to ensure that through its government it lifted the veil on what an independent government could do in the world. That opportunity came in August 2009, when Kenny MacAskill, the Justice Minister announced that Abdelbaset Mohmed Ali Al Megrahi, who had been convicted of the bombing of the Pan American plane which had come down over the town of Lockerbie in Dumfriesshire, would be released on compassionate grounds and allowed to go home to Libya. Al Megrahi was suffering from terminal prostate cancer.

Not everyone in Scotland, the UK and the world generally was as compassionate! Notwithstanding that the Blair Government had previously done a prisoner deal with the Libyan government for Megrahi's transfer in order to win contracts for British industry, the new Conservative Government thought otherwise, deeming it presumptuous of a provincial government to interfere in foreign affairs which were the preserve of London. There was uproar. Condemnations flooded in from England and especially from the United States of America which had lost a high proportion of passengers in the bombing.

With US elections pending, the matter became a political controversy for US Senators representing east coast states about to face re-election. They put pressure on the US Government. President Obama criticised the move. Other parts of the world supported the actions of the Scottish Government. Nelson Mandela backed the decision. MacAskill and the Scottish Government stood firm. The Justice Secretary declared he had made a quasi-judicial decision based on medical reports obtained to validate Megrahi's state of health. When I complimented Kenny on his courage and the way he had stood up to hostile opinion, he said he had received full support from his civil servants amid the attacks. He had made his decision correctly in terms of the UK statute that had invested him with the discretion. London could not interfere because the Scottish legal system was fully under the control of Holyrood and administered from within Scotland.

This dispute with the US and London would rumble on. When Megrahi stepped off the plane in Libya he was welcomed by a crowd flying the Scottish flag and repeatedly this was shown worldwide on television. More importantly, this incident had given the impression to many countries that Scotland was now a country to be reckoned with. The Edinburgh Parliament may have been a provincial one, acting under devolved powers. Yet, it had stood up to the might of the United States and had snubbed London. In short, Scotland had acted as if it were an independent country with determination, courage and compassion. Many of those in Scotland who had opposed the transfer of a convicted terrorist had to confess to some pride in the actions of their own government on the world stage. For the future, the incident added to the status of the Scottish Government and made its leader recognised world-wide.

For the Party, normal politics continued in what had become a strange new environment of needing to defend the actions of a government rather than attacking it – a form of culture shock. And defending a government changed the conditions under which the Party fought by-elections. The SNP was much stronger in fundraising capability. Its membership post the 2007 election had risen to over 15,000. Success had bred success. Yet the Labour Party was still strong and was going to be difficult to dislodge in its heartlands.

By December 2007, the Party had adapted to the new position by regularising the right of council groups to enter into joint administrations with other parties. There was a successful amendment from Govan restricting coalitions to those not involving Conservative Councillors. National Council also elected David Alexander as Local Government Convener. The June meeting backed the Scottish Futures Trust with non-controversial amendments.

The principal preoccupation of 2008 was the fighting of elections in two Westminster constituencies. The first of these in Glasgow East was a victory for the SNP Candidate, John Mason – one of those rare occasions where the SNP came out on top. The second in Glenrothes took place in the autumn when the SNP Candidate was Peter Grant. It provided evidence - if it were needed - that the Westminster nut had still to be fully cracked.

Glasgow East By-election (Westminster) - 24 July 2008

Party	Votes	Percentage
SNP	11,277	43.1%
Labour	10,912	41.7%
Conservative	1,639	6.3%
Liberal Democrats	915	3.5%
Scottish Socialist	555	2.1%
Solidarity	512	2.0%
Others (3)	464 votes (Greens 232)	
Turnout		42.3%

The 365 majority was very narrow and even then it represented a huge 22% swing. In the run in to the Glenrothes contest, SNP hopes were high. The Party had done well in the local elections of the previous year. The SNP ran the Fife Council in coalition with the Liberal Democrats. At first glance, there were hopes that seat would be winnable if the momentum of Glasgow East were maintained. There was a nuance – the Liberal Democrats had also some considerable success in Fife – and Fife was proving to be an area where canvassing assessment was problematical as to accuracy! The SNP had a strong local councillor, Peter Grant as its candidate. Labour had Lindsay Roy, a local headmaster. The question was: which would trump the other.

Glenrothes By-election (Westminster) - 6 November 2008

Party	Votes	Percentage
Labour	19,946	55.1%
SNP	13,209	36.5%
Conservative	1,381	3.8%
Liberal Democrat	947	2.6%
Others (4)	712	
Turnout		52.4%

The SNP grew its share of the vote by a creditable 13.1% only to find that Labour, too, managed a 3.2% up-rating, both at the expense of the Liberal Democrats and Conservatives. Labour won!

It was also evident that traumatic changes in Britain's financial structures were taking place as the UK suffered from international pressures. Credit had dried up leading to banking failures at home and abroad. The great credit boom masterminded by Labour to end the cycle of 'boom and bust' was going to end in an almighty slump. The extent of the crisis and its longevity could not be foretold. Scotland, as an integral part of the UK, could not escape. Nevertheless, it was evident that the UK would need to close the borrowing gap and Scotland could expect swingeing cuts in its funding from the Treasury. It was not a good time to form your first government.

There were some political problems, too. Alex Salmond and the SNP had long prayed in aid of the benefits of independence an 'arc of prosperity' which included Iceland and Ireland as well as the Scandinavian countries. Both Ireland and Iceland had runs on their banks and had to be rescued. Ireland found it necessary to seek comfort from the European Union while the Icelandic people resolutely refused to insure the international losses of their banks. The SNP Government was curiously passive in relation to the collapse of HBOS (which included the Bank of Scotland) and the Royal Bank of Scotland. It was perhaps embarrassed that its support for light regulation of the banks in the preceding decade left it exposed.

Also, the SNP had not discouraged the potentially dangerous RBS reverse take-over of the much larger Nat West in England – dangerous because of the imbalance in size of the respective institutions. Alex Salmond had also supported the RBS take-over of ABN-Amro the debt laden Dutch bank which finally brought about the collapse of RBS. The Party had been uncharacteristically silent when the Bank of Scotland had been acquired by Halifax some 10 years previously. In previous decades it had zealously campaigned against the take-over of RBS by HKSB, now HSBC and the privatisation of the Trustee Savings Bank to protect the integrity of the Scottish banking system.

A problem for the SNP and the Government was that the banking collapses were used by unionist politicians to decry the financial security of a Scottish state. How could a small country like Scotland pay for the rescue of large international banks, they asked? And yes, with the example of

Ireland before them, they had a point - or would have had, if the corporate debts related largely to operations inside Scotland rather than had arisen externally.

Most other countries in similar situations were bullied by fear and non-co-operation from the EU or the US into having their citizens accept liability for the misdeeds of the banking sector. The problem for governments is that they feel forced to act reasonably to their neighbours even if they cripple their own economies in doing so. Greece is the prime example. Ireland, Portugal and Spain in the EU followed closely behind. It is distressingly likely that an independent Government would have behaved similarly. Certainly, the devolved Scottish Government gave a convincing impression of a rabbit in the middle of a road facing the headlights of an oncoming vehicle – and largely said nothing.

This was wrong. Even if a Scottish Government agreed to a bail out – and if a member of the Euro system would have been forced to - it should have been more positive. For example, it could have declared that an independent Government could have nationalised the Scottish operations of the banks and faced with that threat, England would have been forced to pick up the tab for non-Scottish debts incurred by the operations of HBOS and RBS/Nat West there. Co-operation had taken place as between the Benelux countries in dealing with problems with the Fortis bank whose operations straddled their countries.

It would have been unreasonable for Scotland to have refused to assist with a wider bail-out, it could be argued. Icelandic governments wanted to do so but in a referendum and elections, the Icelandic people said no - and were not to be refused, perhaps made even more determined when the UK used anti-terrorist legislation to seize funds of Icelandic banks deposited in the UK. There were consequences in toughing it out. The Icelandic currency plummeted but with an absence of the burden of huge debt, their economy had no handicaps against growth. The depreciation of the currency proved to be a great boon in making the country competitive. Six years later with growth over 2.5%, the damage has been repaired, they are in course of rejoining the 'arc of prosperity' and are voluntarily repaying some overseas debt! The Icelanders are a tough people, much hardier and more independent than the Scots. They did not care about being popular or 'communitaire'. And they have two major advantages. They have their own currency and they are members of EFTA and not the EU. If they had been in the EU, their scope for independent action would have been compromised.

In the meantime, the minority SNP Government had to shelter the Scottish economy from the full impact of the London cuts, especially after the Conservative Government came into power in 2010. It was no easy task and again the credit for balancing the budget and minimising the risk fell upon the shoulders of John Swinney. The opposition parties were largely neutered by the threat from the First Minister to place the SNP in election readiness if the budget and other critical policies failed. In June, 2009 after the European Parliament Elections , the Headquarters of the Party were transferred from McDonald Road to Gordon Lamb House, near the Scottish Parliament building. These elections paid off, showing that the performance of the SNP Government had achieved widespread popularity. There was the added satisfaction of pushing Labour into second place by quite a margin

European Parliament Election - 2009

Party	Votes	Percentage	Seats
SNP	321,007	29.1%	2
Labour	229,853	20.8%	2
Conservative	185,794	16.8%	1
Liberal Democrat	127,038	11.5%	1
Green Party	80,442	7.3%	0
UKIP	57,788	5.2%	0
BNP	27,174	2.5%	0
Socialist Labour Party	22,135	2%	0
Christian Party	16,738	1.5%	0

After a relatively quiet summer, the SNP was faced with yet another by-election, this time in Glasgow North East. It followed the resignation of Michael Martin, (Labour) who was the first post-union Speaker to be forced from office. There was a huge number of candidates.

That was the end of the excitement. On polling day, the turn-out was 33%, the lowest ever Scottish by-election figure. David Kerr did his best in the circumstances but was without the benefit of the constituency connection enjoyed by John Mason in the neighbouring constituency, Glasgow East, won for the SNP in 2008.

Glasgow North East By-election (Westminster)
- 12 November 2009

Party	Votes	Percentage
Labour	12,231	59.4%
SNP	4,120	20%
Conservative	1,075	5.2%
BNP	1,013	4.9%
Solidarity	794	3.9%
Liberal Democrat	474	2.3%
Scottish Green	332	1.6%
Jury Team	258	1.2%
Others (5)	298	
Turnout		33.2%

Labour were difficult to shift in Glasgow. Comfort was taken by an Ipsos Mori Poll also in November showing that throughout the country the SNP held the lead for voting intentions. For Westminster, the SNP had a narrow lead of 34% to Labour's 32% and for Holyrood the tallies were slightly wider 36% to 32%. The SNP gain came from all parties with a huge drop in support for the Lib Dems for Westminster and slightly less of a decline for Labour. When it came to issues, the poll showed that the first two areas of importance to the electorate were unemployment and the economy, followed by health and education. Constitutional matters had moved up in ranking to fifth. Alex Salmond's popularity ratings exceeded those of Gordon Brown and David Cameron.

Some signs of 'stroppiness' emerged at the December National Council when Council remitted back resolutions on by-election levies and health. The main business was the White Paper setting out the terms of the independence debate and presentation of the campaign for the 2010 Westminster General Election. The theme of the campaign was based on Scotland's need for more champions – in parliament and in communities. The Party had set a target to win 20 Westminster seats. The narrative ran that without a strong team of SNP MPs in the House of Commons, and a strong Scottish voice, the London Parties would target Scotland. Deep cuts in essential services would follow at a time when billions would be spent on replacement of the Trident missile system.

There was no mention to members that a large vote for the SNP would advance independence. Instead MPs, as both national and local champions, would work to safeguard Scotland's interests, particularly local jobs and local services and argue for a fair deal on fuel prices and pensions. The aim was to represent the people in the House of Commons; certainly not to withdraw from it by winning Scotland's independence.

So with this 'inspiring' call to arms, the SNP went into battle. The result was a very modest 2.3% up-rating of the share of the vote, largely at the expense of the Liberal Democrats. Labour did marginally better with an increase of 2.5%. Even the Conservatives posted almost 1% up. As for seats won, these remained stubbornly at 6.

General Election (Westminster) - 6 May 2010

Party	Votes	Percentage Vote	Seats
Labour	1,035,528	42%	41
Liberal Democrat	465,471	18.9%	11
SNP	491,386	19.9%	6
Conservative	412,855	16.7%	1
Turnout			63.8%

This election was unusual since for the first time it presented the leaders of the UK political parties in televised debates as if they were presidential candidates. The power of this presentation was shown in the first of the three debates when Nick Clegg, Leader of the Liberal Democrats emerged as the winner. This gave a forward thrust to the Lib Dem campaign for a time until the momentum was lost in the remaining battles.

Despite strong protests, the UK parties in collaboration with the UK broadcasters refused to permit the SNP Leader and Scotland's First Minister to appear. This discrimination against the SNP in election broadcasts is traced thoroughly in 'SNP: The Turbulent Years 1960-1990'. The breakthrough of the SNP to become Scotland's government changed nothing in English terms. The same discrimination applied to party leaders in Wales and Northern Ireland, leaving the brutal and unavoidable conclusion that unless you challenged in England, you counted for nothing. Nothing had changed.

The eyes of the Party were firmly focused on the next Scottish General Election due in 2011 so despite a well justified grievance that the dice had been loaded against the SNP, the June meeting of National Council showed little sign of protest. The decision to exclude Scotland's first Minister appeared more a slap to the face of Scotland than to the SNP.

Interestingly, following the June 2010 meeting of National Council the National Secretary, William Henderson responded by letter to the redoubtable Gerry Fisher on the subject of Europe and ensured that the Party's policy passed at Conference in 2002 was enshrined in the Minutes for reference, a novel procedure. In addition to the policy statement it gave the text of the 2009 Conference Resolution as it related to the Party's position on the Euro.

> "The SNP notes that it is only with the full powers of independence that Scotland would have the maximum flexibility to protect Scotland from the current recession, take the necessary steps to create the circumstances for sustainable economic recovery and to play our part in co-ordinated global policies to both stabilise and grow the global economy whilst creating an appropriate regulatory framework.
>
> The SNP further recognises that the interests of the people of Scotland would be best served by an independent Scotland becoming a member of the Euro should the economic conditions be right and following a referendum of the Scottish people. Membership of the Euro would allow an independent Scotland to participate and engage in the debate for effective financial regulation in Scotland and Europe."

The National Secretary added that the pledge to have a referendum on the Euro did not extend to membership of the Union itself. The lack of protest over broadcasting in June was not replicated in December when the Party entered the strongest possible objection to the Westminster decision to hold a referendum on the Alternative Vote on the same day as the devolved parliamentary elections. It took the opportunity to advocate the Single Transferable Vote system now operative for Scottish council elections.

Chapter 10:

A MIRACULOUS MAJORITY

The SNP Government had survived for three and a half years despite all the predictions that it would fall. It had governed well and now enjoyed widespread support to the chagrin of the Labour Party. Yet all good times come to an end and the end of this first term was on the horizon.

The re-election campaign was launched at the Annual Conference in October. Every member was determined to see Alex Salmond returned as First Minister for another term. Indeed, ambitions went further. The minority Government had been unable to make any progress in delivering the Grail of an independence referendum in face of opposition from the unionist parties. The aim was to secure an increased mandate although nobody expected to win a majority since the electoral rules had been devised at the outset to prevent the SNP from ever achieving full victory.

No expense was to be spared. Ultimately, the SNP spent £1,141,662 on a five month campaign, including £300,000 on advertising. Labour spent £816,889, the Conservatives £273,462 and the Liberal Democrats £176,300. (Electoral Commission for Scotland) To put this into context, the SNP spent £240,000 less than it did in 2007. (Guardian) In implementing the campaign, the SNP distributed 1.4million of their Saltire newspaper, 1 million copies of cards with the words, 'Alex Salmond for First Minister', had 200 billboard adverts and canvassed 25,000 electors a week. 10,000 party workers were out on polling day. (Scotsman Digital)

The SNP campaign was also in front by providing an Iphone app for volunteers that would give them access to the SNP's on line canvass system and social media networks. It would also provide SNP information and policies on tap, daily campaign updates, breaking news and events. SNP Campaign Director, Angus Robertson claimed in October when rolling out the app that this was a groundbreaking system that had been trialled in the 2010 Westminster election for canvassers going round the doors.

The Manifesto itself explicitly promised to give the Scots an opportunity to decide their nation's future. The theme was 'Re-elect a Scottish

Government working for Scotland'. It included promises to freeze the Council Tax for the duration of the parliamentary term and to protect the NHS budget and police numbers. The Government would unify the fire service (with no mention of the police). There were also promises on jobs, training and minimum pricing of alcohol. An essential message was the record of the first SNP Government and the competence of SNP Ministers.

Labour was the principal opponent as always. Under their Leader Iain Gray, who did not have the same recognition or charisma of Alex Salmond, their campaign initially was based around opposition to the Westminster Coalition cuts, deploying the successful campaign strategy used in the 2010 General Election the previous year. To begin with they had reason to expect a good result. At the end of February, a YouGov study claimed that Labour was heading for a comfortable victory ahead of the SNP by 41% to 32%. Yet by the middle of April, a ScotPulse survey gave the SNP an 11 point lead in the constituency vote and a 10 point lead on the list vote suggesting that the SNP could be 4 seats short of a majority.

The Labour Party had to change tack. It went negative on independence and Alex Salmond. It was too late. The televised leadership debates had cemented a growing view of the inadequacy of the Labour leadership. The SNP entered into the last stages in a comfortable position. Observing the campaign, I heard stories of how good the canvassing was in former mining communities of North Lanarkshire and the higher echelons of the Edinburgh establishment. It was not difficult to form the conclusion that hundreds of thousands of other voters might be turning the same way. The SNP was now unable to use the sobriquet 'Alex Salmond for First Minister' used last time on the ballot papers for the list vote. With ingenuity the SNP had the obligatory 'Scottish National Party' along with 'Alex Salmond for First Minister' beneath.

Scottish Parliament General Election - 5 May 2011

Party	Constituency	%	Seats	Region	%	Seats	Total
SNP	902,915	45.4	53	876,421	44	16	69
Labour	630,461	31.7	15	523,559	26.3	22	37
Conservative	276,652	13.9	3	245,967	12.4	12	15
Liberal Democrat	157,714	7.9	2	103,472	5.2	3	5
Scottish Green				87,060	4.4	2	2
Independent	12,357	0.6	0	22,306	1.1	1	1
Scottish Senior Citizens	1,618	0.8	0	33,253	1.7	0	0
Turnout							50%

None of the many other contestants achieved more than 1% of the vote. The independent elected on the list vote for the Lothians was the redoubtable and long lasting Margo MacDonald. For the SNP it was a landslide triumph, seizing most of the first past the post seats from Labour and clocking up a huge electoral vote. For the first time, there would be a Scottish Government with a parliamentary majority. For Labour which had dominated Scottish politics for a half century it was a disaster as one by one its central Scotland citadels fell to the SNP. The Conservatives lost 5 seats and the Liberal Democrats paid the price of their coalition with the Tories at Westminster and were humiliated with the loss of 12 of their MSPs.

Alex Salmond arrived in presidential style by helicopter the following day at an Edinburgh hotel to be met his deputy Leader, Nicola Sturgeon and to greet the massive line up of media.

Then the message hit home. Whereas there was no possibility in the previous parliament for the SNP to advance the case for an independence referendum, now the Party had both a mandate and the majority to deliver it. The next three years were to be interesting! Scotland had the opportunity to become independent after 300 years of union with England.

On 18 May 2011, Alex Salmond was elected by a clear majority on the first ballot to serve as First Minister for a second term and immediately set out his goals in his acceptance speech.

"Scotland's strength has always lain in its diversity. In the poem, 'Scotland Small?' Hugh MacDiarmid challenged those who would diminish us with stereotype. He asked:

Scotland small? Our multiform, our infinite Scotland small? Only as a patch of hillside may be a cliché corner to a fool who cries 'Nothing but heather!

The point is that even the smallest patch of hillside contains enormous variation: bluebells, blaeberries and mosses. To describe Scotland as nothing but heather is, as MacDiarmid said, marvellously descriptive but totally incomplete.

To describe Scotland as small is similarly misleading: Scotland is not small. It is not small in imagination, and it is not short on ambition. It is infinite in its diversity, and it is alive with possibility.

Two weeks ago the voters of Scotland - the people of Scotland - embraced that possibility. They like what this Parliament has done within the devolved settlement that Donald Dewar negotiated. They like what the first minority SNP Government achieved, and now they want more. They want Scotland to have the economic levers to prosper in this century, and they are excited by the opportunity to reindustrialise our country through marine renewable energy, which offers skilled, satisfying work to school leavers and graduates alike. However, they know that we need tools to do the job properly, and I believe that this chamber understands that as well.

My message today is, let us act as one and demand Scotland's right. Let us build a better future for our young people by gaining the powers that we need to speed recovery and to create jobs. Let us wipe away past equivocation and ensure that the present Scotland Act is worthy of its name.

There is actually a great deal on which we are agreed. Occasionally in the hurly-burly of an election campaign - and I am as guilty of this as anyone else - we tend to forget that, so let us just remember the extent of the agreement that we share across the Parliament.

The three economic changes that I have already promoted

to the Scotland Bill were chosen certainly from the SNP manifesto, but also because they command and have commanded support from other parties across the chamber. All sides of the Parliament support the need for additional and immediate capital borrowing powers so that we can invest in an infrastructure and continue the growth in our economy, and I am very hopeful that that will be delivered.

The Liberal Democrats, the Greens and many in the Labour Party agree that the Crown estate revenues should be repatriated to Scottish communities; we await Westminster's reply. Our leading job creators back this Government's call for control of corporation tax to be included in the Scotland Bill. The Secretary of State for Northern Ireland - a Conservative - supports the devolution of that tax, and the cross-party committee that met in the last session of this Parliament agreed unanimously that if the principle was conceded in Northern Ireland, Scotland must have the same rights.

However, those are not the only issues that carry support across this chamber: there are three more to which I want to draw attention.

Why not give us control of our own excise? We in this Government have a mandate to implement a minimum price for alcohol. We intend to pursue that in this Parliament, come what may. Although our Labour colleagues agree that it is correct to set a minimum price, they were concerned about where the revenues would go. Gaining control of excise answers that question. It means that we can tackle our country's alcohol problem and invest any additional revenue in public services. I ask Labour members to join me in calling for control of alcohol taxes so that together we can face down Scotland's issue with booze.

Another key aspect of our national life controlled by Westminster is broadcasting. All of Scotland is poorly served as a result. If we had some influence over that currently reserved area, we could, for example, create a Scottish digital channel, something that all parties and every member in the last session of Parliament supported as long ago as 8

October 2008. We agree that such a platform would promote our artistic talent and hold up a mirror to this nation. How Scotland promotes itself to the world is important; how we talk to each other is also critical. These are exciting times for our country. We need more space for our cultural riches and for a lively, intelligent discourse about the nation we are and the nation that we aspire to be.

Finally, many of us - a great number of us, I think - believe that in this globalised era Scotland needs more influence in the European Union, particularly in the Council of Ministers. At the moment, that is in the gift of Westminster. Sometimes it is forthcoming; more often it is withheld. We in the Scottish National Party argue - and will continue to argue - for full sovereignty, which would give us an independent voice in the European Union. However, short of that, the Scotland Bill could be changed to improve our current position. When the first Scotland Act was debated back in 1998, there was, as I remember it, a proposal from the Liberal Democrats to include a mechanism that would give Scotland more power to influence European policy. It was defeated then but why not re-visit that proposal from 1998 to give Scotland a guaranteed say in the forums where decisions are made that shape our industries and, increasingly, our laws?

I have outlined six areas of potential common ground that stretch across this Parliament to a greater or lesser extent: borrowing powers; corporation tax; the Crown estate; excise duty; digital broadcasting; and a stronger say in European policy. I think that we should seize the moment and act together to bring these powers back home. Let this Parliament move forward as one to make Scotland better.

Norman MacCaig observed that when you swish your hand in a stream the waters are muddied but then settle all the clearer. On 5 May, the people of our country swished up the stream and now the way ahead is becoming clear. We see our nation emerge from the glaur of self-doubt and negativity. A change is coming and the people are ready. They put ambition ahead of hesitation.

The process is not about endings; it is about beginnings. Whatever changes take place in our constitution, we will remain close to our neighbours. We will continue to share a landmass, a language and a wealth of experience and history with the other peoples of these islands. My dearest wish is to see the countries of Scotland and England stand together as equals. There is a difference between partnership and subordination: the first encourages mutual respect, and the second breeds resentment.

Let me finish with the words of Fletcher of Saltoun who addressed this Parliament in 1706, before it was adjourned for almost 300 years. He observed:

> 'All nations are dependent; the one upon the many, this we know.'

However, he warned that if

> 'the greater must always swallow the lesser',

we are all diminished. His fears were realised in 1707. However, the age of empires is over. Now we determine our own future based on our own needs. We know our worth - we should take pride in it - so let us heed the words of Saltoun and go forward into the community of nations to lend our own, independent weight to the world."

A week later, the First Minister announced his government team in which Alex Neil was promoted to the Cabinet.

SNP Scottish Cabinet 2011

First Minister	Alex Salmond
Deputy First Minister and Cabinet Secretary for Health & Wellbeing	Nicola Sturgeon

Cabinet Secretaries

Finance, Employment & Sustainable Growth	John Swinney

Education & Lifelong Learning	Michael Russell
Parliamentary Business & Government Strategy	Bruce Crawford
Justice	Kenny MacAskill
Rural Affairs & the Environment	Richard Lochhead
Culture & External Affairs	Fiona Hyslop
Infrastructure & Capital Investment	Alex Neil

Junior Ministers

Commonwealth Games & Sport	Shona Robison
Public Health	Michael Matheson
Energy, Enterprise & Tourism	Fergus Ewing
Local Government & Planning	Aileen Campbell
Children & Young People	Angela Constance
Learning and Skills (including Gaelic & Scots)	Alasdair Allan
Parliamentary Business & Chief Whip	Brian Adam
Community Safety & legal Affairs (including tackling sectarianism)	Roseanna Cunningham
Environment & Climate Change	Stewart Stevenson
Housing & Transport	Keith Brown

Shortly after the formation of Alex Salmond's second period in government, there was yet another Westminster by-election (Westminster seemingly having a high degree of morbidity)! In this case it was Inverclyde, following upon the unfortunate death of Labour MP, David Cairns, at a relatively early age. For a change, the contest was not in Glasgow or Fife. Historically the old Greenock seat had been a contest between Labour and the Liberals. Even at the General Election a year previously, the Liberal Democrats had come third with the Conservatives close behind. More importantly, the SNP had done poorly getting only 17.5% of the vote. No doubt there were hopes within the Party that the landslide in the Scottish election would translate into victory in Inverclyde. In the event, the SNP candidate Anne McLaughlin did very well doubling the SNP share. Unfortunately, this increase came almost entirely from the Liberal Democrats and the Conservatives, demonstrating that despite their collapse the previous month, Labour in British contests still held a strong position.

Inverclyde By-election (Westminster) - 30 June 2011

Party	Votes	Percentage
Labour	15,118	53.8%
SNP	9,280	33%
Conservative	2,784	9.9%
Liberal Democrat	627	2.2%
UKIP	288	1%
Turnout		45.4%

The Party could relax. The electoral contests were over for the time being. It was back to humdrum housekeeping with the main challenge arising from accommodating a huge surge of new members. Membership had risen to over 25,000 - almost a threefold increase from 2005. Save in times of adversity or crisis, Conference had become like those of the other parliamentary parties, a show event with a succession of Ministerial speeches, anodyne motions and acclamations for the leadership. Nor did the membership wish anything more. They trusted the leadership. The leadership had delivered more than they had expected. Conference was a great gathering of the members and the last thing they wished in the new climate was something that disturbed their peace. And the 2011 Conference could be none other than a wonderful celebration of having achieved the impossible to wrest majority control of the Parliament in the face of an electoral system that had been specifically designed to prevent the SNP from forming a majority government. Above all, SNP members now believed that they were on the way to winning independence through the referendum the Government could now deliver.

Changes were made to the ministerial team on 5 September. Nicola Sturgeon transferred the Health brief to Alex Neil in exchange for Infrastructure and Economic Development. In addition to being Depute First Minister, she was allocated the major role of overseeing the independence referendum. Bruce Crawford, Stewart Stevenson and Brian Adam retired from office. In came Paul Wheelhouse (Environment), Joe Fitzpatrick (Parliamentary Business), Hamza Yousaf (External Affairs & International Development) and Margaret Burgess (Housing and Welfare)

Within the Party, Derek Mackay had succeeded Bruce Crawford as Business Convener in June and with the nomination from Alex Salmond had the blessing of the leader and good prospects for the future. The June meeting of National Council was held in Greenock to encourage members to work in the election with most of the office bearers being in the field and not in attendance to deliver their reports. By December there was a gripe from Glasgow Cathcart Constituency Branch complaining of a drop in the number of SNP women MSPs and calling for positive action. The resolution passed on the nod as did all others.

The Party was preparing for the Council elections. The objective was to retain or win control of Councils. There was an interesting Council resolution from Alyn Smith MEP and Angus Robertson MP drawing attention to an EU strategy for the High North and Arctic Ocean to deal with issues of relevance to Scotland and our Scandinavian neighbours, Iceland and Norway with whom we should collaborate. The Party agreed. In December, there was a resolution from Cathcart reminding the Party to remember the deceits of Westminster in the seventies when a report from civil servant economist Dr Gavin McCone revealing the wealth of Scotland's oil resources was suppressed. It hinted that there was a need to educate the Scottish people in preparation for the Yes campaign in the coming Referendum.

As a cure to any criticism of the SNP Conference having become neutered by comforting political warmth, it flared into life in dramatic fashion at the October 2012 Conference. In the summer, Angus Robertson, the Party's Defence spokesman indicated that the Party should review its policy on non-membership of NATO. For decades the SNP had been resolutely opposed to this defence organisation, mainly but not exclusively, on the basis that it had nuclear weapons in its arsenal. Nuclear disarmament was almost as part of the ark of the covenant of the Scottish National Party as independence – and sometimes it felt that there was more vehemence amongst Party cadres against nuclear weapons (housed in the Firth of Clyde at Faslane) than there was support for self-government. As Party Chairman in the eighties I had attempted to modernise the NATO policy and had received a dunt on my behind for my pains. This time, the Government was preparing for a referendum on independence and was anxious to neuter the issue of opposition to NATO as an impediment to the campaign.

Immediately, all hell broke loose. It was clear that the Party leadership intended to force through a policy amendment and that a resolution would be brought before Conference in October. It was going to be a bloody affair. There were strong opinions on both sides of the debate.

After acceptance of minor amendments, the NATO resolution before Conference was:

SNP Foreign, Security and Defence Policy Update

1. Conference believes that the Foreign, Security and Defence Policy of Scotland be determined by the Scottish Government and Scottish Parliament and always reflect the priorities of people living in Scotland.

2. An independent Scotland will be an outward-looking nation which is open, fair and tolerant, contributing to peace, justice and equality. By mobilising our assets and the goodwill and recognition that Scotland enjoys in the world, we will provide sustainable access to natural resources to tackle need and prevent insecurity in the world for this and future generations.

3. The SNP re-iterates its commitment to non-nuclear defence, international law and the United Nations and supporting multilateral solutions to regional and global challenges.

4. While conventional military threats to Scotland are low, it is important to maintain appropriate security and defence arrangements and capabilities. This includes a cyber security and intelligence infrastructure to deal with new threats and protect key national economic and social infrastructure.

5. Scotland is (a) maritime nation with more than 11,000 miles of coastline, including nearly 800 islands, critical under-sea and offshore infrastructure and an area of responsibility extending far into the North Sea and Atlantic Ocean. The SNP recognises our national responsibilities as a northern European nation to work with our neighbours to fulfil current defence and security responsibilities and improve collective regional arrangements. Environmental changes to the High North and Arctic Region raise major regional challenges and responsibilities which Scotland shares.

6. Scotland will require military capabilities to fulfil these responsibilities. These will be provided by the Scottish defence and peacekeeping services answerable to the Scottish Government and Scottish Parliament. An independent Scottish Government led by the SNP will commit to an annual defence and security budget of £2.5bn, an annual increase of more than £500m on recent UK levels of defence spending in Scotland but nearly £1bn less than Scottish taxpayers currently contribute to UK defence spending.

7. The Scottish armed forces will comprise 15,000 regular and 5,000 reserve personnel, operating under Joint Forces Headquarters based at Faslane, which will be Scotland's main conventional naval facility. All current bases will be maintained to accommodate units, which will be organised into one regular and one reserve Multi Role Brigade (MRB). The air force will operate from Lossiemouth and Leuchars.

8. Regular ground forces will include current Scottish raised and restored UK regiments, support units as well

as Special Forces and Royal Marines, who will retain responsibility for offshore protection.

9. The Scottish armed forces will be focused on territorial defence, aid to the civil power and also support for the international community. The Multi Role Brigade structure and interoperable air and sea assets will provide deployable capabilities for United Nations sanctioned missions and support for humanitarian, peacekeeping and peace-making 'Petersburg Tasks'.

10. The Scottish defence and peacekeeping forces will initially be equipped with Scotland's share of current assets including ocean going vessels, fast jets for domestic air patrol duties, transport aircraft and helicopters as well as army vehicles, artillery and air defence systems. A Scottish defence industrial strategy and procurement plan will fill UK capability gaps in Scotland addressing the lack of new frigates, conventional submarines and maritime patrol aircraft.

11. Joint procurement will be pursued with the rest of the UK and other allies as well as shared conventional basing, training and logistics arrangements, fulfilling shared priorities in 'Smart Defence'. This includes sharing conventional military capabilities, setting priorities and better coordinating efforts providing economic synergies, job stability and taxpayer value for money.

12. A long-standing national consensus has existed that Scotland should not host nuclear weapons and a sovereign SNP government will negotiate the speediest safe transition of the nuclear fleet from Faslane which will be replaced by conventional naval forces.

13. Security cooperation in our regions functions primarily through NATO, which is regarded as the keystone defence organisation by Denmark, Norway, Iceland and the United Kingdom. The SNP wishes Scotland to fulfil its obligations to neighbours and allies. On independence Scotland will inherit its treaty obligations

with NATO. An SNP Government will maintain NATO membership subject to an agreement that Scotland will not host nuclear weapons and NATO takes all possible steps to bring about nuclear disarmament as required by the Nuclear Non Proliferation Treaty of which all its members are signatories and further that NATO continues to respect the right of members to only take part in UN sanctioned operations. In the absence of such an agreement, Scotland will work with NATO as a member of the Partnership for Peace programme like Sweden, Finland, Austria and Ireland. Scotland will be a full member of the Common Security and Defence Policy (CSDP) of the European Union and the Organisation for Cooperation and Security in Europe (OSCE).

For old stagers, it was a welcome return of party democracy. Angus Robertson moved the resolution and assured delegates that any decision to apply to join NATO would be dependent on the removal of nuclear weapons which Scotland would not host. He had had meetings with neighbouring countries whose security interests were similar to our own. He told the delegates: 'This defence policy sends a very important message to people in Scotland and to friends, neighbours and allies. We are preparing for a referendum and for a sovereign, independent Scotland, with a defence and security policy that is best for Scotland'. The speech was met with applause and booing. Tempers were high. The resolution was opposed by list MSP for the Highlands and Islands, John Finnie who looked over to Alex Salmond and Nicola Sturgeon and declared pointedly: 'If you vote to join NATO, you will not get rid of Trident.' The resolution was backed by government ministers and senior spokesmen. It was opposed by 8 MSPs amongst others. With the pressure of the referendum, the resolution went to the vote on a critical negative amendment which was defeated by only 394 votes to 365. A motion to remit back the whole resolution was defeated by 425 votes to 360. The resolution was carried by 426 votes to 332.

Two MSPs, John Finnie and Jean Urquhart, also a list MSP in the Highlands and Islands, resigned from the SNP and became independent MSPs.

Despite this turbulence, the Party remained strong. Colin Beattie, the National Treasurer and now an MSP, reported that the national finances were in a sound state. The position was recorded by the Electoral Commission for Scotland.

	2008	2009	2010	2011	2012
Income	£1,768,384	1,842,127	1,861,595	5,030,916	2,300,459
Expenditure	1,700,401	1,737,609	2,167,720	3,453,882	2,656,059
Net assets/ (Liabilities)	(516,831)	(412,313)	(718,038)	858,996	503,396

The SNP majority in Parliament was slim. Fortunately, the two defected MSPs continued to give broad support to the administration. Bill Walker MSP was suspended while facing trial on multiple charges of wife assault. And then the big blow, the death of Brian Adam, MSP for Aberdeen Donside. Brian had been a long time activist prior to his election and had built up the SNP in the city and constituency. He was very well regarded amongst all parties and his electorate.

The by-election was one that the SNP had to win. It was expected that the Unionists would mount a major challenge both to give a knock-back to the SNP and also to try to stymie the independence referendum. The SNP chose one of their list MSPs, Mark McDonald to be the candidate and after a fierce battle, mainly on local issues, he emerged the winner. The share of the vote was down although given Brian Adam's personal popularity, this was not unexpected.

Aberdeen Donside By-election (Scottish Parliament) - 20 June 2013

Party	Votes	Percentage
SNP	9,814	42%
Labour	7,789	33.3%
Liberal Democrat	1,940	8.3%
Conservative	1,791	7.7%
UKIP	1,128	4.8%
Scottish Green	410	1.8%
National Front	249	1.1%
Others (2)	257	
Turnout		38.8%

Later in 2013, there was to be a by-election for the Scottish Parliament seat of Dunfermline. This had been one of many seats won in the landslide of 2011. The sitting MSP was Bill Walker who had been suspended from the SNP while awaiting trial on multiple charges of domestic abuse. He had vacated the seat on conviction. With this background, the chances of winning were slim. The Party had to make the best go of it and selected a former MSP, Shirley-Anne Somerville as its candidate. Labour also wanted to win back one of its traditional constituencies and threw everything into a contest which was dominated by local issues. It was a tousy contest which Labour won with a swing of 7% from the SNP. The Liberal Democrat share of the vote decreased by 8%.

Dunfermline By-election (Scottish Parliament)
- 23 October 2013

Party	Votes	Percentage
Labour	10,275	42.5%
SNP	7,402	30.6%
Liberal Democrats	2,852	11.8%
Conservative	2,009	8.3%
UKIP	908	3.8%
Greens	593	2.4%
Other	161	
Turnout		42.7%

The sudden death from cancer of the sitting MSP, Helen Eadie provoked another by-election in Cowdenbeath. This was a heartland Labour seat that had withstood the SNP onrush of three years before. There was not much chance of winning it in a short campaign in the depths of winter but the SNP candidate, Natalie McGarry took on the fight. Labour won with an increased majority and a strong swing from the SNP which still achieved its 2007 level.

Cowdenbeath By-election (Scottish Parliament)
- 23 January 2014

Party	Votes	Percentage
Labour	11,192	55.8%
SNP	5,704	28.4%
Conservative	1,893	9.4%
UKIP	610	3%
Liberal Democrat	425	2.1%
Others (2)	238	
Turnout		34.8%

A reminder of the Party's roots was given with the passing in the spring of Margo MacDonald who had won the pivotal by-election of Glasgow Govan in 1973 and Hamish Watt, MP for Banff from 1974 to 1979. Too often the contribution of pioneers such as these is overshadowed by later events. Like many others, they did not survive to vote for independence in the referendum.

The final electoral test before the referendum arrived on 22 May 2014 with the holding of the European Parliament election. By then the SNP Government had been in power for seven years and was still holding a lead over Labour for the Scottish Parliament. The SNP was clearly the establishment party of Scotland. It had traditionally done well in these elections and had previously topped the poll in 2009 with 29.1% when the Party had secured its usual total of 2 MEPs. The election was overshadowed by the referendum campaign and the aim was to increase the vote to 33% and win a third seat for Tasmina Ahmad-Sheikh. The polls gave reason for this confidence. But as the election developed, massive publicity for UKIP (the UK Independence Party) made it a wild card.

Neither of the two objectives was achievable given the wall of media publicity beamed to Scotland from broadcasters in London. Two other factors were apparent. The SNP had underestimated the degree of dislike for the EU arising from the recession and although this was less by 8 percentage points compared to England, it was seriously underestimated by SNP strategists who were engaged in a fire-fight over Scotland's admission to the EU. It was only in the last week that mild Euro-sceptic noises were heard and this was too late too correct a view that the SNP was too slavishly European. Secondly, with western European establishment parties about to be given a kicking, the context made it difficult for the SNP to increase its vote.

When the votes were counted, the SNP had done well to hold its share of the vote with a modest decline to 28.9% and the two serving MEPs, Ian Hudghton and Alyn Smith. Labour increased its share to 25.9% and remained at 2 MEPs. The Conservatives retained their seat with 17.2%. UKIP doubled its vote to elect one MEP with 10.4%. The Greens advanced to 8%, displacing the Liberal Democrats whose vote collapsed to 7.1% and surrender of its seat to UKIP. The adverse factor for the SNP was that having talked up its likelihood of getting an additional MEP, its good performance in the circumstance did little to advance the momentum of the Yes vote in the referendum. The SNP was blamed for its concentration on UKIP in the last few days but it is unlikely the late tactic had much impact either way.

European Parliament Election 2014

Party	Votes	Percentage	Seats
SNP	389,503	29%	2
Labour	348,219	25.9%	2
Conservative	231,330	17.2%	1
UKIP	140,534	10.5%	1
Green Party	108,305	8.1%	0
Liberal Democrat	95,319	7.1%	0
Britain First	13,639	1%	0
BNP	10,216	0.8%	0
NO2EU	6,418	0.5%	0
Turnout			33.5%

By the beginning of 2014, the SNP was in good shape although it had seen its election performance fade against Labour. Overall for a government in its sixth year, it seemed to have avoided the mid-term recession that political commentators had come to expect. Indeed, in late 2013, it was polling 48%, above its landslide performance of 2011. Its Ministers' performances were strong. Decisive interventions by Alex Salmond to save the Grangemouth petro-chemical facility threatened by closure and a fighting response by Nicola Sturgeon as Deputy First Minister and local MSP to threats to naval shipbuilding on the Clyde did much to secure the reputation of the Government as a defender of Scottish interests. In the Cabinet, Nicola Sturgeon took over primary responsibility for the referendum and constitutional affairs on 5 September 2012 and soon established herself as the dominant debater. Her successor as Health Secretary was Alex Neil who managed that difficult brief with panache. One of the most effective Ministers was Richard Lochhead. Quietly with little fuss and attention seeking, he won support from both the agricultural and fishing communities. He delivered because he 'listened'!

As with all governments, there was controversy over its programme. The decision to progress same sex marriage legislation was calculated to obtain the support of younger generations and worth the disapproval of the middle aged and old. Leaving aside the arguments, it was a curious priority to introduce a controversial marginal issue in the run-up to the referendum on independence when it would alienate the churches and Muslims alike. Also there was disquiet over the amalgamation of the police and fire services as the SNP had always previously been opposed to centralisation both within and outwith Scotland.

Likewise, the highly controversial decision to dilute Scots criminal law by abolishing the need for corroboration of evidence as a pre-requisite for conviction (and opening up the prospect of increased wrong convictions) suggested that the SNP had lost some of the sensitivity stemming from minority government. This did not appear to worry the public as a Panelbase poll commissioned by the Party in late February showed that a third of Labour voters were less likely to vote for Labour while another indicated that the SNP was 9 points ahead of Labour for the next Holyrood General Election. By July, this had widened with the SNP standing at 43%, a remarkable level for a Party in its seventh year in Government and busy putting at risk support from those approving of the Government but not of its promotion of independence during a fraught referendum! Perhaps this was why support in the YouGov Poll of late August had slipped to 39% but so had that of Labour.

What of the contribution of the SNP leader, Alex Salmond? With only the short inter-regnum of John Swinney, he was in charge of the SNP for twenty years. Even without the independence referendum – a major achievement - he is undeniably the most dominant and successful leader the Party has known. This is can be truly said without diminishing the contribution made by predecessors, now dead, who in difficult times ploughed a nationalist furrow in unforgiving soil, at a time when Scotland was part of the British nexus and hostile to any kind of self-government. In their day, they laid the foundations. For example, there was John MacCormick in the twenties and thirties founder of the Party and a National Secretary every much in control as Alex. Or Robert McIntyre elected as the first SNP MP in 1945 and a resolute influence in days of despair. Then, Jimmy Halliday, witty and intelligent, leading the SNP out of the nadir of the late fifties. And Arthur Donaldson who gave inspiration at a critical time in the sixties as the Party advanced or Billy Wolfe who brought creativity in policy and presentation, instrumental to the election of the 7 and 11 MPs in 1974. It was remarkable how their different accomplishments matched the needs of the time. And that was the just the Party leaders. There were many others like Winnie Ewing and Margo MacDonald who played a critical role.

So far, David Torrance is the only person to have written a biography of Alex Salmond (Against the Odds *infra*). It is illuminating yet it was written without Alex's co-operation. Rarely for a politician, Alex Salmond has been careful to screen his private persona from open gaze. His achievements speak for him instead. If he struggled to make a go of the SNP in his first five years when facing problems similar to those of his predecessors, he surpassed them later. Through debates over devolution, he established himself as a pre-eminent figure in Scottish politics and rallied the Party behind him.

Alex is not perfect – few people are. Some internal critics have focused on his shyness to operate collegially other than through a narrow circle of loyalists and a perceived failure to develop policy or accept criticism (not an uncommon feature in political leaders!). Leadership can lead to strains on friendship. He has been at pains to stand by his associates in Government so long as they were loyal to him, even when some selective pruning would be appropriate.

That, however, is his style. Any minor flaws are overwhelmed by strengths – power of communication, his ability to exude confidence and mastery of opponents through charisma and chutzpah. It is remarkable how as First Minister of a devolved Scotland, he managed to gain UK and international identification, something that no other First Minister in

Scotland, Wales and Northern Ireland had succeeded in doing. For some watching from aboard, he seemed to be Prime Minister of an independent country.

Such was his popularity that the SNP took the remarkable step of fighting and winning the 2007 election (diminishing its own brand) by contesting under the sobriquet of 'Alex Salmond for First Minister'. It worked and he became First Minister of a minority Government. His crowning achievement in 2011 was forming the first majority Scottish Government, something that nobody thought possible under a proportional system of election devised to prevent any political party achieving a majority.

Alex Salmond was not alone. In September 2014, he and Nicola Sturgeon celebrated the 10th anniversary of their leadership. It had been a remarkable partnership. In the initial stages when Alex was an MP in Westminster, it was Nicola who had fronted First Minister's Questions in the Scottish parliament. Later she was Deputy First Minister. There was no sign of any material fall out between them – something remarkable in politics. She grew into the jobs of both Depute leader of the SNP and as a Minister and with that confidence became more relaxed, developing a style which although forthright and occasionally aggressive was accepted without any measured public downside. Her ratings during the referendum campaign where she bore most of the burden of presentation in the early stages came close to equalling those of 'the boss'.

These successes of Alex Salmond and his colleagues, Nicola Sturgeon and John Swinney paled before the challenge to win a Yes vote in the independence referendum. That battle would make or mar the reputation of the SNP Government as well as dictate the future path of Scotland. Would Alex enter the pantheon of those Scottish heroes who had secured Scotland's freedom in the past? Referendum day beckoned.

Chapter 11:

RIDING TWO HORSES

In the battle for Scotland's freedom from British rule, the SNP had long since dropped any strategy other than that of achieving independence through a referendum. In fact so predominant was this approach that the Party could be described more as a 'referendum' than as an 'independence' party. Not that this was either stated or understood. The Party membership would never have condoned the abandoning of the 'ark of the covenant' of independence. It sensed that the leadership's main goal was independence and accepted that the only possible practicable route lay through a referendum of the Scottish people. So far as they were concerned, the SNP leaders were delivering political progress and that this would lead eventually to Scotland re-entering the world as a fully self-governing nation.

Even if there was no other ball-game in town – and other solutions were scarce on the ground – the referendum route did pose political problems. In the democratic pantheon, the use of direct consultation of people through plebiscites had attained the status of sanctity . Could there be any better way of achieving popular sanction for constitutional change than by a referendum? Parliamentary democracy where decisions are taken by legislators under delegated powers from the electorate was the only other route and naturally, the political parties and the politicians preferred to keep decisions to themselves on the basis that they knew best. Hence in Britain, even the power to wage war was held by the Government acting under Crown prerogative powers until recently.

Also one does not have to be a Machiavelli to realise that however sanctified a referendum may be, the motives for holding one could be deeply political. In the forty years since the process of direct consultation was first introduced, there have been only four outwith Northern Ireland. In 1975, the referendum on staying in the Common Market was held by Labour to reaffirm the decision of the previous Conservative Government to join in 1973. In 1979, the Labour Government abandoned a straight manifesto commitment to set up a Scottish Assembly and held a referendum on Scottish and Welsh devolution accepting a pre-condition that 40% of the electorate, alive, dead or moved away, had to vote in favour (failure to vote was classified as a NO vote for this purpose). Even after an admittedly narrow YES vote, Parliament disregarded the outcome and repealed the Scottish Assembly legislation.

In 1996, the Labour Party abandoned yet another pledge to establish a Scottish Parliament by insisting on a referendum and was mortified when a year later the Scottish public voted overwhelmingly for a parliament with tax raising powers. And the alternative vote referendum of 2011 was held by the Conservative/Liberal Democrat Coalition to keep the Lib Dems quiet and in the government. In that referendum the proposal to change the British electoral system from 'first-past-the-post to one nobody wanted was soundly thrashed. Yet it succeeded in its principal goal of keeping the Lib Dems in the Coalition dominated by the Conservatives. The referendum was used as a political tool in all cases.

So without being too cynical, it could be reasonably argued that the purist view of consulting the people was not used in Britain for that purpose. Instead referendums were held to oppose something governments did not want (i.e. Scottish Parliaments or voting reform) or to ratify a controversial action by a Government by giving it popular camouflage (EU referendum of 1975) or to resolve internal divisions (1975, 1979, 1987 and the proposed EU referendum, to appease Conservative backbenchers and deflect UKIP votes back to the Tories, scheduled for 2017. There will always be the odd exception and that had now occurred when an incoming SNP Government proposed to put the question of independence to the Scottish people on a matter of principle!

The Scottish Parliament electoral system had been intended to make it impossible under a multi-party system to elect a Government with a majority. Indeed it had been designed explicitly by Labour to prevent the SNP from entering into government with a majority. It showed real dedication to the Union by Labour since in most normal circumstances, given its huge tally of Westminster MPS from 'first-past-the-post', it would have formed majority governments on a semi-permanent scale.

It looked impossible. Yet SNP members expected action and the Government would lose credibility if it failed to make progress. Strangely enough, there was another problem which went unnoticed in the first term or if noticed, was ignored, presumably on the basis that there would be no prospect of holding a referendum in that session of Parliament. What if a referendum bill squeaked through because the Liberal Democrats had repented and entered into coalition with the SNP?

And this is where the referendum strategy could founder. There had been little evidence over the last forty years that the Scottish people would be willing to vote for full self-government. Apart from a few rogue polls, all others had shown support for independence no larger than 36% and frequently at lower levels. Thus the conundrum facing the SNP Government was how to raise support for independence to give a YES campaign a realistic chance of winning. Otherwise, there would be little advantage in holding a referendum which was bound to fail. It could set back the cause for a generation.

With his customary political flexibility, Alex Salmond found a solution. All the political polling had shown that there was a large majority of people who wanted to extend the powers of the Scottish Parliament short of independence. Inaction on the part of an SNP Government was not feasible. There was pressure on all sides for him and his Government do something constructive or to bridge the gap. And he had given himself a target of 100 days for a response.

That came on 14 August 2007 when the First Minister launched the publication of a White Paper, 'Choosing Scotland's Future' to an assembly of media representatives. In the foreword, he accepted that there was a division of opinion as to the way forward. He set his cards on the table:

> "As First Minister of Scotland, it is my responsibility to explore and lead discussion on the options for constitutional change. I lead the first Scottish National Party Government to be elected in a devolved Scotland, so I will put the case for independence, its benefits and opportunities. However, I also recognise there is a range of other views in our country, and represented in the Parliament.
>
> Scotland's long-standing union with the other nations of the United Kingdom is based on the Union of the Crowns of 1603 and the Acts of Union of 1707 and 1801. The 1801 Union with Ireland has already undergone substantial change. The political debate in Scotland concerns the 1707 political Union, the amendment or repeal of which would still leave

the Union of the Crowns intact.

I therefore propose that we have a national conversation on our future to allow the people of Scotland to debate, reflect and then decide on the type of government that best equips us for the future. This paper is intended as a starting point and inspiration for that conversation. It explores the areas in which Scotland could take on further responsibilities – such as employment, our national finances, or legislation on public safety such as firearms – as well as the concept of independence, and wider constitutional developments in Britain.

It is now ten years since the referendum to establish the Scottish Parliament. We have seen its potential to respond to the wishes and needs of the people of this country. But we have also seen the limitations of its current responsibilities. I believe it is now time for us, the people of Scotland, to consider and choose our future in the modern world."

The White Paper was largely analytical. It was composed by civil servants on behalf of the SNP Government, illustrating the resources now available. Whereas civil servants in the seventies acted on behalf of the UK Government as in the notorious case when the McCrone Report into the value of Scotland's oil and gas resources was hidden from Scotland's people, now they were required to assist the SNP as the elected Government of Scotland.

There were no great surprises as to the contents. It defined the options such as enhanced devolution through expanded powers, possible fiscal autonomy and independence. It was nevertheless good to see Scotland's claims to liberty laid out succinctly. For example it asserted the sovereignty of the Scottish people and their right to determine their own future. It declared that Scotland was a national political and territorial entity with many of the institutions of a state. It left room for transfer or renunciation of powers for the attainment of independence.

The White Paper accepted that the assumption of independence would require the transfer of powers by Westminster. Certainly this would be a common-sense way of creating the Scottish state. This assumption flew in the face of the constitutional doctrine that the Scottish people, and the Scottish people alone, were sovereign so that theoretically no Westminster

Act would have been necessary. The absence of any precautionary statement is important since it implicitly conceded that the rest of the UK remained the continuing state. It was arguable for negotiating purposes, if none other, to claim that rUK as it came to be known would also become a new entity and have to apply to the UN or EU for recognition. In reaching an agreed settlement, this would give enormous leverage to the Scottish negotiators since they could give assent, say to rUK remaining on the Security Council.

The White Paper also recognised the importance of an independent Scotland acceding to the Nuclear Non-Proliferation Treaty as a non-nuclear weapon state as this would compel the nuclear Trident submarines to depart from their Scottish base. It closed with a draft Referendum Bill. To keep within the legislative competence of the Scottish Parliament, a referendum would be held to consult the Scottish people on the Scottish Government's proposal to negotiate with the Government of the United Kingdom to achieve independence.

The questions were to be decided by the ticking of an appropriate box and were stated as:

> "I AGREE that the Scottish Government should negotiate a settlement with the Government of the United Kingdom so that Scotland becomes an independent state" or "I DO NOT AGREE that the Scottish Government should negotiate a settlement with the Government of the United Kingdom so that Scotland should become an independent state".

The key strategy was to hold the National Conversation for which the White Paper paved the way. Over the next two years, in between carrying out their ministerial duties, SNP ministers individually and sometimes through public meetings of the Scottish Cabinet on tour, would carry out 59 visits and make speeches while the Minister for Enterprise, Energy and Tourism alone would be at 130 National Conversation economy-based events. Around 15,000 people were consulted. Most of the respondents who provided evidence and papers were public sector bodies, NGOs, charities and churches with a smattering of companies although it was clear that commercial firms did not wish to be drawn into making comment.

During the period of consultation, the Government published a series of papers. These included

- Fiscal Autonomy in Scotland: The case for change and options for reform.

- Europe and Foreign Affairs: Taking forward our National Conversation.

- Opportunities for Broadcasting: Taking forward our National Conversation.

- An Oil Fund for Scotland: Taking forward our National Conversation.

- People and Communities: Taking forward our National Conversation.

- Rural Affairs, the Environment and Climate Change: Taking forward our National Conversation.

The outcome of all this activity led to the publication of a second White Paper in November 2009, entitled 'Your Scotland, Your Voice'. Presenting the Paper, the First Minister wrote that there had been significant contributions from experts, academics, journalists and think-tanks on a range of subjects from which two things were clear from the National Conversation. First, there was a demand in Scotland to consider and debate our national future. Second, that the current arrangements did not meet the ambitions of our nation. Ten years on from devolution, almost all agreed that it was time to expand the responsibilities of our Parliament. He closed by declaring that it was time that Scotland reclaimed its place among the nations of Europe and the world. The intended date for the referendum was November 2010.

The Paper defined the options facing Scotland as:

- the *status quo*: Scotland retains its current responsibilities with gradual evolution in response to particular events or pressures

- implementing the recommendations of the Commission on Scottish Devolution *(Note: this was the Calman Commission established by the unionist parties as their contribution to the debate, some of whose conclusions subsequently led to legislation. The SNP had not participated. Independence was excluded from the terms of reference)*

- full devolution of the maximum range of responsibilities to Scotland while remaining in the United Kingdom (sometimes called 'devolution max' and shortened to devo. max)

- independence: Scotland has all the rights and responsibilities of a normal independent state.

Leaving aside the constitutional issues, the White Paper laid stress on the need for powers to encourage economic development and amend the tax system, especially in securing powers to borrow for infrastructural improvements. It narrated what should be a vital part of the case for independence in these terms:

> "For over a generation, the growth rate of the Scottish economy has been lower than that of the United Kingdom and other comparable European countries. In the 30 years to 2007, Scotland's average annual GDP growth rate was 2.0% - lower than the United Kingdom economy as a whole (2.4%) and well behind Ireland (5.3%), Norway (3.1%) and Finland (2.9%). As a result of being locked into a low-growth cycle for so long, Scotland now trails many comparable European countries across a range of economic indicators."

In the absence of a claim for self-government based on identity, the economic case would be paramount. And although the White Paper was published in circumstances when a referendum was unlikely to be held, it was no bad thing that it set out the failure of the Scottish economy under economic management from Whitehall to keep pace with England and other comparable European states. In seeking independence, any YES campaign would have to explain WHY independence was necessary in order to succeed. Economic issues would be paramount.

Unwittingly, the Paper gave as reasons for change the necessity for the UK to set inflation targets to suit the UK economy as a whole and how this did not allow through monetary policy for variations in prices, demand or economic cycles within the United Kingdom. With later decisions to forsake a Scottish currency and thus Scottish management of economic cycles in favour of remaining in the sterling zone, it created an incongruity which any NO campaign could latch on to if it did its homework.

This problem also extended into White Paper claims that infrastructural investment restraints and a macro-economic policy were subject to a range of 'one size fits all' policies that did not meet Scotland's needs. This was made opaque by subsequent reliance on tax changes through fiscal autonomy alone. In short, the Paper confusingly straddled the distinction between independence and devo.max when the economic section concluded:

> "Finally, fundamental decisions such as the choice of currency and the overall balance of taxation lie outwith the remit of the Scottish Parliament. The Scottish Government cannot adopt macroeconomic policies to address the weaknesses of the current United Kingdom framework, such as the limitations of the financial regulation and fiscal frameworks."

Perhaps this critique is too harsh. After all the White Paper was contrasting the options available and at the same time looking at the alternative options suggested by the Calman Commission which were being canvassed by the unionist parties. Yet, the suspicion remains that the authors found it difficult to attack devo.max since they considered it a realistic fall-back substitute for independence. Eventually, in para. 3.32, there is the almost reluctant admission that it would be difficult to devolve monetary policy effectively while Scotland remained part of the United Kingdom as a common currency is a feature of a unified state! All compounded by para 3.33, indicating that under independence, Scotland would have the power to choose the monetary framework and currency that best suited the needs of the Scottish economy. Despite this, the section on independence concluded that Scotland would continue to operate within the sterling system until a decision to join the Euro by the people of Scotland through a referendum when the economic conditions were right – almost prescient with the worst of the Euro zone tsunami still to reach the shore, and yet in the knowledge that there was an ongoing global credit crunch!

The reason for riding two horses at the same time soon became apparent when the White Paper reached the stage of what now? It briefly specified in two paragraphs the Government's preferred option of independence in which it defined sovereignty as including all decisions on economic and fiscal affairs, currency, the constitution, foreign affairs, security and defence with Scotland being recognised as a state by the international community and be part of the European Union as a full member state. It then engaged in an extended discussion of whether it was possible to include options from the Calman Commission or devo.max in the referendum. Those wanting no change would be able to express that view and the Paper posited the possibilities of a question approving the Calman suggestions for enhancing devolution or devolution max. The Government were willing to consider proposals that would extend the powers of the Scottish Parliament, short of independence. It conjectured that transfers of powers would primarily include broadcasting, taxation and social benefits.

The practical problem was that none of the civic organisations had worked out detailed proposals that would produce broad support. Nevertheless the Government would proceed with a Referendum Bill to be introduced in Parliament early in 2010 and would consider amendments from one or more of the opposition parties for insertion of an additional question in the legislation.

Naturally, the SNP Government made it clear that it did not favour a mid-way option and would not campaign for it. Nevertheless, it was a remarkable concession for a nationalist Party whose *raison d'etre* was obtaining national independence to allow an escape clause. Undoubtedly, given the opinion polls where people preferred enhancement of the powers of the devolved parliament to the concept of independence, the middle way would certainly triumph. It was, however, a solution to the vexed problem of securing progress at a time when the SNP formed a minority government and was unable to legislate without the support of one or more of the main opposition parties.

In the end, parliamentary support had been lacking. The proposed Referendum Bill fell by the wayside. Some, but not all, of the Calman proposals were approved by the London Government and a Scotland Bill was introduced at Westminster. All that remained was for the Scottish Government to prepare for the coming election. Given the SNP's poor standing in opinion polls, it was by no means certain that the SNP would remain in office to take the referendum further.

Chapter 12:

A PERPLEXING BEGINNING

The 2011 Campaign ended in a tremendous victory for the Scottish National Party. It was still in office. It had achieved a result which everybody had deemed impossible under the proportional voting system. It had won an overall majority. Progress on an independence referendum could not be avoided. The shutter of the trap had dropped.

Majority or not, there were substantial problems to be surmounted. Constitutionally speaking, the Scottish Parliament controlled by the SNP did not have the power to hold an independence referendum. The powers of the Parliament were fixed by an Act of the Westminster Parliament. The power to amend the Act was reserved to Westminster. If the Parliament proceeded with holding a determinative plebiscite, rather than the one previously envisaged of asking the people whether they wished independence negotiations to proceed, then it could be struck down by the Supreme Court as *ultra vires* – and given that of the twelve justices in the Supreme Court, only two were Scots whereas nine were English lawyers and two from Northern Ireland, the outcome was certain. Nor could resistance from the Scottish justices be expected!

Potentially, this hindrance could have forced the Government to go to the fundamentals of the Scottish constitutional law which the President of the Court of Session in 1953 had made clear was different from that of England. In England since the Conquest, sovereignty had rested with the Crown, and then with the Crown in Parliament whereas it had long been established that in Scotland sovereignty was vested in the people. Here this debate was notional; there was no evidence that the Scottish people either knew of their constitutional rights or if they did were in a sufficiently revolutionary mood to invoke them.

It all came down to politics. For Westminster, the problem was that the SNP had secured a mandate to hold a referendum on independence. If Downing Street mounted a 'high horse' and denied this mandate, it could easily stir up passions amongst the Scots which they would rather not wish to see. Any English arrogance would certainly have the adverse impact of seeing support for independence rocket upwards. For the Scottish Ministers, under constant attack and jeers from the opposition parties, the important thing was to evoke confidence in the legality of the referendum.

The end result after stiff negotiation was agreement by Deputy First Minister, Nicola Sturgeon and Secretary of State for Scotland, John Moore to use Westminster's reserved powers to enable the Scottish Parliament to legislate to hold a referendum on independence without fear of court action being taken to declare the Act *ultra vires* and therefore null and void. Such an action would have provoked hostility between the British and Scottish Governments even if any court action had been raised by an individual citizen objector. The agreement was remarkable. It gave the SNP most of what it wanted. On the part of the British Government, it agreed to break up the British state if that is what the people of Scotland wanted and unlike the devolution referendum of 1979, there was no attempt to require a 40% of the Scottish electorate threshold to vote YES. While it is likely the British Government was confident on the basis of the polls that the Scottish people would vote NO at the end of the day, it would be churlish not to congratulate them on their maturity.

The 'Edinburgh Agreement' as it came to be known. was signed by Prime Minister, David Cameron, First Minister, Alex Salmond, Secretary of State, John Moore and Deputy First Minister, Nicola Sturgeon at Edinburgh on 15 October 2012.

Agreement between the United Kingdom Government and the Scottish Government on a referendum on independence for Scotland.

Edinburgh 12 October 2012

The United Kingdom Government and the Scottish Government have agreed to work together to ensure that a referendum on Scottish independence can take place.

The governments are agreed that the referendum should:

- have a clear legal base

- be legislated by the Scottish Parliament

- be conducted so as to command the confidence of the parliaments, governments and people

- deliver a fair test and a decisive expression of the views of people in Scotland and a result that everyone will respect

The governments have agreed to promote an Order in Council under Section 30 of of the Scotland Act 1998 in the United Kingdom and Scottish Parliaments to allow a single-question referendum on Scottish independence to be held before the end of 2014. The Order will put it beyond doubt that the Scottish Parliament can legislate for that referendum.

It will then be for the Scottish Government to promote legislation in the Scottish Parliament for a referendum on independence. The governments are agreed that the referendum should meet the highest standards of fairness, transparency and propriety, informed by consultation and independent legal advice. The referendum legislation will set out:

- the date of the referendum

- the franchise

- the wording of the question

- rules on campaign financing

- other rules for the conduct of the referendum

The details of the agreement between the governments are set out in the following memorandum and draft Order which form part of this agreement.

An important restriction in the agreement was that the referendum would have only a single question, YES or NO to independence. In the memorandum there was a further requirement that the wording of the question and other practicalities had to be submitted to the Electoral Commission. The restriction to one question had strategic and tactical consequences. In the White Paper published two years earlier, there had been a willingness on the part of the SNP Government to have a multi-option referendum. From a principled viewpoint this was heresy since it meant effectively reduction of a question on independence to nominal importance.

Pragmatically, it was another matter. After five years of an SNP government performing creditably on the devolution stage, there had been no movement towards increasing support for independence in the polls, thus making an independence referendum a considerable gamble. Looked at in terms of the strategy of the Scottish Government, developed since 1990, that independence should be secured on a salami basis with incremental transfers of power and the campaign for a multi-option referendum, the gradualist approach was logical. Yet reliance on a referendum on independence was as much of a trap as an opportunity At least with a successful compromise option of devo.max, the Scottish Parliament could emerge with enhanced powers. Spared the set-back of a No vote, if not political humiliation, the SNP could return to the independence trail at a later time.

Unfortunately, the Westminster Government did not wish to allow the SNP to escape. It wanted the SNP to encounter a crushing defeat. Nor did its reluctance to implement all of the modest Calman Commission recommendations indicate a likelihood of transfers of greater powers to the Scottish Parliament. The object of the Agreement was to forestall any further demands for devo.max. If that question appeared on the the ballot paper and was backed by popular support, it would make it difficult (although not impossible) to withstand the pressure. In Scotland, the Scottish Parliament had prestige. In London, it was seen as an impertinent nuisance to the good government of the UK as an integrated state by Westminster and Whitehall. After all, unionist politicians at Westminster - including the powerful bloc of Scottish Labour MPs – believed that if the Scottish Parliament had accepted its limited provincial role, there would have been no problem. Its ambition to increase its powers at the expense of London had made it 'too big for its boots'. It must be stopped!

Initially, I had expressed support for the multi-option approach of the Scottish Government. I had long suspected the pre-legislative referendum strategy adopted by the Party. Little good could come from a referendum where independence was defeated. Devo.max appeared to offer a tactical consolation even if it deferred a real decision on Scotland's future until later. Politics after all, they say, is the art of the possible. But nothing is ever in isolation. The global credit squeeze and the failure of the banks had diminished the credit worthiness of the British state and the proposed cut backs if properly focused could make independence look more attractive. More vitally, Scotland could expect less power transferred from London if it voted NO to independence.

And with Scotland no longer having any clout in British politics, the Westminster Government could rest easy. The British state would ignore devo.max and rub in the failure of the SNP. If the aftermath of the 1979 Referendum when a YES majority for devolution was ignored, was repeated, it was likely a defeated Scotland would become passive. Publicly in an article in the Sunday Mail, I expressed the view that a multi-option referendum was not a valid choice and that Scotland had to be given a challenge.

One other matter of interest appeared in the memorandum. The franchise for the Scottish Parliament elections was to be adopted. This gave the right to vote to British, Irish, qualifying Commonwealth citizens and European citizens provided they were resident in Scotland. It removed all British citizens and expatriate Scots from a say in determining Scotland's future, even though dissolution of the Union would impact on the rest of the United Kingdom. The future of Scotland would be determined by those who lived in Scotland.

By November 2013, all the pieces in the procedural jigsaw were in place. The franchise was to be extended to include young people aged 16 (down from the usual 18). The single question would be:

"Should Scotland be an independent country?"

Fifty per cent of the vote plus one (a bare majority) would be sufficient with no qualified majority imposed. Polling Day (or Scotland's date with destiny) would be Thursday, 18 September 2014. With an affirmative vote, Scotland's independence day would be in March 2016, taking effect after conclusion of negotiations and the passage of enabling legislation in both the Westminster and Scottish Parliaments.

With the procedural issues systematically attended to, all that remained was the campaign. Here is where it gets perplexing. When did the campaign start and when should it have started?

Let us put it into an historical context. From 1934 when it was formed, the Scottish National Party had by and large, mainly from a position of weakness and occasionally with some success, fought an incessant battle to convince the Scottish people of the benefits of their country resuming its independence as a state. From the sixties onwards, partly as a result of Britain's decline and the wrapping up of the colonial empire combined with a growing disparity in wealth between the north and south as the old heavy industries declined, social opinion in Scotland began to change. Until then, most people in Scotland regarded themselves as British and reserved their Scottish identity for sporting contests with the auld enemy, England. Gradually, as the generations changed, the unity induced by Britain's former greatness and the Second World War weakened. Some now thought of themselves as exclusively Scottish; the majority found it possible to have a shared identity as both Scottish and British with the primary emphasis on their Scottish identity. Immigrants found it possible to describe themselves as being say, Scottish Asians or whatever, without difficulty.

In 1997, the SNP committed itself to progressing the path to independence through the establishment of a Scottish Parliament and this was accentuated in 1999 when, the Party found itself in the Scottish parliament with a large group of MSPs. Implicit in this change was the strategy to win power by persuading the people that the SNP was fit to govern and should become the Scottish Government. The path to this goal was achievable by fighting elections on the basis of expanding the powers of the Parliament gradually until it became a short step to cross the line and convert Holyrood from being a provincial assembly into a fully sovereign parliament. Indeed in the 1999 Manifesto, out of the ten priorities, independence came last in tenth place. And so as not to frighten the horses, a vote for the Party was for a referendum for independence, not for independence itself.

It was hardly surprising that when the SNP came into government in 2007, it settled into a new, gradualist establishment. By showing that it was skilled in administration, it was hoped to build confidence and to demonstrate that it was safe to vote SNP. Certainly, the landslide victory of 2011 was ample proof that the strategy could work. Any fears that there was too big a gap between YES and NO were dispelled by the SNP coming from behind to overtake Labour to win the majority. If it could be done in 2011, it was argued, there should be no problem in doing the same in the referendum campaign. Most assuredly, those of us who were worried by the difference in support for independence and staying in the Union, hoped that they were right.

An alternative strategy was for the Government to have used every opportunity to show how Scotland was being held back by the Union instead of clapping itself on its back as it had to do when under constant attack from all sides. Paradoxically, the success of the SNP made devolution work and independence unnecessary for many. Thus the opinion polls repeatedly placed the SNP Government at a high level, contrasting with no improvement in support for independence. All theory, but what other reason can there be for the disparity in support between the two objectives?

The SNP should have sustained its attacks on the Union when it came to power. If independence was the goal then it was essential to raise the profile of Scottish identity and dissipate British identity. In most cases when countries gain their independence it is because of identity. Win the argument on identity and then everything falls into place automatically. Of course, the plain fact is that nobody expected the SNP to win a majority in 2011. It was not until the closing weeks of the campaign that the SNP also began to believe.

2011 changed the game. The referendum was now a reality. Campaigning organisations, YES Scotland (with Blair Jenkins as Chief Executive) and Better Together (led by Blair McDougall) were set up to project the cases. In the background were the SNP and the SNP Government on the one hand and the unionist parties on the other. YES Scotland had Advisory Board representatives from the Green and Socialist Parties and independents. In reality, it was funded by the SNP and totally dominated by the policies of the Scottish Government.

Better Together, whose main spokesman was former Labour Chancellor of the Exchequer, Alistair Darling MP was broadly a front for the Conservative/Liberal Democrat Coalition Government with many Labour activists being unhappy at being associated with the Tories. The Conservatives having no credence in Scotland were happy to allow the Liberal Democrats to do their dirty work. It is difficult to see what benefit the Lib Dems would see in this arrangement as it made them appear anti-Scottish. The lesson of the wipe out of the Scottish Tories for similar misconduct should have exercised their minds.

The Conservative led Coalition Government at Cabinet Office level was aware of the threat posed to their prestige and authority worldwide. A working group was established to attack the nationalist case, using the whole resources of the British state and Treasury. It did not assume that this matter should be left to the Scots. The idea that Scotland should cease to be part of the UK was unthinkable and had to be resisted. The departure of Scotland would make the decline of Britain over the previous 50 years since the loss of the colonies brutally transparent. So far as the power brokers of the world were concerned, the UK was an 'empty drum', all sound and brave talk to disguise its weakening economy and reduced military capability.

And so within six months of the 2011 victory, the UK Government rolled out its self-styled 'Project Fear' campaign. Initially, the concentration was on major issues such as defence, admission to the European Union and NATO, and the currency. The problem with a pre-legislative referendum is that the electorate would have to vote for unknown outcomes. The SNP and YES Scotland countered that common sense dictated that these matters would be solved easily after independence. There would be 'hard pounding' over the details but at the end of the day common interest would ensure that the UK Government would do a deal. The same answer was advanced over entry to the EU and NATO. The constant questioning was intended to cause uncertainty and did so, leaving the YES movement looking more like a punch bag, absorbing blows defensively over an 18 months time-span.

It was difficult to discern the strategy of the YES movement during this period. The polls continued to show the YES vote trailing. Sooner or later the YES campaigners would have to come out to fight. There was no indication of when this would be and with every month passing nearer to polling day, the time to shift public opinion shortened.

The trouble with YES Scotland was that it was not independent. It was funded and had staff seconded from the SNP and Government. It was also overshadowed by the Scottish Government whose Ministers set the pace, leaving little latitude for striking a different posture.

The SNP vote was not large enough to win, especially with up to one third of its voters being against independence. To carry the day, it was necessary to obtain the support from adherents of the other parties and those who did not vote. Many of these would not wish to be associated with the Scottish National Party when their party loyalties lay elsewhere. This was particularly true of Labour voters who favoured independence. If they saw the referendum was genuinely non-party political and Scotland's referendum, it would be easier for them to cast their vote FOR. Conversely, if it was perceived as the SNP's referendum, then they might vote No or abstain.

As the SNP called the shots, YES Scotland found that the battlefield was based on SNP policy. The Scottish Government would have found it difficult to divert from its own policies since it was the campaign master. Finding a broader solution would have been easier if another of the major parties had been onside as occurred, for example, in the 1997 referendum on devolution.

The only practical alternative was to fight the case on general principles such as Scottish democracy or the needs of the Scottish economy and not to rise defensively to every jibe or claim posed by London or Better Together. By giving the Scottish people an assured right to a second vote on the major issues after the negotiations were concluded, it could have campaigned positively in favour of Scottish democracy and eased potential fears. This could be done in two ways.

The first was through the old device of a 'multi-option' referendum where the people would decide directly on Europe and the currency, for instance. The second was to emphasise that electors would be free to vote on these critical issues at the first general election after independence through the Party of their choice. The SNP Government or its negotiators would promise dual track negotiations and lay out the options available so that Scotland's political parties could make a choice for their manifestos. If not direct democracy, it would at least transfer some of the flak to the unionists for their unpreparedness and distance the referendum from too close an association with the SNP.

Take one example, the promise that Scotland would join the European Union. Nobody seriously doubted that an independent Scotland with its resources would be refused entry. Nevertheless, London claimed that there could be delay of years in limbo, that Scotland could lose its share of the British rebate and that Scotland could be forced to join the Euro. All of these arguments were advanced to cause uncertainty. It is also undeniable that while Scotland was less Europhobe than England, there was a significant minority who were unhappy with the way the EU had centralised. An IPSOS-Mori survey in February 2013 found that 53% of Scots would vote for the UK to remain in the EU, with 34% opposed. 61% thought an independent Scotland should be a member.

34% is a big figure to ignore. A sensible course, appealing to both views would be to negotiate with both the European Union and EFTA (the European Free Trade Association comprising Norway, Switzerland,

Liechtenstein and Iceland). EFTA has full access to the single market without the burden of EU bureaucracy. At the very least, the EU Commission and Council of Ministers seeing that Scotland had a valid alternative would be less likely to impose problematical conditions. And a nation securing its freedom might find joining the bloc of small prosperous EFTA countries (the millionaires club!) highly attractive!

A similar course of action could be followed in respect of the currency negotiations with London on access to the sterling zone as against a separate currency pegged in the first instance to GB pounds. Not only would this be good politics, it would be an example of the transparent democracy to be adopted in the new Scotland and a far cry from the political elitism practised at Westminster.

What was particularly worrying in the opening stages of the campaign were signs that the SNP, perhaps taken by surprise by the victories of 2007 and 2011, did not have a coherent plan of action. It seemed obsessed with the processes and protocols while the UK Government and other unionists launched propaganda attack after attack. Both it and YES Scotland were passive to a fault. They seemed to be scratching for ideas and more concerned with making an independent Scotland seem a cut-down version of the UK as if that would confuse die-hard unionists into casting their vote for Independence

The Party did have an impressive blueprint, The Transition to Independence. It had been prepared in the late nineties by Dr Allan Macartney and a distinguished team of academics. It set out the basis for dissolution of the Union of Parliaments of England and Scotland of 1707, the preparation of the Constitution by a Constituent Assembly, accession to the European Union, international issues, the status of the monarchy, assumption of existing treaty obligations, division of public utilities, debts and assets, broadcasting and pensions – all the matters now under scrutiny. The document even listed the terms of two Vienna Conventions on Succession of States in respect of Treaties (1972) and in respect of State Property, Archives and Debts (1983). When I made a copy available to the Party, I was surprised to learn it had slipped from its collective memory. This was unfortunate as it supplied the SNP and YES Scotland with much of the ammunition it desperately needed.

One interesting proposition in the Macartney paper was that it would be wrong to treat Scotland as seceding from the United Kingdom. With

Scotland being a high contracting party to the Union, it had the right to dissolve the partnership. Thus England, Wales and Northern Ireland (EWNI) would also have to seek recognition by Europe and other bodies as a separate entity. By consent (on suitable terms), Scotland could agree to secede so that EWNI could be treated as a continuation of the UK and inherit the UK seat on the Security Council. Such an option would strengthen Scotland's hand in negotiations.

In the event, this view did not meet with support from the SNP leadership which adopted a more diplomatic stance. No doubt after carefully studying attitude polls which showed that the Scottish public wanted change though not at any price, it presented a different face. Scotland would still be in the British social union. Scotland would keep the monarchy. Scotland would keep sterling. Nothing too dramatic would cause alarm. Scotland could have its political independence, yet to all extents and purposes would still be British. At this point, some activists began to wonder where independence and freedom had gone. Indeed, if devo.max was not an option, perhaps it had become 'Independence Lite'. What was the difference between devo.max and Independence Lite, it was asked. What then was the point of an independence referendum?

Meantime, the British and European economies were in deep recession with massive cuts in public expenditure planned by both the Labour and Conservative Parties. Despite this, the YES campaign was curiously inactive in focussing attention on Britain's high ratio of debt and continuing economic mismanagement. Still more cuts in public expenditure were coming. By now retired and having more time to assess the position, it seemed to me that the obvious tack was to pin the blame for all this on London. Why independence? This was the vital question and one that had to be answered if the people of Scotland were to be given strong reasons for change.

There was no attempt to use negative campaigning against London's control of the economy. Sometimes, it appeared that the SNP's victory in 2011 in a positive campaign set against the failure of Labour's contrasting negativity had caused the Party to believe that a positive presentation was the only working formula.

I disagreed and over a three year period wrote a series of articles, mainly in the Scots Independent, which advanced a more aggressive approach highlighting the dangers of continued London rule. The titles sum it up – British Bankruptcy Ruining Scotland, the Great British Delusion, Grow Independence, It's the Economy, Stupid and Last Chance Saloon.

I did two other things. Firstly, in initial association with Jim Sillars in November 2012, I set up a think-tank, Options for Scotland. This was designed to look at the far side of a YES vote and creatively set out the options which independent Scottish Governments could adopt. Starting in November 2012, there was a statement with Jim Sillars on the EU/EFTA issues. In 2013, Options published expert papers on Electricity Generating Policies for an Independent Scotland (by Nick Dekker), A National Plan for Scotland's Oil and Gas Industry (by Martyn Tulloch and myself), Economic Options for an Independent Scotland (by economists, Jim & Margaret Cuthbert) in joint association with the Jimmy Reid Foundation, Aviation Policy Options for Scotland (by Iain Lawson), Location of New Ministries (by Roy MacIver and Gordon Wilson), Emigration and Immigration Policy Options for an Independent Scotland (by Gordon Wilson and Nick Dekker) and Banking in an Independent Scotland (Ian Blackford). There were also frequent, shorter articles including one on Defence by Stuart Crawford, another on a socialist future by John McAllion and currency by Jim Fairlie.

Secondly, sensing growing apprehension amongst the public about the absence of public campaign, I made my exasperation known to the media. When there was no seeming end to the drift, I wrote on 12 June 2013 to Dennis Canavan, the former Labour MP and Chairman of YES Scotland in the following terms:

> "While I am less than happy with the current YES vote campaign, I believe that you can turn things round. The present defensive approach is a failure. With your extensive political experience, you must be fed up with being a 'punch-bag' for the NO campaign. If you are content, you are not the pugnacious Dennis Canavan, I broke a lance with in the Commons so many years ago
>
> I shall put my views as succinctly as I can:
>
> 1. So far the presentation has all the emotional content of a calculator. It is almost as if we are fighting a local government election rather than one giving Scots an historic chance to secure full self-government. We must up the tempo and create excitement. If Catalonia can

put 1.5 million on the streets, why should we be coy to assert our nationhood. Currently, there is more passion amongst supporters of the Union than those who seek independence. Odd, that!

2. People I speak to want to hear the facts. This is problematical since the debate has caused confusion. On the major issues like Europe, the currency and defence, it is assumed that if Scotland votes YES, then SNP policy on these matters is unquestionable. But this is Scotland's referendum. While the SNP deserves every credit for securing the referendum, it would be wrong for one political party to dictate the issues on which the public and other supporters of independence have different views. These matters are so strategically critical to Scotland's future that the people of Scotland who are constitutionally sovereign must be consulted in a second multi-choice referendum on the outcomes of the post-independence negotiations conducted by representatives of the Scottish Parliament. That way the people will know the facts and be reassured that they will have direct say when a choice can be made. Perhaps we should follow the model of prosperous, democratic Switzerland that allows its people to make principled decisions. You will also recall that when Norway obtained its independence, it held a referendum to choose its King – at the request of the Danish prince who had been invited by the Storting to fill the office. Psychologically, this will give our people more confidence to vote YES and the campaign will be given a boost.

3. So far the Scottish people have not been given the facts. Yes, in a scatter-gun fashion, some of the benefits of independence have been outlined but there has been no coherent, systematic presentation. The real choice is between Independence and the Union. So far, the NO campaign has launched attack after attack on Scotland's confidence. Nowhere have they been challenged to justify why Scotland should **remain** in the Union. Their assumption is that Scotland benefits from membership.

Or our jobs depend on it. Or that without 'big brother', our society would collapse. Also, many Scots will be irritated by the constant negative out-pourings from London that assume we are a nation of half-wits, unable like other nations to govern ourselves. Likewise, given the hostility from Westminster, YES For Scotland (sic) should be asking the question: if those attitudes represent London's pre-referendum stance, what penalties will Scotland face, if we vote NO. Assimilation to England will follow under the guise of one nation Britishness, be sure of it – and fear it!

4. We need a hard-hitting sustained attack on the British economy. A quick glance at the excellent paper by Margaret Cuthbert on the management of the British Economy published by the Jimmy Reid Foundation two weeks ago shows that any benefits from the faltering economy of the UK, go not to the Union as a whole but to London and the South of England. That is where the prosperity and jobs go. London is the leech that has sucked away the lifeblood of Scotland over decades. With similar growth, Scotland's economy would have been 25% higher.

   There are alleged to be around 800,000 Scots in other parts of the UK. Most are not there by choice. They had to emigrate because British mismanagement of the Scottish economy did not provide them with opportunities in their own country. Under London management, the British standard of living has sunk to 2003 levels. There is a threat of seven more years of austerity. The economic dangers of **remaining** in the Union should be emphasised.

5. Scotland is not the only country or region affected. Northern England suffers particularly badly. If Scotland votes NO, the one area that will benefit is London and the South. Why the English regions do not rebel, I do not know as they are faced with continued comparative decline as London grows. Scotland has a remedy – and that is independence. Without it, the advice to our children or grand children is to emigrate. After a NO vote, Scotland

will have little future. To attack the octopus of London and the South is not to attack England as conceivably the changes brought about by Scottish independence will have a beneficial impact on the North. The counter-weight of the prosperous expanding economy of an independent Scotland would give Northern England a fighting chance.

I appreciate that all the tools are not in the YES (For) Scotland basket or indeed the cash. But you are the official campaign and have more clout that you think. I hope that there will be a serious rethink over the summer and that you come out fighting. If the Scottish football team can beat Croatia, you still have a chance. But you must fight!"

Given the pressures on YES (for) Scotland, I did not expect a direct response. Nevertheless, it was my hope that the issues would be addressed. Sources inside the campaigning organisation indicated that the same paralysis was continuing.

I gave it time. Eventually, in August, I published through Options for Scotland a half time critique that drew remarkable publicity. As can be seen, I did not pull my punches, yet tried to make it constructive:

"The independence referendum campaign is unusual. Amongst the modern countries seeking their independence, the arguments were simple and effective – independent self-government is the form of government that is the essence of national freedom – the democratic expression of the will of the nation. So there is little argument over the case. Instead there is an enthusiastic vision of what the new nation can do with independence once it joins or rejoins the family of nations within the UN.

Then there is absence of vision, passion and emotion. National freedom does not exist in a sterile environment. Yet in Scotland there is little such expression and the politicians, particularly on the YES side, prefer to argue a case with all the excitement of a robot. As for nationalism this has been successfully given the homeopathic treatment so that it has been successively diluted beyond trace, and with it the strong card of Scotland's national identity! The dynamic of nationalism has seemingly been dulled by doses of devolutionary 'mogadon'. George Robertson (former Labour Minister) may have overstated his case that devolution would kill nationalism stone dead, but he clearly had a point.

<u>Temper of the Nation</u>

So where are we now? In Catalonia, much larger than Scotland with 7.5 million people, over one and a half million have demonstrated on the streets in favour of Catalan independence in Europe. YES supporters would be delirious if a fraction of that, say 20,000 to 30,000 instead of a comparable one million, turned out in Scotland.

Neal Ascherson once compared the nationalisms of Poland (messianic) and Czechoslovakia (reluctant), it would appear that Scotland is more in the Czech mould. Rather than looking ahead confidently, many of our people are frightened of change. But if they realise that there is no equality, fairness or future under the Union with England given the disparate sizes of both populations, they may reluctantly, accept that the best prospect is with independence.

Nevertheless, it is surprising that a referendum is being held at all without the due preparation of public opinion that would lead to a resounding victory – and when you are 9 points behind, the judgement and strategy look adventurous at best and reckless at worst. But you can only build with the clay you have!

At half time, all is not lost. But where do we go from here?

<u>The Rival Campaigns</u>

<u>Yes for Scotland/SNP Government</u>

For a start, has there been a campaign? No doubt YES (for) Scotland has been 'beavering' away at the important organisational and social media campaign and is getting ready for the work on the ground. The impression given to the public and media is one of lack of strategic vision and general unreadiness to face issues such as Europe, the currency and defence. Instead, the YES side has shiftily moved position under pressure from Better Together. Why the stance on these issues was not worked out earlier is one aspect historians will be anxious to explore!

There seems to have been an uneasy and certainly listless response to the attacks from the other side. Political punch-bags do not usually win votes. The campaign seems to be a two headed affair with the larger head of the SNP dominating. If so, that structural imbalance needs to be sorted out as a matter of urgency!

What is surprising is that the YES campaign has found itself bogged down in trench warfare over topics like Europe etc where the outcome cannot be known in detail until the negotiations take place after the vote in principle. There are political stratagems that could easily have been put in place, and still can, to allow the Scottish people a vote on options or choices after independence to ratify the solutions that they consider best for Scotland.

It has not been made clear that the Scots will have an immediate general election after independence takes effect. Instead, the impression given is that the choice lies only with SNP or Scottish Government policy. That is clearly not the case as this is Scotland's referendum even if the SNP deserves the credit for achieving it and negotiating the terms. And it also has to be said that the manoeuvring of the British Government into signing the Edinburgh Agreement was a political triumph for Scotland since it dispelled any doubts over the legitimacy of the process.

Nevertheless, there has been little systematic effort to persuade the people of the weaknesses in devolution and advantages of independence – almost as if the message of good government at Holyrood in itself is an argument for independence. Paradoxically, the converse may be true.

Also from YES Scotland and the Government, there is the peculiar notion that negative politics does not work –

something the Americans would find strange. Of course, positivism worked in the Scottish elections of 2007 and 2011. But negative campaigns torpedoed the 1975 EU referendum, 1979 referendum, the SNP in the Scottish Elections of 1999 and 2003 and the SNP in most Westminster elections.

There has to be a balance but the YES campaign has been silent on the issue of why the Union is bad for Scotland as well as why independence is good.

So, three out of ten so far.

<u>The NO Campaign</u>

Without doubt the NO campaign has been better prepared, better organised and more effective – hardly surprising since it exercises the power of the British state within its weaponry. It has taken the attack and forced an ill-prepared YES side into defensive reactions. Of course, it has benefited from the support of a predominantly Unionist media. Yet with the SNP Government polling at a record 48%, this is not as potent as it seems. Still, for activity and direction, one can admire the superior staff work of the Cabinet Office compared to that of the Scottish civil service.

If reports are correct, the Conservative controlled Cabinet Office set up a team to defend the Union as soon as the SNP won an overall majority in the 2011 election and set out to use British state institutions like the Commons and Lords Select Committees (some 13 adverse reports) and other governmental agencies to argue against Scottish independence.

Little attempt was made to show the benefits of the Union other than in cursory terms. Instead from November 2011, there was an offensive on what were perceived to be weak points such as Europe, the currency and defence. Since then there has been a constant stream of negativity. The Scots, they said, would be isolated from Europe (and coming from the 'little Englanderism' of London, that was rich). The Bank of England would not play ball over Scotland's inclusion in a sterling zone (despite us owning 9% of the Bank). And as for defence, unlike other small European nations, Scotland would be prey to large, unidentified predator countries). Again rich coming from the UK which is building aircraft carriers with few aircraft and which has notified NATO that it cannot fulfil its naval commitments!

But then the campaign ran out of control. The incessant attacks lost punch. They began to look anti-Scottish, disparaging to the point of racism. Indeed, the anti-Scottish tone caused people to wonder are these rancorous people in London on our side? If not, what will happen to us if we vote NO? If this is London's snide wooing when they want us to stay, what will happen to Scotland if we make ourselves defenceless with no influence after remaining in the Union? That coin has still to drop, but when it does, the impact will be potent.

So, for aggression, direction and impact, Better Together should have won hands down. Against that, they lacked subtlety and while succeeding in creating doubt as to how Scotland can manage, they have over-stated their case. Bluntly they have shot their bolt. Project Fear has become Project Ridiculous. They will be in a difficult position to maintain their momentum once the YES campaign (hopefully) gets its act together. Sooner or later they will have to demonstrate what benefits Scotland will get as a minority partner within the Union in circumstances where Scotland will have no political relevance after a NO vote.

Gauged alone for causing doubt, they are worth four out of ten!

What Should The Yes Campaign Do Now?

1. Operational Control

The imbalance between the SNP Government and the campaign body YES Scotland is wrong and both the governmental politicians and the leaders of the wider campaign must redefine their roles and become more effective. It is confusing to have YES for Scotland having independent and other Party representatives forced to adopt policies on Europe, defence and the currency to suit SNP policy with which they do not agree.

2. Vision and Strategic Direction

If the Campaign leaders have imagination and boldness, they could immediately gain momentum by outflanking Better Together and its negativity by proposing that the two salient issues of Europe (EU or EFTA) and the currency go to the Scottish people for decision in a second referendum after the negotiations are concluded. This will be ultimate democracy and difficult for the NO campaign to argue against. Relatively consequential issues like defence, NATO and Trident can be matters for the first Scottish government elected after independence. In the current set-up, the issue of the monarchy is aberrational to the campaign and if Scotland adopts a Swiss style constitution, it will potentially be a matter for resolution by referendum on a monarchical accession on the far side of independence. In any event, the people would decide. This is the right thing to do.

Freeing up these issues would allow independent i.e. non-SNP representatives to speak up. Although I am a member of the SNP, I concede that this Referendum belongs to the Scottish people rather than to the SNP although the SNP deserves the credit for securing a mandate for it and for its resolve and astuteness that led to the Edinburgh Agreement with the UK Government that removed any questions as to legitimacy.

3. Stating the Benefits

This should largely be the task of SNP Government Ministers backed by the Scottish civil service. They have the senior public presence and the back up to make this their role. They will, however, have to sharpen the pedestrian caution of civil servants, some of whose loyalties will be dubious. The business of administration will need to be reorganised to allow space for Ministers to act as politicians almost as if this was an election to give some dynamism to the campaign. It should be for YES for Scotland to secure independent experts/reports and endorsing celebrities to back up the ministerial effort.

4. Attacking the Union

This is where YES for Scotland and SNP MSPs, MEP's and MPs should be deployed as soon as possible in a managed offensive. The theme is obvious. The enemy of the British Union is London and the South of England which from Thatcher's day has been gobbling up the wealth of the UK to the hurt of the rUK, in this case Wales, Northern Ireland, Northern England and Scotland. Thanks to the Scottish Parliament and the strength of a good Scottish Government, Scotland has fared less badly, but even there our rate of economic growth has been constrained by the fact that British economic and monetary policy under Labour Ministers like Brown and Darling and the Coalition of Southern Tory and Liberal millionaires, has been managed for the benefit of the City of London and the south.

There is plenty of ammunition but the central buttress is the recent report on the mismanagement of the British economy by Margaret Cuthbert and published in July 2013 by The Jimmy Reid Foundation. Few people in Scotland are aware that there had been no industrial policy in the UK for thirty years designed to neuter the rapacious greed of southern England.

Here we share the problems with other parts of rUK as the economy of the North of England has atrophied while London has boomed. So Scotland should go out of its way to establish strong contacts with the Northern English Councils who are beginning to sense the economic benefits to their region of having a strong independent Scottish economy as a counterweight to London.

Scotland, with the moral support of the North, should strike at the southern cancer. For Scottish people the lesson should be made clear. London and the South are holding Scotland back. London got more benefit from Scotland's oil than Scotland did. Freed from London control, Scotland will be set for expansion. Under the London straitjacket, continuing mismanagement of the British economy favouring the south of England cannot be withstood by the limited powers of the Scottish Parliament.

What Happens If Scotland Votes NO?

There is a naive notion that if Scotland votes no, Westminster will give additional powers to the Scottish Parliament. No doubt devolution carrots will be dangled in the run-up to the Referendum. The evidence runs to the contrary. In 1945, 1969, 1974 and again in 1979 successive UK Governments reneged on promises of Home Rule, industrial powers based on North Sea Oil and 'better' schemes of devolution as soon as pressure from Scotland eased. It is not in the nature of the British beast to change its nature.

Objective analysis of what happened in Canada after Quebec narrowly voted against independence in the last referendum has recently been published. After the referendum, Quebec lost political influence within Canada and Canadian centralisation increased.

This will happen here. As a matter of strategy, the UK Government will move to trim the powers of the Scottish parliament to ensure no further moves towards independence. The Barnett formula will be scrapped. The revenues of the Scottish government will be reduced proportionately to the English average. Scots law will come under attack from the Supreme Court whose President has declared in a speech that he expects the Court to be more active on devolution matters if Scotland votes NO.

There will be a process of assimilation of Scottish institutions to an Anglo/British mode and deviations from English models, including the NHS will not be tolerated in the interests of equality and rationalisation. Nor could Scotland object, having voted to remain within the British polity.

One thing assured is that Scotland's influence will be reduced domestically and worldwide for a generation. If you aim for the stars and crash, no one will take you seriously and it is likely the trend of positive foreign investment seen during the independence debate will reverse

This issue has not yet surfaced but when it does, it will have impact. Most of those intending to vote NO expect the *status quo* to continue. It will not. The tail of the British lion has been tweaked and there will be uncomfortable consequences.

Recognition of this by the wider Scottish electorate could be a game changer.

Options

This article is intended to be an analysis of progress so far and outline possible future options for the YES campaign. It is not a blueprint, something far beyond the scope of Options for Scotland.. What it does is to inject new ideas and themes at a mid-term turning point. At the very least, it is to be hoped that the YES Campaign will be more visionary and assertive."

This message was not greeted with joy by the official campaign or the SNP. It did however say what had to be said and responded to a deep apprehension amongst many of those favouring the campaign for independence. There was also a dawning understanding amongst the leadership that a new phase was necessary. The SNP Government had secured a major tactical success the previous year when it had manoeuvred the UK Government into signing the Edinburgh Agreement. This had demolished a major area of doubt as to the legitimacy of the referendum and the consent of the UK to working constructively in the event of a YES vote was not unharmful. Yet the message of Scottish democracy was not 'cutting the mustard' with the Scottish electorate.

There were some bright points. Despite the battering from Better Together, Westminster and Whitehall over a sustained period of two years, the impact of the negative attacks had been muted. Although the opinion polls put the No vote in a commanding lead and the YES vote trailing consistently, there were indications that the No vote was softening and the Don't Knows growing.

Some columnists, mainly Iain MacWhirter and Ian Bell of the Herald began pointing to the comparison between the prosperity of the city state of London and the South of England and the rest of the UK. By 18

September 2013, only 1 year from polling, the campaign intensified. There was no weakening of hostility from the printed news media but now radio and television got into the act with debates where Nicola Sturgeon consistently demolished the opposition to the dismay of the unionists. So too at the SNP Annual Conference in October, she took up the theme of what would happen if Scotland said NO.

The great counter-offensive of the SNP Government was to be a White Paper answering all the difficult questions and giving the YES campaign a major boost. And with the polls still showing support for independence in minority, great hopes were placed on the White Paper. It was intended to be a substantial game changer.

Chapter 13:

HARD POUNDING

Under the title of 'Scotland's Future', the White Paper was published by the Scottish Government in November 2013 amidst a blaze of publicity. The Media Conference featuring the First Minister, Alex Salmond and Depute First Minister, Nicola Sturgeon was attended by a large turn-out of journalists from home and abroad. Cheekily, London media representatives were given international accreditation.

The White Paper was intended to set out Scotland's case for independence and to answer the questions that had been raised. The aim was to remove the uncertainty created by the Better Together NO campaign. It therefore opened with the case for independence. It set out the democratic imperative that decisions currently taken at Westminster would be taken instead by the people of Scotland. At the centre of the case was the proposition that with independence, Scotland would always get governments it voted for. The country would have control of its resources, make its own decisions and decide its own social and economic priorities.

It concentrated on the practical and pragmatic aspects of the case. It was unrelentingly positive and at times carried civil service blandness to an extreme. It contained questions and answers for every disputation and was of impressive length – a veritable encyclopaedia! The arguments were still based on Scotland's opportunities and a real criticism was that it was perfunctory in its criticism of the economic treatment of Scotland under the Union. It contented itself, as the summary shows, with a brief critique:

> "The economic choice in the independence referendum is therefore how to build on this sound economic base to create sustainable jobs, ensure that more people share in Scotland's wealth and build long-term resilience and security in our economy.
>
> Under the Westminster system Scotland is treated as a regional economy within the UK. Our ability to meet future challenges and seize opportunities is constrained and many

major decisions are taken by Westminster. Currently, the Scottish parliament is responsible for just 7 per cent of taxes raised in Scotland; new tax powers will only increase this to around 15%. With independence Scotland will control 100% of our resources.

Under the Westminster system Scotland is also locked in to one of the most unequal economic models in the developed world: since 1975 income inequality among working-age people has increased faster in the UK than in any other country in the OECD. The increasing geographical imbalance concentrates jobs, population growth and investment in London and the South East of England, but no action has been taken to address this by successive Westminster governments."

In a nutshell, this was the economic case against the Union. It is the economic 'WHY' independence was vital for without it wealth and population would continue to flow south. There were 800,000 people of Scots birth already living in England. That was no accident. Without proper economic policies devised for Scottish needs, there were already insufficient jobs here. Without independence that out flow of educated skilled younger people would continue. The time imperative for urging people to act now before it was too late was not developed in terms people could understand.

If one did not examine the White Paper as a campaigning tool there was much to be satisfied with. It was a substantial, well argued contribution to the debate. It achieved substantial television and press coverage – even from London, and to that extent achieved its purpose. It fell prey to expected criticism from the UK Government and Better Together. It did not answer the questions about accession to the European Union or the sterling currency zone, they said. And how could it, the unionist critics were not only refusing to pre-negotiate. Instead, they were rubbishing the Scottish Government proposals and refusing to have pre-negotiation discussions which could have ironed out some of the main divisions .

A criticism made by the opposition was that the White Paper read like an SNP manifesto for the first independence election. If so, it created an unexpected difficulty. Although the referendum was   Scotland's referendum, the White Paper gave the impression that independence was to be on SNP policy and terms. It consolidated a view that the referendum was the SNP's referendum and not that of the Scottish people as a whole. There was a danger that if this aspect took hold, people supporting other parties could be put off voting Yes.

Nonetheless, the White Paper was a massive achievement. Even the arithmetic is impressive – 10 chapters, 650 pages and 170,000 words; altogether a huge amount of work had gone into the preparation of the document. It was in demand with a final print run of 100,000. The Paper asserted SNP Government policy on Europe, the currency, immigration and other matters. It could not do otherwise without running foul of the rules regarding political partisanship. White Papers do not have to be non-political as they set out Government policy established by the political party in Government. Nevertheless there is a boundary and the SNP came close to it. One of its star policies was vastly increased child care with independence, regarded as a political master stroke.

The acid test of the 'game-changing' objective of the White Paper was the impact it would have on support for independence. As Prof John Curtice of Strathclyde University said prior to its publication, the essential element of the multitude of the opinion polls was how little they had changed during the first phase of the campaign. Individual polls differed but by and large the message was the same. Support for the Union was well in the lead and the Yes vote trailed. The fact that Project Fear had had little sustained impact was little consolation to independence voters when their figures remained static. Despite the pro-British enthusiasm whipped up in 2011 for the Queen's Jubilee (less in Scotland than in England although the display of Union Flags - who provided and paid for them is a question - outnumbered Saltire Flags), the display of British togetherness in the London Olympics and the subliminal seeping of 'Great British' programmes on BBC TV, there was little change.

All this was denting the morale of SNP activists. Nothing seemed to work. In January 2013, the Social Attitudes Survey recorded that only 23% of Scots supported independence, down 9 points from 2011. In February, 2013 an Angus Reid Opinion Poll put out the settled referendum question to survey and found independence support at 32% and the NO vote 47%. Both surveys had divergent questions, yet recorded a huge gulf. Although the SNP claimed the tide was turning in favour of a YES vote later in the month with publication of an Ipsos Mori poll (Herald 14 February 2013), the result was 34% YES to 55% NO.

Naturally, with the campaign failing to close or extend the gap on either side, there were criticisms during the summer. On the YES side apart from my own exasperations earlier, First Minister Alex Salmond was on record to steady the troops that the campaign had not yet begun. In the New Statesman (20 June 2013), he declared:

> "This is the phoney war. This is not the campaign. I went into an election in 2011, 20 points behind in the polls and ended up 15 in front. The real game hasn't even started. We are just clearing the ground."

Given that the UK Government Campaign had commenced as soon as the SNP had achieved a parliamentary majority in 2011, this comment displayed a bullish confidence remarkable even for the First Minister who was rarely short of that commodity! From the distant ramparts of the BBC in London, self-exiled Dundonian, Andrew Marr who had updated his 1992 book, 'The Battle for Scotland' was reported in the Herald as saying:

> "Andrew Marr has questioned the tactics of both the pro- and anti- independence camps and predicted the outcome could be closer than many outside Scotland think.
>
> The broadcaster suggested the No campaign could be making a 'mistake' by 'playing the fear card' highlighting the potentially negative consequences of leaving the UK.
>
> However, he also suggested the nationalists could do more to set out their vision of the future, adding 'so far we have heard surprisingly little about exactly how an independent Scotland would differ from a Scotland inside the UK."

This view was widely shared. In the course of the campaign, Scotland on Sunday quoted Professor Curtice, by now the prime expert in interpreting the referendum polls, as indicating in relation to the latest Social Attitudes Survey:

> "The referendum campaign is at risk of short-changing the people of Scotland. So far it appears to have done little to help them be clear and confident about the decision they have to make. Many of the issues that preoccupy those campaigning for independence are apparently of peripheral interest to voters.

Voters want to hear about the economic and financial consequences of the choice they make, and it is on the outcome of that debate that the result of the referendum is likely to turn."

Those survey data related to a period before publication of the White Paper, yet earlier polls had spotlighted the importance of economic factors. The hotly contested battlegrounds of the EU, the currency and welfare appeared to have little impact.

Yet as the summer rolled into the autumn, some of us intuitively felt that all was not lost. There was a perceptible current suggesting that hostility to independence was softening with some movement to the Don't Know category. The media began noticing the issue of the danger of London to the UK – and Scotland. On 15 August there was a major article in the Herald exposing the danger of accelerating growth of London at the expense of other parts of the UK – something that the YES campaign had failed to do.

In a rare positive tabloid involvement, the Sunday Mail came out with an Opinion feature in favour of independence and calling for more adventure. 'Say Yes to Adventure' it said on 15 September:

"With a year before Scotland votes on independence, there are many on his own side who fear the First Minister is taking too many small steps, hedging too many small bets, draining away too much passion and encouraging too many Scots to believe they will even notice if they are independent or not." And, continuing the argument. 'But how can a campaign that seems designed to suck the passion from the vision and drain the colour from the banner for independence ever end with a vote for Yes." It concluded with a call to accentuate change:

"Barack Obama, no slouch at making electoral history, knows its power. 'Hope' and 'Change' was the slogan that took him into the White House in 2008 and spin doctors and pollsters around the world say the words hold a special kind of magic for voters.

So maybe it is time for the Nats to stop kicking the tyres and poking about under the bonnet of this old banger of a debate and start telling us about the exciting journey ahead of us, of the things we'll see and the things we'll do, if only we turn the key in the engine and get moving."

With the referendum only a year away, there was considerable coverage of both the issue and campaign. In August, Scotland on Sunday had run an Ipsos Mori poll concentrating on certainty to vote with a consequent 67% NO to 33% YES ratio. Gloomy at first reading but bringing out that 44% had still to decide. A month later, it published an ICM/Scotsman poll showing that although the division remained the same, there was evidence that Scotland would become an independent country in 12 month's time if voters could be convinced over the next year that a YES vote would make them better off although this suggestion lost credibility by being based on a preposterous level of £500 – an insult to both political cases for the Union and for Independence! What price independence or the Union if only £500 would sway the outcome? In a commentary, John Curtice believed the poll would give comfort to both sides as it was the middle vote for advanced devo.max that was the target for the winning side.

Despite a very successful SNP Conference in October, there was little sign of impetus and it looked as if indeed the White Paper would have to be the 'game-changer'. There were some small harbingers of change. A Panelbase Poll was slightly double-edged. The gap had narrowed to 8 points with a reduction of 4 points in support for NO counter poised with a lesser drop of 2 point for YES compared with a survey in September. Nevertheless, a four point swing could bring independence victory.

The New Statesman rolling political blog gave a favourable and fair-minded analysis of the White Paper. It had passed the political test, despite having some worrying political insistencies on the currency issue. The Paper, it said, reflected the SNP's ideological ambiguity.

> "It is a solid but not inspiring prospectus for independence. In fact the whole document is designed to highlight the government-focused nature of modern Scottish nationalism – and largely succeeds in doing so. The challenge now for supporters of independence is to marry the White Paper's pragmatism with RIC's (Radical Independence Conference) sense of urgency. One without the other isn't going to be enough, but together they present a formidable challenge to the unionists' increasingly lacklustre and repetitive campaign."

There was very little sign after publication of Scotland's Future that it had made a measurable change to public opinion. It had had a good reception by and large. There were three reprints to bring the hard copy total to 40,000. It had been downloaded to a degree unimaginable for a standard government publication. It had obviously been taken seriously by those of the general public interested in political issues. There was no immediate change in support for independence although a side benefit was that the lack of a positive response from Better Together indicated just how worn and threadbare their opposition narrative had become. This showed in a TNS BRMB poll published in the Herald on 19 December when support for the Union had dropped three points from 44% in September to 41%, closing the gap to 14% with Yes at 27%, up 1 point from November. So, no 'game changer' evident there!

During the festive period there was little sign of a downturn in the volume of activity on both sides nor any indication of major change of emphasis. Having tired of the currency issue, the debate swung to Europe with the Spanish Prime Minister causing trouble by predicting that Scotland's accession to the EU would not be as swift as the Scottish Government had predicted. Much of the opposition was now coming from the UK Government rather than from Better Together which had run into problems when Alistair Darling, their principal spokesman, was attacked by London Conservative sources as ineffective and 'comatose'. This was unfair. The term more accurately described the Better Together presentation.

And then breakthrough! On 27 January 2014, Scotland on Sunday published an ICM poll showing 37% would vote YES compared with 44% for NO. In September before the White Paper, the figures were 49% and 32%. The poll also showed growing support amongst women (up 5%) and young people (up 26%).

The blink of light only served to engender further activity on the part of the UK Government which had been in attack mode from November 2011. Prime Minister David Cameron, having conceded the Edinburgh Agreement, refused repeated requests by Alex Salmond for a televised debate when he would be able to defend the Union and Salmond advance the case for independence. Cameron claimed disingenuously that the vote had everything to with Scotland and that it would be wrong for the UK Prime Minister to take part.

It was a threadbare argument. The rest of the UK may not have had a vote. It most certainly had an interest strategically, fiscally and economically. In reality, the UK Government had been better prepared for the contest than the SNP Government. The SNP Government had underestimated the power of the British state to defend itself ruthlessly and unrelentingly. The generation of nationalists which had experienced similar pressures in the seventies had aged, died or were no longer active.

For Westminster to have treated Scotland as if it were a colony would have been immediately fatal for the Union as it would have scunnered a large section of Unionist voters who clung to the belief that Scotland was an equal partner. Yet, some of the principles in dealing with colonies or provinces seeking their freedom were still applicable. The first weapon was to 'divide' opinion. This meant that the fight should be led by Scots so that it would appear that there was internal opposition rather than English intervention. Secondly, the Government would pray in aid of their cause the unity of all the peoples of the UK to disguise that the 'British Union' is England with over 80% of the population. Thirdly, the Government should stress the benefits of remaining in the Union while simultaneously endeavouring to create fear of change.

Whitehall does this well. They had a lot of experience during the break-up of the British Empire! Nationalists get uptight when they encounter British civil servants and politicians having no conscience or sense of British fairness when they act to defend the interests of the British state. This was particularly true in the seventies when Ministers, MPs and civil servants connived to disguise the value of Scotland's oil revenues going to London to derail the Labour Government's half hearted attempts to produce a Scottish Assembly.

Why ever should London not do this? If there is a British state, then it is there to be defended at all costs. The essence of that state is that it is unitary not federal. The standard governing that state is that its Government should act for the greater good of the greater number. The fact that Scotland had special needs or rights to assets is irrelevant. Scotland with its small population could never be 'the greater number' and logically, could benefit only by trickle down largesse or by a conscious decision of 'the greater number'. There was nothing unethical in this as Britain was the political unit. If you are British, then those are the laws of the game. From a Scottish angle, there is only a come-back if you assert a change of identity from British to Scottish. Automatically with independence, Scottish democracy and priorities come into play. This was the whole point of the independence referendum.

So although the Prime Minister would not debate, it did not stop other ministers from making carefully orchestrated visits clutching the latest report from some 'independent' body or government department casting doubt on Scotland's viability or on the objective for co-operation advanced by the Scottish Government. Every other organ of state was encouraged to join the hunt. By 21 December 2012, a number of Westminster Committee reports (committees on which there were no SNP representatives) were under preparation. For example, a House of Lords Select Committee on the Constitution was investigating 'The Agreement on a referendum on independence for Scotland' (HL Paper 62) and another Select Committee on Economic Affairs was examining the 'Economic implications for the United Kingdom of Scottish independence'.

The House of Commons was also in on the act. The Defence Committee was looking into the 'Defence implications of possible Scottish independence' while the Energy and Climate Change Committee was casting its eye on 'The impact of potential Scottish independence on energy and climate change', the Foreign Affairs Committee felt inclined to look at the 'Foreign Policy implications of and for a separate Scotland' and then not to be left out there was an enquiry by the Scottish Select Committee on 'The Referendum on Separation for Scotland' (whose choice of title is indicative of its open-mindedness and lack of prejudice)! All of these reports would naturally be released under the authority of parliament. It would be miraculous if any was favourable to Scottish self-government.

Additionally, between October 2011 and December 2012 (there were six debates in the Commons on the Constitutional Status of Scotland (HC Deb 25 October 2011 vol 534 c288-94)), Scottish Separation (HL Deb 10 July 2012 vol 548 cc24-49WH), Referendum (Scotland) (HC Deb 15 October 2012 vol 551 cc 63-80), Scottish Separation (BBC) (HC Deb 16 October 2012 vol 551 cc22-31WH), UK Constituent Parts (EU) (HC Deb 21 November 2012 vol 553 cc141-167WH) and Scotland and the Union (HC Deb 29 November 2012 vol 554 cc405-440). The House of Lords also stuck in its undemocratic oar (undemocratic since it was not elected). There were no SNP Lords to put Scotland's case. This did not stop their Lordships on two occasions such as : Constitutional Settlement (HL Deb 15 October 2012 vol 739 cc1168-1203) and Scotland: Referendum (HL Deb 15 October 2012 vol 739 cc1310-1321). (Source; Letter from the House of Commons Library to Stewart Hosie MP 21 December 2012 – Appendix 1)

As indicated there could be no objection to these interventions (save out of democratic objection to the existence of the House of Lords).

The Westminster MPs had a role while Scotland was part of the Union. Now they faced unemployment. An imminent hanging is supposed to concentrate the mind wonderfully, so Scottish independence would lead to their expulsion from membership of the House of Commons and the House of Lords. They would have to compete within their Scottish Parties to be selected as candidates for election to the new independent Parliament. It would be surprising if feelings did not ride high!

Then what was the UK Government up to abroad? It was not inactive. When Options for Scotland in late 2012 raised the possibility of Scotland joining EFTA, there was an immediate welcome for the prospects of Scottish membership from the EFTA press office. This was followed by the entry of Icelandic President, Olafur Grimmson to the debate in a BBC Newsnight interview on 15 December 2012 when he declared:

> "Independence is not a disaster" and "could be the road towards prosperity and a good society". He told the BBC that small countries in northern Europe have fared well. Iceland was surrounded by an arc of successful, small nations in the North Sea who were all doing relatively well. If you take a long term view of about 100 years or so, the history of northern Europe is that countries have become independent one after the other. Whether Scotland will follow that route is a decision for the Scots to take. But despite the difficulties we have all faced (and Iceland had been praised by the IMF for its recovery having spared its citizens many of the austerity measures felt elsewhere in Europe) the moral of the story of independence in the Atlantic – from Norway, through Iceland and growing self rule in the Faroes, and Greenland – is of course that the nations have fared quite well."

Several months later, when Options for Scotland applied to EFTA and Iceland for briefings on the advantages and disadvantages of EFTA membership it met a wall of silence. There was a simple explanation, support for independence was running at too low a level and it was natural that they should ca' canny until the outcome was known. But was this the sole reason? During 2013, there emerged voices in the EU, NATO and Spain pointing to difficulties in an independent Scotland being admitted smoothly to membership of these bodies. It was, of course, paranoid to assume that our friends in London would ever get up to dirty tricks or seek to persuade foreign countries or institutions such as the EU (of which

Scotland was currently a member as part of the UK) against the case for Scottish independence.

And yet, the French had not awarded England the title of 'perfidious Albion' for nothing and the Foreign Office was not known for its ethical foreign policies. So what did happen?

The truth 'outed' on 12 January 2014 when the Sunday Herald splashed a major exclusive story that Prime Minister Cameron had sought the support of the Russian President Vladimir Putin. The TASS News Agency report ran:

> "Great Britain is extremely interested in the support of Russia, as holder of the G8 presidency, in two vital areas in 2014: the Afghan pull-out and the Scottish independence referendum."

TASS claimed that a UK Government 'insider' had said: 'We believe the G8 could become one of the main political platforms where London will find backing." Obviously, the British Government had not been put out by the appearance over Christmas 2013 of the Admiral Kuznetsov Russian carrier group in the Moray Firth in Scottish waters. There is, of course, no truth in the rumour that they were on a reconnaissance mission in case Prime Minister Cameron sought the aid of Russia to help restore London rule in Scotland in the event of Britain reneging on the Edinburgh Agreement! Still Britain despatched a naval surface vessel from Portsmouth, one of the few left, as there was no Royal Navy surface presence in Scotland! It was comforting to know the Royal Navy still existed even if Scotland did not form part of their normal patrols.

First Minister, Alex Salmond responded more seriously:

> "This report from Russia raises serious questions about the UK Government's underhand tactics. If this is accurate then Westminster has been caught red-handed trying to stir up hostility to Scotland instead of representing Scotland's interests – it seems the NO campaign's self-named 'Project Fear' has now gone global."

The story seemed to have died yet exploded into life once more in an article by Tom Gordon, Scottish Political Editor of the Sunday Herald on 26 January 2014 when he disclosed that the Devolution Unit created by the Foreign and Commonwealth Office to represent the interests of the devolved administrations overseas had now been deployed against the Scottish referendum. Based on diplomatic cables, it appeared that the FCO had contacted the governments of China, Russia, the US, New Zealand, Australia and Canada and the 28 EU nations about the Scottish referendum in a global search for allies who might oppose independence.

One recent cable showed UK embassies being ordered to forward a Westminster paper critical of independence to their host governments and other local contacts' and then feed their comments back to the Devolution Unit ASAP! It was understood that this would help the Unionist cause if countries raised their concerns about an independent Scotland joining international bodies such as the EU and NATO. Further activism of the Foreign Office asking the Spanish press to undermine Scottish independence also materialised (Sunday Herald 9 February 2014).

The SNP Government did not take this lying down and made its own international contacts. Most countries appeared willing to keep their views to themselves while awaiting the outcome.

As the Campaign entered the last eight months, things were certainly heating up.

Chapter 14:

THE GREAT BRITISH BOMBARDMENT

Could it really be true? Was the huge gamble succeeding? Six successive opinion polls showed a trend of a strengthening of the independence vote, a weakening of that for the Union and a corresponding closing of the gap. The changes were small. It seemed momentum lay with YES Scotland at long last.

Opponents of independence observed the movement and their confidence ebbed. At the end of January 2014 as Scotland began the year of the great referendum, the mask began to slip. It manifested itself first in a Debate in the House of Lords initiated by Lord Lang, a former Secretary of State for Scotland, who distastefully dragged in the sacrifice of Scottish soldiers when he declared:

> "Must we now, both Scotland and England, disavow that shared history? Would that not dishonour the sacrifice made in common cause if those who died for the United Kingdom, a nation now to be cut in two, if the present generation of Scottish nationalists have their way? I earnestly hope not."

He was followed by a succession of other speakers mostly all against although there were one or two neutrally raising technical points relating to medical and university research. There were so many former Ministers and MPs, refugees from the House of Commons as to be a reminder of the observation of a sitting MP looking up at the Commons Gallery reserved for Lords that 'it gave proof of life after political death.'

These were mere pricks. Nobody gave much attention to this unelected chamber of the British Parliament regarded widely as a parasite on democracy. The real counter-offensive waited. It would be launched not by the Scottish front campaign Better Together but by the London Tory/ Liberal Democrat Government with all the resources of the British state. The chosen ground of battle would be the currency and whether the SNP Government's preference for a shared sterling currency zone was feasible.

The scene was set with a visit to Scotland the day before the Lord's debate by the Canadian, Mark Carney who was Governor of the Bank of England which despite its ancient title described itself on its website as the Central Bank of the United Kingdom. In an address to an invited business audience, Dr Carney went into the technicalities of having such a zone, describing the difficulties and warning that Scotland would have to cede power to the Bank of England and other UK bodies to make the arrangement work. As to feasibility, he indicated that if the Bank were instructed to make arrangements, it would do so. One YES supporter said this was a 'score draw'. Rather optimistic I thought, it was more like a defeat by 2 goals to 1. Nevertheless, it could have been far more damaging. Being a Canadian, Mark Carney was well aware of the issue from the experience of Quebec and chose his words delicately.

Shortly after, the Chief Executive of BP (no longer British Petroleum but badged in the USA), Bob Dudley, an American this time, with less delicacy attacked the uncertainties of independence and the currency situation, the extra costs for business, a threat to European links and a new tax regime. All this he said could impact on future investment. He did not seem to see the incongruity when at the same time he confirmed BP's intention to invest £10 billion in the North Sea between 2011 and 2016, its highest ever investment in the area. With the Clare Field west of Shetland having 7 billion barrels of oil, it was even more surprising that in an off the cuff remark he gratuitously added: 'My personal view is Great Britain is great and it ought to stay together'. Only one specialist journal quoted former Chief Executive, Tony Hayward a week later at International Petroleum Week in London when asked about the impact of independence:

> "None whatsoever. Our industry is very good at working with whoever happens to be in power. It's what the industry does. My view is the industry will continue to invest and life will continue."

These other adverse reports received wide coverage in both the Scottish and UK media, mostly negative to the concept of Scottish independence. Then the Ministers arrived. Off the block to open the February offensive was Vince Cable, the Business Secretary who gave a warning in early February that if Scotland became independent then RBS (the Royal Bank of Scotland) in state ownership, would be forced to relocate to London to ensure it was 'protected against the risk of collapse.' The Bank was already largely managed from London. The impression was given jobs would be at stake. At the same meeting of the Scottish Select Committee, Professor Ranald Macdonald, of the Economics Department of Glasgow University said that a currency union could result in another Black Wednesday (the day the pound was forced out of the European Monetary System). (Herald 6 February 2014). He thought a separate currency would give Scotland greater flexibility.

That report in the Herald had the headline, 'Cable: YES vote will force RBS to London. The Scotsman went further 'Scottish independence: 25 years of misery'. Intrigued I looked further at the report for the origin of the headline. When the expert witnesses said that Scotland would need long term adjustments when adjustment meant more taxes or reductions in spending over a generation, the Chairman Ian Davidson (Labour) queried the meaning of generation by asking, "Do you mean 25 years of misery?' Prof MacDonald replied 'Possibly, Yes'.

Soon after English Conservative MPs had claimed that the English would demand a poll on a currency union, there was concern on high that the Scots might feel unwanted by all these negative bashings and being hurt, might be inclined to vote YES. So on 7 February 2014 came an extraordinary intervention by the Prime Minister, David Cameron. According to reports, the British Government had been studying an independence referendum in Quebec when it was judged that the knife edge majority to keep Quebec within Canada had come about because Canadians in other Provinces had 'love-bombed' Quebec to persuade them to stay in the federation.

The speech by Cameron was remarkable because of its emotive content. From the safety of London in an empty stadium in Olympic Park to a small audience of athletes, he addressed his remarks to people living in other parts of the UK – all '63' million of them who were profoundly affected by the referendum. Not a heart string was spared as can be seen from these phrases culled from the BBC report, 'Scottish Independence: Seven months to save UK, says Cameron':

- We would be deeply diminished without Scotland

- For me, the best thing about the Olympics wasn't the winning. It was the red, white and blue

- It was the summer patriotism came out of the shadows and into the sun, everyone cheering as one for Team GB

- Separating Scotland out of that brand (UK institutions) would be like separating the waters of the River Tweed and the North Sea

- If we lost Scotland, if the UK changed, we would rip the rug from under our own reputation. The plain fact is that we matter more in the world together.

- So let other UK citizens phone a relative or friend to persuade them to stay in the UK

Love-bombing can be double edged if you do it at a distance from your subject. Initial 'vox pops' in the media suggested that far from being impressed, his declaration from the far south in face of repeated challenges from Alex Salmond to debate with him in Scotland inclined votes towards Yes. Scotland was never enthusiastic about challenges from Conservative prime ministers at any time, let alone those issued from the imperial capital!

The First Minister's comment in an article in the Sunday Herald (9 February 2014) was scathing about David Cameron's motives as it indicated a sense of deep, deep unease was beginning to engulf the NO campaign as poll after poll showed the gap between Yes and No closing. He further related:

> "But the things he spoke about also showed that he fundamentally misunderstood what the independence debate was about. Ill-judged remarks about 'bloodlines and D-Day are frankly insulting to an electorate that is far more concerned about the future for them and their families.
>
> Ironically, Mr Cameron's speech this week embodied the democratic case for a Yes vote. Lecturing Scots from London has never gone well for the Tories – and by doing so on Friday, the Prime Minister simply reminded the people of Scotland where power currently lies.
>
> Highlighting Scotland's immense economic strengths and contribution to the world reaffirms that Scotland has what it takes to be a successful independent country – something which even the most ardent Unionists now admit.

> There is no reason why an independent Scotland and the rest
> of the UK cannot continue to share what works well for us
> all – the currency, the Common Travel Area, the social union,
> the monarchy and much more."

Yet who could tell. Scots are as open to suggestion as any even the
novel experience of being noticed by the greater English public, something
rarely apparent from coverage on the BBC or ITV from London. So everyone
waited for opinion polls to tell whether Cameron's 'love in' had hit or
missed the mark.

The riposte came fast. Before the Scots could react to this show of
'affection', the love fest was sharply displaced by a display of political brute
force. Up came George Osborne, the Chancellor of the Exchequer from
London on a brief visit to Edinburgh. He delivered an ultimatum, backed by
a Treasury report. He was nothing if not explicit (Herald 14 February 2014).

> "If Scotland's walks away from the UK, it walks away from
> the UK pound."

Nothing could be plainer although he did his best to make it so.

> "The SNP says that if Scotland becomes independent there
> will be a currency union and Scotland will share the pound.
> People need to know – that is not going to happen. .... It is
> clear to me I could not, as Chancellor, recommend that we
> could share the pound with an independent Scotland. The
> evidence shows that it wouldn't work. It would cost jobs
> and cost money. It wouldn't provide economic security for
> Scotland or the rest of the United Kingdom.
>
> I don't think any other Chancellor of the Exchequer would
> come to a different view."

And to back up the Conservative Chancellor in his anti-independence
referendum demarche there came the even more remarkable support
from his arch-enemy Labour Shadow Chancellor, Ed Balls who stated:

> "Alex Salmond is saying to people you can have independence
> and keep the pound and the Bank of England: that is not
> going to happen.

And after declaring such a sterling zone would place an unacceptable burden on the UK taxpayer and repeat the mistakes of the Euro zone:

"In fact worse, you'd be trying to negotiate a monetary union as Scotland is pulling away from the UK."

Alex Salmond was not slow in denouncing this salvo from London as bluff and bullying, calling it:

'a concerted bid by a Tory-led Westminster establishment to bully and intimidate' and that this would backfire spectacularly in terms of the reaction from the people of Scotland who knew that the pound was as much theirs as it was George Osborne's.

All the debt accrued up to the point of independence belongs legally to the Treasury as they confirmed last month – and Scotland can't default on debt that's not legally ours.

However we have always taken the reasonable position that Scotland should meet a fair share of the costs of that debt. But assets and liabilities go hand in hand, and - contrary to the assertions today, sterling and the Bank of England are clearly shared assets."

Finance Secretary John Swinney added, after insisting that the Treasury analysis was flawed and backward looking and took no account of the comprehensive evidence provided by the independent economic experts of the Fiscal Commission: (The currency union) would ensure financial stability and allow both governments autonomy over economic and social policies, including fiscal policy, before noting how Mark Carney, Governor of the Bank of England had confirmed the Bank would deliver a currency union if it was agreed by both Governments.

Having delivered his threats, George Osborne departed forthwith to London without having the grace to hold a media conference for the Scottish press and television journalists – a display of contempt and arrogance that went unappreciated.

It was a major step in the referendum campaign and was covered as a prime story by the UK and Scotland, being first item on all bulletins and discussed in depth on television. The international press adjudged the manner and peremptory tone of George Osborne as indeed an effort to bully and intimidate.

What was very strange was that this intervention came so soon after the attempt by the Prime Minister to be 'nice'. It was always on the cards that the UK Government would attempt, probably at a later stage in the campaign, to shoot down the currency union assurances from the Scottish Government. And why was the Exocet currency missile launched just then?

Kieran Andrews, Political Editor of the Courier, saying that the move was politically fascinating and took him by surprise, had a view:

> "There's an image I can't get out of my head. It's a 'Scotland' alarm at Downing Street, the fear and ...alarm, if you will. I also can't help but feel someone must have smashed the glass and pressed the big red (white and blue?) button this week prompting George Osborne to finally agree with Ed Balls about something, make sure Danny Alexander (Lib Dem Chief Secretary to the Treasury) was on board and fly up to Scotland to say 'naw' to a currency union in the event of a YES vote."

While not sure it would be effective, he did add that it certainly posed massive questions for the Yes campaign, questions neither Alex Salmond nor Nicola Sturgeon seemed desperate to answer during TV and radio interviews in the ensuing hours.

There was no time to take breath. Every day brought a new salvo from the London 'big guns'. On Friday 14 February, the next detonation hit Scotland's independence 'war zone'. In the Herald a front page exclusive by Michael Settle, their UK political editor ran the story that London was effectively tearing up the Edinburgh Agreement to accept the outcome of the referendum. The banner headline, 'Yes does not mean Yes' said it all. According to a senior Coalition source, a referendum Yes vote would not guarantee Scottish independence and the status quo would be maintained if the talks (negotiations) did not go smoothly. The planned Independence Day of March 24, 2016 would not happen, leaving the current set-up as the 'default option' unless negotiations between Edinburgh and London were completed satisfactorily, according to one of Prime Minister David Cameron's most senior colleagues.

"Dismissing the SNP Government's 18-month timescale for completing negotiations as 'totally unrealistic', the source said: 'A Yes vote in the referendum would be the start of a process not the end of one; we would start negotiations. But if Alex Salmond made impossible demands, we would not just roll over and agree to everything he wanted."

This stark warning was fit to remove any naive expectations that England would easily allow Scotland to leave its control. Leaving aside the promises in the Edinburgh Agreement to respect the outcome of the referendum, it was apparent that the SNP Government had been misled. What was offered was a legal referendum, not one that was legally binding, a point made earlier in David Torrance's book; The Battle for Britain (2013). 'Perfidious Albion' had not gone away. The glove may have been clothed in deeper velvet but it still housed a steel gauntlet! And if this anonymous briefing was distrusted, it was borne out by similar objections from Baroness Jay, daughter of former Labour Prime Minister James Callaghan and Chair of the Lords Constitution Committee. The Westminster establishment of Conservative, Labour and Liberal were united in deep opposition.

The Sunday Herald quoted an article by former Conservative Defence Minister, Michael Portillo in the Financial Times which summed up the attitude: 'Having lost Ireland, then Scotland, where would the disintegration end? Sneering enemies would join up some dots to draw an unflattering picture'.

Scotland's departure would reveal Britain for what it had become - a small country with little power and diminishing influence, other than in financial markets where it still had some strength. The armed forces had been run down until they had difficulty in coping. The Empire and 'big power' status had gone. The Emperor would be revealed to have no clothes. The seat on the UN Security Council was at risk. The loss of prestige would be crippling to London. This realisation was at the root of the new bitterness and brutality directed towards Scotland as well as to the Scottish Government.

Then came a flanker from the President of the European Commission, Jose Manuel Barroso who stated in a BBC TV interview on 16 February that it would be very difficult, if not impossible for Scotland to get approval from member states for it to join the European Union. He said that an independent Scotland would have to apply for EU membership and obtain the approval of all current member states in the wake of a Yes vote in September's referendum.

Mr Barroso said he respected the ongoing democratic processes surrounding the independence debate and said it was for the Scottish people to decide on their country's future. His view was rendered dubious when he used Kosovo as an example as Kosovo had gone through a unilateral declaration of independence and was not fully recognised as a state. His motives were later questioned by French Socialist MP, Axelle Lemaire who believed that his tactics were to acquire London support for a bid to become secretary general of NATO after stepping down from the Commission in the summer.(Herald 13 March 2014) Then it emerged in a series of articles in the Financial Times in mid-May on How the Euro Was Saved that Mr Barroso as Commission President had told his aides that one of his cardinal duties as guardian of the EU's treaties was to keep the eurozone and EU from losing members, be it Greece from the currency union or Britain from the EU itself. So what price Scotland not being admitted?

This should have been a huge and unwelcome story for the Yes movement but it was dwarfed by the ongoing controversy over the use of the pound. The issue was a curious one for both camps to adopt. Polling had shown that the public regarded the issues of the currency and Europe of little interest. Instead they were more concerned with bread and butter matters such as the economy, employment and prices. If the Scottish public was not exercised by the pound, why then did George Osborne use the British big stick to rule out a currency zone?

It had been made clear by the Governor of the Bank of England that an independent Scotland would need to cede substantial monetary, borrowing and economic power to the Bank and Treasury in London. And to the chagrin of some nationalists, the SNP leadership was prepared to do just that. With these concessions in their pocket, the terms for membership of a sterling zone would have tied everything up tightly – too tightly for many economists as the UK corset would constrain the growth prospects of the Scottish economy to a nugatory extent. The only reason for this pre-emptive attack on the part of the UK Government was the belief that they were losing ground and needed to advance a major piece in the referendum chess game to claim tactical advantage. To induce lack of confidence on the part of those still wavering and to recall some support from Yes voters, it would be necessary to risk that the brutal 'diktat' of the Chancellor would not offend the general public. Also if the SNP Government were seen to be knocked off a major perch that would be a useful side benefit. It was also significant that London had brushed aside Better Together. The battle was now entirely between the two governments! Through Options for Scotland, I issued the following statement designed to point up this change:

> "Has London made a fatal mistake? The story of the last two weeks is not the oiliness of the Cameron 'love-in' or the insufferable arrogance of Osborne's Valentine threats. It is that the London Government in a panic has brushed aside their Scottish front Better Together and entered the campaign directly. The battle for the future of Scotland is not now between Scots. It is between England and Scotland. London has ripped off the veneer that Scotland was a partner in the Union. The evidence from Osborne is that we are not.
>
> A Yes vote in the independence referendum was always dependent on London making serious mistakes. The 'bully-boy' intervention by Osborne has done that. It was not just the arrogant way in which he unilaterally withdrew English approval to Scotland sharing the Pound but his assumption that Scotland had no share in what were always regarded as British institutions and assets. Osborne is the man who has destroyed the Union!
>
> And one other point! Has London considered what they have put on the table for Scotland? It is the opportunity to start the new state with no debt and able to use the Pound with no restrictions of a currency zone or control by the Bank of England until such time as Scotland decides whether to have its own currency. London may not have thought of the consequences. But if I were a member of the Council of State negotiating with England after independence, I would foreclose on that offer immediately. London has given Scotland more than we could ever have asked for."

The SNP Government had made the sterling zone its policy against the views of some of the independent members of the YES Scotland Advisory Board who wished a separate Scottish currency. For the reasons, one has to go back to a report of the Scottish Government's Fiscal Commission published in February 2013 and commented on by a Scottish Government paper two months later. The members of its Working Group were distinguished economists – Professor Andrew Hughes-Hallet, Professor Sir Jim Mirrlees, Professor Frances Ruane and Professor Joseph Stiglitz and it was chaired by Crawford Beveridge. The Group were studiously neutral as to which path Scotland should follow. Presciently they acknowledged that political considerations would play a role and might cloud pre-referendum comments and policy statements. In offering their macroeconomic model, it was their belief that these political responses were likely to differ from the actual decisions taken post-referendum.

The report set out the currency choices for an independent Scotland, the advantages for both parties of retaining sterling in a formal monetary union, why this arrangement would work, plans for the smooth operation of such a system and the opportunities that retaining sterling would bring.

The four options considered were sterling, the Euro, a Scottish currency pegged to sterling and a flexible Scottish currency. They came to the conclusion that Scotland could choose any of these options and be a successful independent country. Nevertheless, they commended to the Scottish Government that the best course was to retain sterling as part of a formal monetary union as this would provide a strong overarching framework for Scotland post-independence.

Given the criticisms made by the SNP regarding the maladministration of the Scottish economy by the Treasury and the Bank of England over decades, it was surprising that the Scottish Government accepted the recommendation to adopt a joint currency zone as the sole option on offer. It ran in the face of repeated assessments by the Party that the Scottish economy should be managed to suit Scotland. The panel of experts did, however, come up with a framework that answered some of the doubts. In a perfect world, there is no doubt that the UK and Scottish Governments could reach a mutually acceptable accommodation. Nevertheless, the weakness was political. An independent Scotland would be only a tenth of the size of England, Wales and Northern Ireland and it was unlikely any agreement could last for long unless mutual self-interest became the dictating factor as the Group thought it would.

From a political point of view the experts were spot on. They predicted that the future currency would be subject to contrary argument – in harsher language from me - a cock pit of feuding during the campaign and so it had proved. Reason would not enter into it. The British Government deployed the Treasury in their nihilistic attack on a currency union. With two Nobel laureates and the wider international experience of the expert panel, the Fiscal Commission Working Group should have had more credence. But they were not known. The Treasury was the accepted authority – even though its management of the British economy over the post-imperial decades had not been a notable success.

The SNP Government accepted the recommendation that the country be in a shared British currency zone . They probably thought that the acceptability of the package on the basis of mutual benefit would ease the way to victory. There was really no alternative. It was a critical issue. They had set up their wider council of experts which had given birth to the Fiscal Commission. Governments can 'punt' some commissioned reports into the long grass if they disagree with the conclusions. In this case, they had to, and indeed were willing, to accept the principal recommendation of the currency zone. For those who preferred a separate Scottish currency, and this included many economists, there was an escape clause. There were viable alternatives such as use of sterling regardless, the Euro (neither politically nor financially possible at this juncture) and a separate currency.

All would depend on the attitude of the UK Government. If it had tied itself into opposition, the simple course would be to use sterling until matters stabilised and then if it were advisable move firstly to a Scottish currency pegged to sterling and subsequently allowed to float. If Scotland and the rest of the UK entered into a currency zone and the conditions were too restrictive or if it broke down through intransigence from London, then it would be open to the Scottish Government to follow the sequence of actions suggested above or to follow subsequent recommendations of the Fiscal Commission.

The SNP Government had also been forced to bypass Yes Scotland and engage the UK Government in 'ship to ship' combat. Its problem with its lesser fire power was how to match the English broadsides. The First Minister was no slouch when dealing with aggression. In a speech in Aberdeen, he fired off his own guns, producing a paper claiming that English business faced a transaction cost of £500 million in cross border trade which he labelled 'the George tax' after Chancellor Osborne. He insisted that the Chancellor would be unable to sell his opposition to English business.

There was a flaw in concentrating his fire on the transaction costs.

If there were transaction costs affecting English trade, would this not also affect Scottish businesses? This was not picked up initially but soon Ministers in the televised debates were being challenged to produce a calculation which they resolutely refused to do. A stronger argument would have been to produce a paper illustrating the likely reaction of money markets as rUK's trading account worsened from the transfer of oil, gas, whisky, manufacturing and food exports to Scotland. Compared to England, our exports would place Scotland in a strong position. Sterling would be in trouble.

By Tuesday 18 – and in this phase of the Great British offensive – each day brought its own surprises, the media had cottoned on to a new development. The Scottish Government had been under substantial pressure. The Prime Minister jeered that Salmond was 'a man without a plan'. There had been calls over the weekend for a Plan B. The Government again resolutely refused to give way instead preferring to conduct trench war on the issue. But seeping out from the rhetoric, came an appreciation that there was some flexibility after all. The Fiscal Commission would be meeting again and it was unlikely that it could ignore the furore arising from their favoured recommendation. Meanwhile as an editorial in the Herald put it:

> "It leaves the voters in a difficult situation. Far from the clarity most folk have been demanding, the game appears to have become a game of bluff and double bluff. The First Minister's best hope of regaining the initiative is by exploring a Plan B for the currency of an independent Scotland. His defence of the currency union was yesterday backed clearly and forcibly by his Fiscal Commission Working Group, the experts who drew up the policy.
>
> But the news it is to meet again and will continue to advise the Scottish Government as the campaign unfolds possibly opens the door to reconsidering the options.
>
> In a statement issued through the Scottish Government, its members saw fit to remind us that their report last year presented a number of currency models that were 'perfectly viable' for an independent Scotland."

Amid the main barrage, there was a fusillade of small arms fire from the Unionists on border control, immigration and pensions. Europe was also in play thanks no doubt to the UK Government's diplomatic efforts. Responding to Cameron's plea for intervention from England, there were sundry declarations of love from obscure celebrities, including some Scots who had shaken off the dust of Scotland from their shoes. Veteran pop star David Bowie entered a call for Scotland to 'stay with us' through a representative before a television audience of millions. And against a poll showing that many people wanted more powers for the Scottish Parliament but were dubious of the benefits of independence, Bruce Crawford MSP warned that any extra powers for child care, pensions, welfare, taxation and financial powers would only be gained by voting Yes.

Although the Scottish Government was on the back foot and counter-punching on the defensive, the position was not black. Many Scots seethed at the arrogant and disrespectful way Osborne had delivered his ultimatum and dashed back to London. Would this anger convert many to voting for independence or would the 'fear' campaign lead to a solidifying of the No vote?

While we waited to find whether the Scottish people were angry or cowed, there was no let up. The UK Government onslaught continued. Unionist ministers and their allies in the Labour Party demanded clarification of the currency issue. 'What is your plan B' was the call directed to the Scottish Government. After the earlier signs that the Government might allow the issue of a Plan B to be referred to the Fiscal Commission Working Group, the line was drawn. So far as the SNP Government was concerned, the UK was bluffing. After a Yes vote, both parties would get down to practical discussions that would produce mutually agreeable solutions to any currency, assets and debts problems.

In the meantime, comments came from members of the Working Group. Sir Jim Mirrlees suggested the alternative would see Scotland launch its own central bank and currency. Professor Andrew Hughes-Hallett insisted there was nothing the Chancellor could do to stop Scotland using the pound although this would deprive Scotland of having a say in the development of monetary policy (Scotsman).

There was a sign of unusual internal SNP discord when a senior SNP figure said:

"It shouldn't exactly have been a surprise that Osborne

would make this announcement. It was more a matter of when rather than if. We should have made sure that we had a stronger alternative to offer, just saying they are 'bluffing' isn't persuasive to the voters we need to win round. It's great for the converted but it's not going to bring don't knows on board.

Alex's line won't hold for seven months. We should have sorted an alternative proposal months ago. Even if his line is that Westminster is bullying Scotland gets any traction, that's not going make people gamble with their mortgage rates or their pensions."

In a sequence of debates and interviews, SNP Ministers took heavy pressure on 'Plan B' and an STV Scotland debate that began reasonably decorously between Nicola Sturgeon as Deputy First Minister and Johann Lamont, the Labour Leader descended into a shouting match that offered heat rather than light. It would have scarcely persuaded the undecided to support either cause – and did both participants damage to their reputations.

Despite this the SNP held the line until a more lethal stage of the Treasury campaign kicked in. Unbeknownst to the Yes side, Osborne had followed through his offensive by making it difficult for transnational big business to avoid commenting – even if they had wanted to. As reported in the Courier Business pages, the Financial Reporting Council had reminded them of the Companies Act and Corporate Guidance Code thus prompting companies to comment on the independence referendum in these terms 'if boards consider that a vote in favour of Scottish independence is a strategic issue or a principal risk, then disclosure should be made'.

Given that the UK Government had been trolling foreign Government and international institutions against independence, a safe assumption can be made that 'nobbling' commercial institutions would have been in their armoury, especially as the responses in the company reporting season were due to come shortly after Osborne's currency demarche.

The fruits of this were soon to be seen. In late February, Robert Peston, BBC Industry Editor, published a report 'leaked' from London that the giant Scottish investment and pensions firm Standard Life (which had previous form hostile to devolution) had set up companies in England because of the uncertainty. The inference was that if there were a Yes vote and no agreement on the currency, funds (and perhaps staff) would be transferred to London as 90% of their business lay in England.

The response from the SNP Government was weak. They were unaware that Standard Life had run large businesses successfully in Canada, Ireland and Germany with no problems over currency. They had also failed to highlight the large number of redundancies carried out by Standard Life at and beyond privatisation from its former mutual status. How any rapid response team was so inadequate is a matter for conjecture but did not offer much confidence for the rest of the battle!

The expectation was that other companies would follow suit in what the UK Government had intended to pulverise the opposition by a series of punches to the solar plexus of the case for independence. And so one of the next into the ring was the Royal Bank of Scotland (RBS) which warned a Yes vote would impact on its business saying in a statement (Herald 28 February 2014)

> "The group's borrowing costs and its access to the debt capital markets and other sources of liquidity depend significantly on its and the UK Government's credit ratings, which would be likely to be negatively affected by political events such as an affirmative outcome of the referendum for the independence of Scotland."

RBS had a joint HQ near Edinburgh and again the impression was given in banner headlines that jobs would be transferred to London (where all the principal managers were already based since the company was owned largely by the UK Government). Likewise when the position of Lloyds Bank came up, the argument was that the large Edinburgh banking and investment industry was at risk. Despite their huge stake in the North Sea, Shell and BP got into the act.

In fact these threats to jobs were spurious. All these companies would incur substantial costs on transfer and would find it impossible to hire staff in hyperactive London in replacement of Scottish staff. Also, RBS when it took over the much larger Nat West in England had become an English bank in practice if not in name. Similarly Lloyds Bank had never been a Scottish Bank. Its 'brass plate' was purely a result of the take-over of TSB where a Scottish domicile had been a pre-condition of privatisation. True, Lloyds had absorbed the Bank of Scotland but it in turn had ceased to be a Scottish bank when it merged with, and was effectively taken over by Halifax to form the recklessly run HBOS. Scotland's problem was no longer the threat of transfer. It was, since Clydesdale was owned by an Australian outfit, that Scotland no longer <u>had</u> an 'independent' bank!

Politically, the situation was far from this reality. Real harm was being done by the sequence of similar noises from Weirs, Aggreko and Alliance Trust of Dundee. The SNP Ministers had their backs to the wall and were in danger of becoming punch drunk. Certainly they looked tired and defensive.

SNP Members and Yes supporters were also feeling the strain. After the succession of polls creating momentum in favour, they were acutely aware that the constant bombardment could slow or reverse the trend. One veteran, an experienced and very tough activist confessed that on going down with a severe cold, she was looking forward to absence from television and the social media to avoid the constant drip of negative announcements. I was more concerned with morale. Those who had not undergone similar organised hostility in the seventies would be ill-placed in 2014. To address the context and stiffen resolve, I prepared an article which appeared slightly trimmed as a lead letter in the Herald and later published in full in the Scots Independent.

"With the turn of the year, the referendum campaign has entered another and perhaps decisive stage, reminiscent in many ways of the 1979 referendum campaign for a Scottish Assembly. In 1979, the No campaign was run by the same commercial and political forces now in play. The Labour Government was notionally in favour of its own legislation which it had allowed to be crippled by the 40% rule. It sat passive, leaving the Trade Unions and opposing Labour MPs to join with the Conservatives in opposing the creation of an Assembly with minimal powers.

Yet the deceptions and threats were still being made. The Assembly, they said, would lead to a wholesale withdrawal of Scottish industry with loss of jobs. The oil located in Scotland's waters was British. It wasn't all that valuable. It would run out and where would Scotland be then? Impoverished and ruined was the answer. And weren't we under a duty to be selfless and help out England's poor. Further generations of those English poor – and Scotland's too - are still with us and using food banks for survival!

Today, 15 years after the setting up of the Scottish Parliament, the disaster has not happened. None of Scotland's companies kept to their threats to pull out. Instead many of the objectors have prospered. If there has been any problem affecting Scottish commerce it has come from the mismanagement of the British economy and its cataclysmic failure to control the credit explosion from which came the 2008 depression. As for oil, the tax revenues went south causing huge expansion in London at the expense of the rest of the UK. In reality, Scotland's oil became London's oil and the cash was squandered there.

It's all happening again. Standard Life says it 'may' transfer jobs and capital south. Not again, you may ask. Then there is the Weir Group which is to produce an 'independent' report to assess the advantages and disadvantages of independence. Some with long memories may remember the then Chairman, Lord Weir being amongst the most militantly opposed of Scotland's industrialists.

In 2014, there are differences. Until January, London thought it had the result in the bag. Then six polls charted growing support for Yes. Abruptly, the Unionist campaign became aggressive and the 'great British' bombardment commenced. The figment that Better Together was running a purely Scottish campaign was brushed aside. Alistair Darling had been sidelined. In came the main armament of the British state. As revealed in the Herald, the British Government had actively canvassed support from other countries, including Russia and Spain to collate opposition that would be published.

Then there was the Cameron 'love - bombing', the Osborne and Balls blitzkrieg on the currency, followed by the President of the EU Commission saying that Scotland (unlike the Ukraine whose independence from Russia is guaranteed by the UK and the USA – shades of 1914!) would have difficulty becoming a member of the EU and a rare meeting of the Cabinet in Scotland to proclaim Scotland's remaining oil was better in London's hands.

The timing and sequences demonstrate that although the British Government claimed it was not involved in the debate, it had laid the ground work for its direct intervention through a series of political hammer blows. The tactics as in 1979 are simple – destroy Scottish self-confidence and morale. There is no attempt to put forward constructive reasons for Scotland to stay in the Union. Promises for more devolution may be made at the Scottish Party Conferences. Do not believe them! In the aftermath of a NO vote, London will see no need to give more powers to Scotland. Why should they? They will have won!

If the Scottish people are as gullible as in 1979, there is not much that can be done. They will pay the price. The budget of the Scottish Government will be slashed when the Barnett revenue formula is abolished and £25 billion of cuts come down the line. In that case, the harsh experience that follows will induce Scotland to win independence in 10 years time.

But why wait? The evidence from 1979 is that these threats never come to anything. They are propaganda only. What is a reality is that Food Bank Britain is crumbling. The bubble of accelerating growth of London and the South East of England will provoke increases in interest rates that will reverse today's shallow recovery and induce a further recession. This will hit people's standard of living. There is an economic case to be made for independence and so far it has not been projected strongly enough. Time for Yes Scotland to move from defence to counter attack!"

The Government's political adversaries in the Scottish Parliament crowed at their discomfort. Joanne Lamont taunted Alex Salmond at First Minister's Questions: 'Standard Life No More; RBS No More, Shipbuilding No More' to be met by Alex Salmond's crushing rejoinder, 'Labour No More'.

The problem was two-fold. As above, in the anonymous SNP criticism, the SNP had failed to have a proper defensive strategy over the currency in play. More importantly, over the years, it had dispensed with its stance of criticising mergers and takeovers of Scottish industry as it became more neo-liberal in its approach to business, economic management and regulation. In the old days, one of the central aspects of SNP campaigns was deeply rooted concern at the takeover and closure of Scottish businesses with resultant unemployment. As strategically important Small and Middle Sized Enterprises (SMEs) were bought out from the south or further afield so their departure diluted the prospects for the reindustrialisation of Scotland. It was part of folk memory from hard experience that large companies were not to be trusted. Their interests were not those of working people and they were run by 'oligarchs' whose loyalties to the people of Scotland were skin deep. It was after all the nobles of Scotland who had sold out their country's freedom in 1707 while the 'non-consulted' ordinary folk had rioted in the streets.

By now Project Fear' had become 'Operation Dambusters' – good old-fashioned British military terminology and indeed the Treasury campaign, aided and abetted by Scots who put Britain first had the character of planning and execution that would not have disgraced the military in its ruthlessness!

Not all the major cards were in the hands of the UK Government. British Airways and Ryan Air declared that Scottish independence could have positive benefits for their businesses if the SNP Government kept to its pledge to reduce Air Passenger Duty. The international credit agency Standard and Poors was encouraging about the investment rating of an independent Scotland. Aviva the giant insurance company with a large presence in Scotland from its takeover of former Scottish insurer General Accident in Perth saw few problems impacting on its business. Crawford Beveridge, Chairman of the Working Group came out with positive endorsements of Plan A for a sterling zone. Yet Citi Bank on 7 March added its weight to the stance of the UK Government that a currency deal was unlikely and warned of higher borrowing costs. It also expressed astonishment that the Scottish Government had not announced an alternative currency plan.

A number of economists flagged up possible benefits of a separate currency through a more flexible economic and monetary policy to suit the needs of the Scottish economy. The Scottish Government had a dilemma. If they moved to a Plan B, whatever it was, they would look weak. They also knew the 'piranhas' on the No side, would set out to rip it apart so they would have confusion added to perceived weakness. Never a good thing – an orderly retreat can lead to a disorderly rout.

The Unionists offensive led by the UK Government was past its zenith. The main objective of causing doubt and uncertainty had succeeded. Despite this there was still a stream of bad news, mainly from the commercial sector. Alliance Trust, an investment company in Dundee, announced that they too had set up subsidiaries in England as had been the case with Standard Life. This was followed by a Survey in a Survation Poll published in the Scottish Mail on Sunday that more than a third of Scottish companies would consider relocating outside Scotland in the event of independence. As summarised by the Courier (10 March 2014):

> "A total of 36% of firms would consider moving following a Yes vote on September, 18, while 40% would not. Only 15% of those surveyed said an independent Scotland would be 'beneficial' to their business, while 45% said separation would be 'harmful'. Three quarters (75%) said it was 'essential' or 'important' for their business that an independent Scotland remain in a currency union with the rest of the UK."

Even allowing for the use of the word 'separation' in the report which may or may not have been deployed in the wording of the questions, it was not good news. Buried at the bottom of the story was a quotation from the controversial industrialist Jim Ratcliffe, whose company Ineos ran the giant petro-chemical plant at Grangemouth who had told the Sunday Times.

> "It will work whether Scotland is part of the UK or independent. It will work as an independent country in the same way as Switzerland works. You don't have to be big to be successful. Switzerland is small and it is very efficient and it has got one of the highest gross domestic products on the planet."

Nevertheless, the Courier headline in what was otherwise a fair and balanced report was, 'Scots firms would move after Yes vote'. Any one casually looking at the page would get an impression at variance with the central thrust of the article. Contrasting reports of evidence given by Bank of England Governor, Mark Carney when giving evidence to the Commons Select Committee were interesting. Dr Carney had indicated that if President Barroso were correct then a condition of entry to the EU would include a commitment to join the Euro in the fullness of time. Under the headline, 'Carney in Scotland Euro claim', the article more encouragingly reported that the Bank of England did not have to be the lender of last resort to Scottish banks if there was no formal currency union. Carney dismissed claims that he thought a currency union was a bad idea for the UK and something he did not support as he pledged to remain neutral on the issue of independence.

By contrast the Herald report, also informative, concentrated on the downside in a headline, 'Carney: joining EU may force RBS to go to London'. Here the Governor as cautious as ever had said 'it was a distinct possibility but I shouldn't prejudge it. It depends on their arrangements'.

There was time for a few more punches. When the Scottish Government published its annual GERS (financial) report, it showed that the Scottish deficit per person had climbed to £283 higher per person than the rest of the UK. This had been caused by a sudden drop in oil revenues of £4.4 billion, partly from an unplanned cut in production from the Elgin Field and increased investment – a surge caused by recovery from disruption from tax changes made in an earlier Coalition budget.

The fact that the drop in oil revenues brought Scotland only slightly above the UK deficit (having had a much better position over the preceding five years) did not register. Better Together spotlighted that this drop represented the whole schools budget, part of the risks of being dependent on a major fluctuating asset. Again the headlines of the Unionist press gleefully recounted the change for the worse. It was too sophisticated for them to come up with a reasonable explanation! The Yes campaign was once again on the back foot with the Chancellor in his Budget Speech of 19 March rubbing it in. Oil expert, Martyn Tulloch put the position succinctly in an email to the author on 13 March:

> "There's been a lot of biased data and coverage of oil lately. The GERS/IFS data that is coming out is a classic example. In addition to taking pessimistic estimates of production and price, they look only at the very short term (next three years) when capital allowances have eaten into tax revenues. However the huge recent capital expenditure will boost production over the next three decades, not just the next three years."

The Yes response was also measured but drowned out by the presentation of the bad news. It clarified that Scotland has generated more tax per head than the rest of the UK for each and every one of the last 33 years and that our finances have been stronger than the UK's over the past five years to the tune of £1,600 per person or £8.3 billion.

A Herald Editorial (13 March 2014) concluded:

"There are specific reasons for the latest deficit figures. They are affected by events that are unlikely to be repeated every year, but they nevertheless highlight how exposed Scotland's finances are to fluctuating oil revenues. This year the disruption is caused by disruption to production and high levels of investment; next year it could be falling oil prices.

The debate about the finances of independence will continue, but this latest GERS report should serve as a cautionary tale for the Yes campaign not to overplay statistics."

There also came signs that the SNP Government was beginning to come out of its defensive bunker and moving to attack. In a speech to the left-leaning New Statesman, in early March, Alex Salmond accused the UK Government of an enormous blunder. He took the fight to this English audience by inveighing against the UK as having the highest levels of regional inequality of any country in the European Union.

And then he highlighted the UK Government's error:

"For the Chancellor to put the rest of the UK into a position where it could be landed with all of the UK's gargantuan debt is at best reckless and at worst totally irresponsible."

It was the turn of the Chancellor to be trapped. What if Scotland became independent? By refusing access to the currency zone and a full sharing of UK assets, he had left it wide open for Scotland to move to independence legitimately able to be free of its share of the frightening overhang of UK debt. So long as Scotland had expressed willingness to assume a fair proportion of the debt and had been refused assets, its refusal to undertake that debt would not be treated by credit markets as reneging on its obligations. It would therefore start its new existence with a clear balance sheet and investment status with cheaper interest rates for future borrowing. Additionally, if RBS and Lloyds were forced to move their brass plate to London by dint of an untested and unimplemented directive from Europe, it would be London that would have to accept future responsibility for their conduct and debt.

UK institutions refused to see the danger their Chancellor had potentially put the rest of the UK into. With some arrogance, and more likely as part of the on-going propaganda war, they still assumed that Scotland would have to take the debt without its share of UK assets and would have difficulty in borrowing. This was seen in one of the regular negative reports from the Institute of Fiscal Studies claiming that Scotland would start life deeper in the red than rUK, although acknowledging that the budgetary position for both parts of the UK had improved with economic growth. Basing its calculations on pessimistic oil revenue estimates from a UK Government quango, the Office of Budget Responsibility (OBR), it reckoned that Scotland's borrowing to plug the current account gap in year 2016/17 was 3.6% of GDP compared with 1.2% for rUK. Thus steep budget cuts under an austerity programme would be necessary. (Herald 5 March 2014). A Scottish Government spokesman countered:

> "There is no doubt that Scotland can more than afford to become an independent country. As Standard and Poor's (sic) noted last week, even without North Sea oil and calculating per capita GDP only by looking at onshore income Scotland would qualify for their highest economic assessment."

All of this high level cerebral exchange in exotic economics was interesting but irrelevant. Few of the general public would find it of interest, let alone comprehensible. What the two campaigns were waiting for were polls signifying the impact on opinion from the Treasury offensive. The earliest TNS poll taken in the immediate aftermath revealed a gap of only nine points amongst those determined to vote Yes, suggesting that the burden still lay with Yes in catch up. (YES Scotland 22 February 2014). A later ICM poll in Scotland on Sunday on the same basis brought out a gap of 14 points and more disturbingly of all those polled (49% No to 37% Yes) a slightly smaller gap of 12 points, masking an increase in No support of 5 points at the expense of those previously undecided. And this was before the warnings issued by banks and investment companies had been fully absorbed. A gallant attempt by the SNP to claim that a poll of polls for February still showing Yes momentum did not succeed as the changes in March had to be factored in.

Not for the last time, the Herald went to Professor John Curtice, this time in a Referendum Special on 19 March. He summed up his views after an analysis of polling developments:

> "Doubtless, the apparent importance of the economy in voters' minds helped persuade the No side to announce an independent Scotland would not be allowed to share the pound. Surely such an announcement would help make the economic risks of independence clear to voters.
>
> It has not worked out that way, however. At 42%, the average Yes tally in the six polls conducted since the currency announcement is actually one point higher than its tally in the polls conducted immediately beforehand. Rather than pushing voters into the No camp, the announcement has simply polarised opinion.
>
> While most No voters agreed that it was not in the interests of the rest of the UK to share the pound, most Yes voters (some of whom do not wish to keep the pound anyway) accepted Alex Salmond's argument that Mr Osborne was bluffing. Meanwhile undecided voters divided more or less evenly down the middle. 'Project Fear' evidently has its limitations."

So, having undergone the Great British Bombardment, the campaign entered the concluding six months. There was a long way to go. The Yes movement still trailed but had gradually reached striking distance of winning. Everything was there to play for.

Yet, it would be wrong to leave this resumé without commenting on the impact of the UK Government attacks on the psychology of Yes activists. Initially, reeling with shell shock, they would have been encouraged by the final outcome. They were however embittered by the one-sidedness of the media. There was evidence of bias within the BBC in presentation of those UK attacks, especially from the London metropolitans who decided news presentation and whose attitudes to the SNP and Scotland had been admitted as a problem by the BBC in years before. On the other side, bitterness as witnessed by the ferocity of the personal attacks on Alex Salmond and Nicola Sturgeon manifested itself amongst supporters of the Union who saw the gap narrowing.

And for the UK Government's onslaught which had abandoned Prime Minister Cameron's love-in in favour of Osborne's brutality there could be post-referendum consequences. From what had been a reasonably amicable though forthright debate within Scotland, there had developed a vicious interference from the largest partner of the UK. Yes, the UK Government saw its need to keep the Union together for its own prestige and its seat on the Security Council of the United Nations. But had they no sense of history. Had they forgotten what England had done to Ireland?

This came to mind when after attempts by the 'three lions' to bully Scotland, David Cameron met the Irish Taoiseach at Downing Street.

> "I think we meet at a time when Anglo-Irish relations are at an all time high. I think relations between our two countries are very strong but I still think there is even more we can do to strengthen our ties and strengthen our relationship.
>
> The economic ties between Britain and Ireland are stronger and getting stronger. In terms of trade, we have realised that one of the goals at the last summit we had when we talked of a joint trade mission between Britain, Northern Ireland and the Republic and we achieved that in Singapore which I welcome"

What a contrast! Praise for Ireland – gall for Scotland. Obviously the imperial lions were not sated!

Chapter 15:

HIGHS AND LOWS

For Yes supporters, it felt like coming out of the valley of the shadow. Not yet reaching the sunny uplands of taking a lead in the polls, they experienced new hope. Conversely, those who supported continuance of the Union no longer had the comfort of ultimate victory. It was all in the balance.

In some ways, the flaws in both campaigns were evident. A 'no score draw' was not enough for the Yes campaign. It had to convince the Scottish public that independence was essential rather than useful. There was still no simple economic narrative WHY the Scottish public should abandon the security of the Union for an unknown future.

The evidence was there. London was too big and hogged the prosperity and capital investment within the UK. The Scottish economy had not over a period of 60 years under Westminster financial management been successful enough to provide a future. An Options for Scotland paper on emigration showed that with migration to England alone the cost of education produced a capital subsidy to the south of around £30billion.

Indeed the position was worse. Over the 20th century, Scotland with a running population of 5million saw a population drain of 2million. If Scotland did not get independence that loss comprising as it did thrusting young ambitious and professionally qualified people would continue. That is a challenge that should have been made and repeated with a demand to Better Together to show how this economic haemorrhage would be stemmed within a Union dominated by the politically powerful London and the south. Strangely other than in a few forays by Alex Salmond and Nicola Sturgeon, the Yes campaign resorted to bland meaningless assertions that things would get better.

Apart from negatively attacking the impact of the Union on Scotland, the Yes campaign could have used more positive ammunition. For example, during the course of the referendum, there was surprise that overseas investment had not declined because of uncertainty. And more to the point, the referendum itself seemed to have energised Scots to start up their own businesses.

As Sheikh Mohammed Al Nahyan, Crown Prince of Abu Dhabi has said, the future of the Emirates lay in its people, not the oil. In Scotland over the last few decades, one of the worrying problems had been the low rate of business start ups. If the Scottish economy was to start a benign cycle of growth it would have to come from a new culture of entrepreneurial activity, whether Scotland was in the Union or independent.

The evidence of a changed attitude was emerging and I wrote to Alex Salmond as SNP leader on 21 March bringing this to his attention in these terms:

> "Success in the referendum campaign will be based on confidence. It is no surprise that Projects Fear and Dambusters from the No campaign have been conceived to damage national self-confidence."

> One of the significant developments during the referendum campaign has been the rise in entrepreneurial activity, almost as if the drive for independence has impacted beneficially on Scotland's psychology. Until now Scotland has had a dependency culture where jobs would depend on the attraction of investment from abroad. Happily foreign investment has not slackened so apart from the politically motivated 'risk' announcements, foreign capital has not taken fright.

> Nevertheless, dependence on incoming investment has been a signal weakness of the Scottish economy over the last seventy years. Some manufacturing industry from abroad comes and goes without putting down roots for the future.

> Can I draw to your attention signs that there is a game changing switch taking place which will aid Scotland to have more small companies. These are the seed corn of growth in the post-union economy.

> More of our people are starting their own businesses. Those registered with Companies House (which can exclude many single traders, small businesses and partnerships) rose

last year by 19% from 25,500 in 2012 to 30,263. Scottish Government figures estimate that more than 340,000 businesses were operating in Scotland in 2013, the highest since records began.

The Scottish Universities have newly released figures that the number of new graduate start-ups rose by 20% between 2011/12 and 2012/13 bringing the total of new active firms to 431. Much of the credit here must go to the universities and the Scottish Funding Council to make courses more relevant to the economy.

More importantly, if you add both developments together, there is evidence of a sea- change in Scotland's dependency culture. Instead of men and women looking for public sector jobs, employment in large companies or careers elsewhere through enforced emigration, there is a new 'get-up-and-go' spirit. There was little sign of this in the early days of the recession so the entrepreneurial shake-up from the referendum must get most of the credit.

As we go into the final phases of the campaign, YES Scotland should highlight the boost to the whole country that would come from the burst of confidence given by independence. It would also do no harm to warn of the damage to Scotland's self-esteem and national self-confidence if Scots were to vote No and see their country decline into the dependency culture of provincialism once more. Dependence on others never works. The price of a No vote will be stagnation at best and economic decline at worst. Emigrant ships would await!"

This last paragraph cursorily mentioned something that was critical. Support for Yes depended on a Scotland with a confident, optimistic outlook. This contrasted with the objects of Project Fear to induce depression and pessimism so that Scotland would not let go of the hand of nurse for fear of something worse! Yet two years into the campaign, it was an issue that had not been discussed in any degree of depth, if mentioned at all.

From the point of view of the British Government and Better Together, there was consternation. They had fired the heavy mortar shell of the currency and far from stoking fear and support for No, it seemed to have stiffened resolve and increased support for Yes.

There was no immediate alternative. The publication of adverse statements from industrial companies would be unstoppable. The Yes side could be sure of publication of statements from industrial companies as to the adverse risks involved to jobs. The Treasury was committed to publishing a series of analytical reports casting a douche of cold water on the economic consequences, including costs to the Scottish public purse involved in setting up new governmental departments and agencies. But increasingly there were calls for more positive responses, particularly on the front of increasing the powers of the Scottish Parliament. This was awkward as the Conservative, Labour and Liberal Parties had different views and could not produce a convincing set of agreed proposals. The seeds of discord had been planted.

By now the campaign was broadening and changing shape. On both sides, there were substantial poster displays – none of them with much humour or bite although the pastel colours were nice to the eye. The nearest to impact was one poster in which the word 'Can't' had the letter 't' crossed out in red to read 'Can'. With the official three months regulated period looming in which there would be strict limits on expenditure, it appeared that there was a loose rein on spending.

Full page advertisements for Yes tended towards the wordy with one towards the end of March with a long heading in white lettering set against a pale blue background bearing the message: 'What would you say to living in one of the world's wealthiest countries?' It was a resource based narrative featuring renewable energy, financial services, whisky, tourism, life sciences and oil. It concluded with a quotation from the Financial Times that an independent Scotland would be richer than the rest of the UK and in the top 20 wealthiest countries globally. Better Together responded with posters declaiming 'More Job Opportunities for Scotland for us as part of the UK (We want the best of both worlds)' and 'More Powers for Scotland Guaranteed – We are better together'.

It was remarkable that it was the Financial Times that had come to the rescue of the beleaguered Yes campaign six weeks earlier. There is nothing better than a good testimonial from a respected source. It gives the smack of veracity to views which if supplied by a politician would be ignored.

It had provided a slew of statistics – with a small population, Scotland was still in the top quarter of GDP economic output and exports ranked at 34 globally, Scotland's national accounts showed the country £1,389 per person healthier than the UK. In terms of tax revenues, the FT calculated that the country raised £12,629 revenue per person compared with £11,381 for the UK.

The paper added:

> "Even excluding the North Sea hydrocarbon bounty, per capita GDP is higher than that of Italy. Oil, whisky and a broad range of manufactured goods mean an independent Scotland would be one of the world's top 35 exporters."

So far the Campaign had been conducted openly through newspapers and broadcasts. These were no longer the prime sources. Beneath the surface a battle raged in the social media. Outlets like Wings over Scotland, Newsnet Scotland and Bella Caledonia had high access rates and provided a complementary counter-point. Intellectually, Scotland was aroused. The Universities and newspapers ran debates and lectures. The University of Dundee had its Five Million Questions series where the respective arguments were given space. Some of these activities were not directly related to the campaign itself but sparked by it. The Jimmy Reid Foundation had a longer range objective of reviving the left. Scottish Global Forum looked at future international issues awaiting an independent Scotland. Options for Scotland concentrated on producing expert papers examining the choices open to independent Scottish Governments of different political persuasions rather than on the trench warfare of the respective campaigns. The National Collective of those involved in the creative arts produced a welcome 'non-economic' approach. It had been a very long time since Scotland had seen such intellectual fervour or so many vigorous arguments raging in the newspaper columns and letter sections.

Even, YES Scotland got its act together on the community side when it spawned branches operating at local level, sometimes alone and sometimes in tandem with the more organised SNP. Severin Carrell, Scottish Correspondent of the Guardian remarked on the changes in his analysis of 18 March.

> "Across Scotland, town halls, community centres and pubs have hosted packed public meetings. Many who go are

non-nationalist voters, people who usually backed Labour, the Scottish Greens, the Liberal Democrats or no party at all. Some listen, arms crossed, not always convinced; many applaud.

Even hardened Scottish National party activists are surprised. They talk of a marked shift in public attitudes in recent months, and a political energy not seen for decades. In many neighbourhoods a switch has been flicked, from off to on. Independence, they argue, no longer belongs to the nationalists.

Voters who once closed the door to Yes Scotland canvassers are now opening them, to talk more, to agree to or even to sign up. Peter Murrell, the Scottish National party's chief executive, estimates that as many as 100,000 people have volunteered, donated money or helped out in some form – a number some four times as large as the SNP's membership."

Better Together did not have the same numbers of people on the ground. It did, however, have the power of the British state behind it and could rely on their resources and the sympathetic manipulation of stories by the Scottish editions of UK tabloid newspapers the Mail and the Express, the Times and the Telegraph. The exceptions were the Guardian and Financial Times which were much more objective.

With no new ideas, the downbeat prospects of Scottish independence continued apace. And so warnings were issued that an independent Scotland would see energy bills rise through having to meet solely the full £1.8billion subsidy bill for renewable energy schemes such as windfarms and wave and tidal schemes. Ed Davey, the UK energy minister declared that the Scottish consumer would see their energy bills rocket while a slump in UK investment would lead to job losses and be bad for clean energy industries and the world's climate!

Jeremy Peat, Director of the David Hume Institute, reported with seeming approval Liberal leader Willie Rennie's views on the fiscal front that Scotland would face competition if it sought to gain advantage via lower rates, even if that was permitted in the context of a currency union. Then there were headlines that a European directive on cross-border pensions would lead, said the National Association of Pension Funds, to 'much more expensive' schemes in Scotland.

As for Defence, Secretary of State Philip Hammond paid his third fraternal visit to Scotland to make a 'positive' case for the union. This meant stressing Scotland's contribution to UK defence with a disproportionate share of bases and greater manpower at Faslane. He decried the SNP budget and promised that a No vote would lead to more powers for Holyrood. His more conciliatory attitude was marred when he visited a Glasgow defence components firm Thales and claimed the creation of a border between that facility and its largest customer would put at jeopardy the future prosperity of that business, the people who worked in it and their families and dependents. He was accused of emotional blackmail. And in a preposterous speech to the Brookings Institution in the US, Lord George Robertson former NATO Secretary General claimed that if Scotland voted to break the Union, the future of the west would be imperilled – a degree of hyperbole that brought derision and embarrassment (for Better Together) in equal portions.

Just to ram home the risks of independence, a Lloyds Bank non-executive Director suggested that financial institutions would desert Scotland if voters opted for Yes in the independence referendum while the Postal Union, the Communications Workers Union urged its members to vote against independence as amongst other factors it would put 'untold pressure' on allied firms and their members working lives.

The whole body politic of Scotland suffered a jolt with the death of SNP and independent legend, Margo MacDonald MSP. In a strange way her passing served to unify the increasingly fractured debate. As Jim Sillars said in the closing paragraph of his eulogy at a celebration of her life in a crowded Church of Scotland Assembly Hall several weeks later, she left a legacy for the future.

> "So, in my final remarks I bring a message from Margo for all engaged in this campaign. There will be harsh statements on both sides. The debate will be fierce. There will be verbal wounds inflicted. But if we conduct ourselves in the run up to 18th. September the Margo MacDonald way, the divisions will be much easier to heal.
>
> The Margo MacDonald way is to recognise that you are dealing with opponents not enemies, not with ogres but with fellow human beings, with whom you can disagree but must do so without malice – and where the exercise of mutual

respect is a civilised corrective to uncivilised abuse, an abuse which, if unchecked by both sides, can so easily mutate into an   irreversible corrosive malign influence on the conduct of public life.

Margo's life's work was a passionate pursuit of Scottish independence. But if she could refuse to sunder friendships with people who fundamentally opposed her on the issue which she spent her life trying to achieve, then so can we all. She could call Alistair Darling the 'Abominable No Man' but continue to like him.

If she could debate without conceding one iota of principle, but do so without venom, so can we all. If she could respect the right of the other side to their opinions, so can we all.

That's what she wanted me to say."

Politicians are rarely given such a memorable send off, especially one like Margo who was certainly no 'patsy' when it came to making a political point in debate. There was a warmth in the proceedings combined with a feeling that someone colourful and valuable had left the political life of Scotland. The warning given that we all had to pull together after the September 18 vote was timely as divisions were growing and opinions hardening.

From April through to mid-May, the activity in the referendum campaign was frenetic with each camp encountering problems. In the Yes campaign, there were a few blips. Alex Salmond normally as surefooted as he was shrewd, made an error when he agreed to do an interview for a magazine with Alastair Campbell, spin-meister to former Labour Prime Minister, Tony Blair. He should have been stopped. There was nothing particularly damaging in his carefully chosen words but in the hands of someone with the tabloid experience and political motivation of Alastair Campbell, it was playing with fire. And so it proved. Campbell managed to produce three headline stories. A cautious compliment to President Vladimir Putin (given before the Russian take-over of Crimea) appeared as a fulsome endorsement. Another arose from a quote from Alex that Scotland had an unfortunate history with alcohol and was characterised and headlined that Scotland was a nation of drunks!

The Yes campaign had regained confidence. The polls were still narrowing. It had received increased funding now at over £5million from Mr & Mrs Weir, SNP benefactors. It launched a new poster campaign on the emotive theme of child poverty showing a waist down image of a little girl in scuffed and battered footwear, dirty ankle socks and a ragged skirt, with the message: 'Let's become independent before 100,000 more children are living in poverty'. What was hard to bear for anyone with a conscience was that such an image in black and white could have graced similar campaigns over the last 100 years. It was Scotland's disgrace. Then, too, the decision of the Sunday Herald to declare itself as a supporter of independence was a real boost to morale. Again, Business for Scotland was proving itself to a powerful counter-weight to the Unionists dismal economic and business forecasts with its spokesmen confidently debunking the scare stories.

For all that, the story was of the disintegration of the Better Together campaign. Leaving aside such oddities as the statement from the credit agency Moody that Scotland's credit would be on par with Botswana, it really ran into crisis when the Confederation of British Industry (CBI) lodged an application with the Electoral Commission to become a registered opponent of independence. This came as little surprise as its Scottish Director, Iain McMillan had long been a vociferous opponent of devolution, never mind independence.

Much to the surprise of many there was an immediate backlash. Some 20 members who wished to or had to be neutral or simply opposed to the CBI stance such as STV, the universities, public bodies such as Scottish Enterprise and Visit Scotland, the Law Society and private companies pulled out or suspended their membership. The CBI went from crisis to farce, destroying its influence and authority in Scotland. Firstly, there was doubt as to whether or not it had consulted its Scottish members. Then, Iain McMillan announced he would retire at the end of the year. Backtracking began when the Director General, John Cridland placed the blame on a junior official in London and sought to have the registration declared void.

By this time, Better Together was in deep trouble. A leader in the Sunday Herald summed up the position on 30 March even before the CBI hammer blow:

> "Rarely has a name been so loaded with irony. Better Together was supposed to convey unity, co-operation and a sense of shared values. This weekend the pro-Union campaign is consumed by rancour, finger pointing and impotent fury.

A single newspaper story triggered the infighting which yesterday broke out between Labour, LibDems and the Tories. But while the Guardian's report of an unnamed Coalition minister saying an independent Scotland could 'of course' share the pound with the UK may have ignited the feud, it is clear the match fell on prime kindling.

Better Together's troubles reflect deeper problems with the organisation, not simply one headline. From the outset, its strategy has been to minimise grass-roots debate – its refusals to supply speakers to public events are notorious – and scare people into voting No before they barely had a chance to consider the issues. The less people chewed over the pros and cons, the better for the No camp it seemed. The upshot has been a campaign over-reliant on negative messages and all but devoid of inspiration. The polls showed where that had got them. They now indicate support for independence rising and backing for the union edging down, a pattern seen across all socio-economic groups, among men and women, and in all age groups bar the over-60s.

Better Together is in trouble, and it knows it. Its job was to deny the Yes camp momentum, but the momentum has developed regardless. The jitters manifested themselves at this week-end's Lib Dem conference as former leader Tavish Scott made it clear Better Together's chair, Alistair Darling, wasn't connecting with Labour voters. And then the Guardian story arrived. It is hard to under-estimate how damaging it is for the No side. The currency issue was Better Together's ace."

The pressure on Alistair Darling continued over the next two months. It had its effect. Normally Darling was calm and reassuring. That was his stock in trade. Yet the New Statesman blog, The Staggers, reported that when he appeared on The Andrew Marr Show in early April he was rattled and put in a tetchy performance rather like 'an embattled football manager giving a post match interview after a bad result'. That jar to his confidence was accentuated by reports that other Labour 'heavies' former ministers such as Lord Reid, Gordon Brown and current shadow foreign minister, Douglas Alexander would be drafted in to take charge. Even by late May he was unable to answer a spirited cross-examination by Joan McAlpine

MSP in one of the Scottish parliament committees that the currency issue was a put up job with the Treasury in which he was involved. The story was denied but so were details of private conversations with Treasury Permanent Secretary, Sir Nicholas McPherson.

John Kay of the Financial Times (30 April 2014) was particularly scathing of the business reservations expressed by Alliance Trust, Standard Life and Weir directed against independence, saying that big corporations and investment managers were accustomed to dealing with currency and regulation matters on a global basis as part of their common business practices and concluded:

> "But these arcane issues are beside the point. People cast votes on major issues by reference to overarching narratives about autonomy, identity and prosperity – a truth the wilting No campaign seems not to have grasped. No one will go to the ballot box in September to express concerns about investment funds custodianship, pension fund actuarial deficits or corporation tax group relief. There are important implications for business in Scotland in the independence debate, but they are not these.
>
> It is possible to describe an independent Scotland which would build a better business sector less focused on London and made more vibrant by the energy and self-confidence which devolution has already brought to Edinburgh. It is also possible to describe an independent Scotland cursed by the entitlement-based culture into which municipal socialism in the west of the country often degenerated, destructively mixed with crony capitalism and overweening ambition which almost destroyed its financial sector. If Scots are to cast their votes on economic issues at all, these competing visions of their country's future should govern their choice."

Yet despite this wise advice, the campaign seemed to continue its dreary way with claim and counterclaim which, if they did not impact on the public, also seemed to make it difficult to distinguish between fact and myth. Returning from a three week family visit to the Middle East – which was both referendum and Scotland free - I found the European Election campaign in full swing. The electorate did not care 'tuppence' about the European Parliament or its elections if the turnout on the day was evidence, but the change of emphasis from Scottish to UK politics and the inexhaustible coverage of UKIP coming through the London broadcasting media seemed to have put a dampener on the referendum campaign.

Also, although the SNP did well to hold its vote its failure to win a much vaunted third seat combined with the success in Scotland of UKIP winning the sixth seat albeit on a third of its vote in England did not produce an acceleration of the Yes position in the referendum as had been hoped. Certainly the improvement in the polls seen during March and April had slowed. At best (TNS mid-May) had brought the gap between the two camps amongst those certain to vote to 44% No, 35% Yes and 20% undecided although the overall gap was 42% NO, 30% Yes and 28% undecided.

It is unlikely given the mess that Better Together were in that the adverse headline coverage given to Alex Salmond's restrained but unwise praise for President Putin had any impact. More likely publicity for UKIP and the SNP's insensitive Europhilia at a time when there was widespread criticism of the EU throughout the continent played its part. Yet as May had progressed there were signs that the Labour Party had become concerned with the inroads which the Yes movement was making on their core vote. Labour was always a Party favouring the Union but it also had a vested interest. If Scotland voted Yes, it would be at the expense of the livelihoods of Labour's 41 Westminster MPs who would be unemployed as would the superannuated, unelected Labour politicians who would also find themselves excluded from the House of Lords. Some no doubt worked but others were 'parasite peers' who infested this 850 strong offence to democracy.

Labour strategists and the shadow Cabinet were more concerned. If Scotland became independent, then the chances of Labour forming a government against the wishes of the majority English electorate would be much diminished. From now on major Labour figures such as former PM Gordon Brown, Douglas Alexander and former Home Secretary Lord Reid intervened. Until then, Labour had been represented by former Chancellor of the Exchequer Alistair Darling, chair of Better Together. From now on, Labour would seize the initiative from Better Together which many regarded as a Tory front, and launch its own anti-independence campaign designed not just to stop independence sentiments amongst its supporters, but also to buttress its support for the Westminster General Election one year away.

Following Douglas Alexander's lead, Labour intended to portray a No vote as something positive. By June, its tone had changed. Both Gordon Brown and Johann Lamont launched a new 'United with Labour – Working Together, Stronger Together' aggressive approach with badges and posters in Labour's colours of red and yellow fostering taking pride in voting No and saying 'No Thanks' to independence. According to Magnus Gardham of The Herald the drive would attempt to rally traditional Labour supporters behind a vision of a fairer Scotland in the UK. Gordon Brown would aim to address 5,000 people at town hall meetings throughout the country over a fourteen day period.

Before the formal onset of the campaign on 30 May when it would be subject to supervision by the Electoral Commission, there was time for a last blaze of expensive advertising on both sides and also by 'Vote NO BORDERS', a stray unionist organisation funded to oppose independence. Likewise the UK Government launched its last offensive from the Treasury on the setting up costs of the new Scottish state. The Treasury got off to a bad start when some of its main costings were repudiated by academics who claimed distortion and misquoting of their research. The Treasury persevered with its original claim of a Union Dividend of £1,400 for each Scot every year by remaining in the Union.

The SNP counter-attacked with its own assessment of a £1,000 benefit from independence only to fall foul when John Swinney in a radio interview, failed to give start-up costs in response to eleven requests to do so. The red faces in the Scottish Government led to a hastily arranged media Conference when Alex Salmond produced his estimate of £250million subject to the outcome of the independence negotiations leading Prof John McLaren of Glasgow University's Adam Smith's Business School to observe that the negotiations over Scotland's inherited share of UK debt had become more 'crucial'. Why the SNP Government had got involved in this stereotyped, unoriginal game of numbers is a mystery. Far better if it had come out then, earlier or later with projections showing the economic and fiscal benefits of the establishment of new government departments in Scotland and resultant increased employment deploying tax moneys Scotland currently sent to London to subsidise public service jobs there. Or highlighted the share of assets Scotland would inherit instead of cowering behind the excuse that all would depend on the negotiations. In other words, employed a bit of vision and showed fight!

On May 30, the structure of the referendum became clearer. The various participants required to register and then abide by fundraising and spending rules set by the Electoral Commission. On the Yes side, the organisations were Business for Scotland Ltd, Christians for Independence, Generation Yes, National Collective (Artists and Creatives for Independence) Ltd, Campaign for Nuclear Disarmament, Scottish Independence Convention, Scottish National Party, Scottish Socialist Party, Women for Independence, Yes Scotland Ltd. And declaring for No, an independent Alistair McConnachie, Better Together (2012) Ltd, Conservative Party, Labour Party and No Borders Campaign Ltd.

With a hundred days to go the battle lines were set. On the Yes side, the opinion polls still stubbornly showed No ahead – between nine and twenty points clear but still within reach. Business for Scotland had begun to play a starring role putting up persuasive speakers and material to the media. The communities' campaign was running full tilt. YES Scotland was becoming more effective. There was still a lot of money in the locker. As for No, it was still the frontrunner. Better Together looked gaffe ridden but it could rely on support from the Coalition Government at Westminster for its heavy armament, and increasingly to Labour which would have more resonance in the deprived areas to which the Yes campaign hoped to draw votes from the disillusioned. Nevertheless, although the Yes momentum had been checked, campaigners for No could no longer assume that victory was certain. They were prey to apprehension, if not neurosis.

Then there were the unknown circumstances. How would the prospect of a Conservative Government propped up by several maverick UKIP MPs after the next election and an in-out referendum on the EU go down with liberal progressive opinion? And would the prospect of another Tory Government itself destroy the appeal by Labour for remaining in the Union? How would the Tory funding cuts of £25billion (supported by Labour) due after the Westminster election, impact on Scottish public opinion? Could Scots take on board the likely impact on services when the Barnett formula is abolished and Scotland's share cut? Would the prospect of additional powers for he Scottish Parliament shoot the independence fox?

There was all to play for.

Chapter 16:

THE HUNDRED DAYS

With the failure of the 'shock and awe' currency offensive, threats from commercial combines at home and abroad to pull out of Scotland with loss of jobs, the fading of the EU membership issue and the deluge of adverse reports from the Treasury, Westminster, academics and quangos, the No campaign was reluctantly faced with having to play its last major card.

When the Coalition Government had entered into the Edinburgh Agreement almost two years before, it had felt confident enough to coerce the SNP Government into dropping a second question on additional powers for the Scottish Parliament. In process of transferring a diluted version of the powers recommended by the Unionist Calman Commission, it was not in the mood to go further. Its aim was to destroy the credibility of the SNP Government by forcing it to face the people on what they perceived as the 'toxic' issue of independence, something that master tactician Alex Salmond had wished to avoid.

During the spring, conscious of the overwhelming negativity of the No Campaign and the closing gap, the Liberal, Labour and Conservative Parties had started to prepare their proposals to expand the scope of the Scottish Parliament. First into the frame were the Liberal Democrats who proposed very widespread taxation powers. Then came Labour. Its proposals went through their Scottish Conference preceded by an almighty internal battle, mainly with the Scottish bloc of MPs fighting tooth and nail to retain their Westminster relevance and promotion prospects in any future Labour Government. Labour promised powers to hike tax rates for those earning over £41,000 a year and the right to vary taxation by 15p. They also wanted fairer property taxes, devolution of housing benefit, a Scottish Health and Safety Executive and more control over the railways.

The Scottish Conservative Conference, to encouraging noises from Prime Minister David Cameron, hinted at further powers and preferred to await the publication of their Strathclyde Commission report. As May passed, Prime Minister Cameron portrayed himself as the guardian of devolution, a claim based on the recent Scotland Act and other powers conferred on the Assemblies of Wales and Northern Ireland. Conservative promises went beyond those of Labour but were less than those of the Liberal Democrats. In taxation terms, they were substantial but failed to permit transfer of corporation tax. Some welfare powers would be conferred. All in all it represented a u-turn by the Scottish Tory leader, Ruth Davidson who had been elected on a pledge to draw the line on devolution and to safeguard the Union. She enjoyed the specific backing of the Prime Minister who promised that if he was re-elected in the oncoming Westminster General Election he could see 'no reason why Holyrood should not gain more powers soon afterwards'.

Under the Strathclyde proposals, National Insurance and state pensions, the vast bulk of the welfare system and income tax bands and personal allowances remained the responsibility of the UK Government. The UK Government did not agree with the recommendation that Air Passenger Duty should be transferred – something already given to the Northern Ireland Assembly.

Yet, there were still problems. The three Unionist Parties had different proposals from each other. Despite gathering on Calton Hill, Edinburgh for a photocall at an incomplete memorial known as 'Scotland's Disgrace', there was no agreed master plan. The outcome was inconclusive and dependent on Scotland voting No. Then, Scotland safely in the bag and completely disarmed from political influence would need to await hearing what proposals would feature in the manifestoes of the three parties. Even then, legislation would permit further changes, restrictions and dilutions to be made.

The SNP was also quick to remind the public of the promise made by Sir Alec Douglas Home on behalf of the Conservative party that they would deliver a better scheme if the Scots voted No in the 1979 referendum – a promise that was reneged on by Prime Minister Thatcher's Conservative Government. For that matter they could have mentioned the various betrayals and dilutions of promises made in 1945, 1968, 1974, 1975, 1978 and 1986 (over the second devolution referendum), as well as the watering down of the Calman proposals. Who would be believed?

On the side of the No Campaign, there was consternation when Gordon Brown now active in 'United with Labour' addressing large meetings broke from the Unionist consensus to campaign on his new book 'My Scotland,

Our Britain', suggesting that Scotland be given more powers over transport, health and land. Then with radical ambition he proposed replacing the House of Lords with an elected Senate and devolution to all English regions and metropolitan areas, including London, as well as Wales and Northern Ireland. Given the reluctance of England to change its constitutional set up, this was a brave foray into constitutional politics.

Away back in the spring, the UK Government had set out to persuade countries in Europe, the Commonwealth, the USA and Russia of the demerits of Scottish independence and to solicit their adverse views for publication. While Mr Putin, the Russian President, did not respond, the campaign bore fruit in other ways. In early June, in a somewhat nervous if not shifty fashion President Obama responded to a question on Scottish independence at a meeting of the G7 summit in Brussels:

> "There is a referendum process in place and it is up to the people of Scotland. The United Kingdom has been an extraordinary partner to us. From the outside at least, it looks like things have worked pretty well.

> And we obviously have deep interest in making sure that one of the closest allies we will ever have remains a strong, robust united and effective partner. But ultimately these are decisions that are to be made by the folks there."

To which First Minister Alex Salmond responded:

> "As President Obama rightly observes, the decision on Scotland's future is up to the people of Scotland. We are deeply fortunate as a nation that we have the opportunity to gain our nation's independence in such a profoundly democratic way as President Obama himself previously acknowledged – and not through conflict as has been the case with so many nations including the United States itself. An independent Scotland will mean that America has two great friends and allies here rather than one."

And rather more sharply, when former US Secretary of State Hillary Clinton came out in favour of the Union, he queried whether she would have given the same advice to General George Washington. There was a further testimonial from the Chinese Premier, Li Keqiang. Pope Francis was more cautious. When questioned about Catalonia he observed that while all division worried him, countries breaking away from larger states should be considered on a case-by-case basis – Scotland, Padania (Northern Italy) and Catalonia. There will be cases that are right and ones that are not. The report in the Herald (14 June 2014) bred the headlines, 'Pope voices fears over division in referendum' and 'Pontiff enters debate with warning'.

Other international comment of a more relevant kind followed. After the No campaign had discarded the Better Together logo in favour of 'No Thanks' derived from the campaign against Quebec independence from Canada where there had been two referendums, a Canadian Liberal Senator Dennis Dawson advised the leaders of the No campaign to keep the tone positive. In the Herald (14 June 2014), he warned:

> "I told them - 'don't undermine Scotland. Scotland could be independent as much as the other 180 countries in the UN. But does it need to be? You can't say that Scotland does not have the economic force to be independent. That is the wrong thing to say. Nobody can prove an independent Scotland would be more prosperous. But nobody can prove it would be in economic turmoil either.
>
> It is quite clear that the biggest risk that the No side have always taken in Canada was to over simplify the negative aspects of independence."

Two days later the Herald returned to the subject of Quebec which narrowly lost the 1995 referendum with a warning from Prof. Alain G. Gagnon, a professor of political science at the University of Montreal in Quebec who said:

> "People need to be aware if you go for a referendum, if you lose it you will have to pay a price. You can't lose the referendum and not lose something else. Scots should be advised that the centre always wants to protect itself. Even if they say they want to consider some devo.max, forget it. They will say 'No we shall not give them more power, look what they have done with the power they have'. They will say 'If we give them more power there will be a slippery slope there'. Their strategy will be to limit the power of Holyrood."

His remarks were echoed by Bernard Drainville, a senior member of the Parti Quebecois, who maintained that Scotland's bargaining power was based on the strength of its nationalist movement. If you did not win as was the case of Quebec, the rest of Canada assumed that losing made the threat of a further independence referendum less credible. Senator Dawson acknowledged that losing a referendum hurt Quebec but blamed his opponents for holding it in the first place!

But at least Kieran Andrews, political editor of the Courier (14 June 2014) said Buckingham Palace had made it clear that the Queen would stay neutral and not publicly back the Union. It appeared two attempts were made to insert gentle references in support of the Union in the Queen's Speech at Westminster and had been rebuffed. Obviously some lesson had been learned from the Crown's partisan behaviour in the Silver Jubilee in the 1970s! And then Magnus Gardham of the Herald quoted Professor Andrew Goudie, former Scottish Office Chief Economist as arguing that the failure of the pro-UK parties to offer a common agreed package of powers raised 'a serious question of credibility'. (Herald 21 June 2014)

As June progressed and the Wold Cup and Wimbledon occupied attention, the pace slackened. Serious points became scarce with the media focusing instead on scraps over social media abuse against No donor J K Rowling and Yes contributors Colin and Chris Weir. Alex Salmond found himself in a stushie when one of his spin doctors briefed the Daily Telegraph inaccurately. There was also a rather strange agreement by the First Minister to debate with Alistair Darling, leader of Better Together rather than targeting the UK Prime Minister. Although this led to bickering over the dates, there was little in it for Alex Salmond. Apart from reducing the status of the office of First Minister, it was expected that he would wipe the floor with any debating opponent. Yet Alistair Darling, still a Westminster MP and former UK Chancellor of the Exchequer was no mean opponent and even a competent performance would take the shine away from the First Minister and the Yes vote case. It also took the heat off the Prime Minister who was seen as running away from a contest. Tactically, Nicola Sturgeon, a very proficient debater, could have been asked to take on Darling with Alex Salmond pursuing David Cameron, especially since Gordon Brown, very much off the No message, had supported a head-to-head between the UK Prime Minister and the Scottish First Minister.

Intriguingly, and this is pure guess-work, it could be that the SNP felt that the independence vote needed a boost. No clear answer could be found in the opinion polls which switched in different directions. On the plus side for Yes was a Sunday Herald poll from Panelbase on 15 June narrowing the gap to 48% Yes against 52% No. This came shortly after a Survation poll showed 47% Yes to 53% No after elimination of those undecided. Even more interestingly, Panelbase indicated 49% were likely to vote Yes if they thought the Tories would win the UK General Election as counter-posed to a figure of 45% if Labour were deemed winnable.

Four days later the Courier reported a YouGov poll where with the removal of undecided voters, the break down was 40% Yes to 60% No, a drop of 2% for Yes since an earlier poll in the spring. So any view as to the extent of the outcome was up in the air. People looked to me as a former MP to say how things were going. This was not easy. Most of my contacts would be of a similar age and background whose identity even where they were SNP voters would be British rather than Scottish – and thus likely No voters. Yet there was no doubt that a class divide was appearing where many of those living in Scotland's housing schemes, and normally Labour voters, were asserting an emerging Scottish identity. They also had nothing to lose from an out of touch Britain and everything to gain from radical change. Those on the No side were confident of carrying the middle classes and rural voters to the extent that they were cocky about it. They clearly were fearful of losing the vote if Scotland's working class urban voters, many of whom had not voted for years, came out for Yes. Such a change in the demographics would blow the opinion polls apart. They could also create a forward surge that would be difficult to counter.

The key strategy for YES Scotland through the Radical Independence campaign, was to canvass the housing schemes, enthuse the electorate there that this time their vote would count and get potential Yes voters to place their names on the Electoral Register. And this was one reason why United with Labour started taking a more prominent role. The ability to sway those who did not vote and those who would normally support Labour was a wild-card that could dictate the outcome. From a view of social and political justice, it was appropriate that the ordinary people of Scotland whose views were ignored in 1707 could now win back the independence the Scottish establishment of the day had thrown away. Gratifying, too, was the news in yet another poll that Scots Asians were favouring independence.

From my experience, the Yes vote had to recognise that it had a way to go. Time was running short. In the run up to polling day, especially from 3 August when the Glasgow Commonwealth Games concluded, the Yes side had to focus its message more sharply and put the No campaign under pressure. Under the banner of Options for Scotland I issued to the media my third and last critique of the campaign giving suggestions for action.

"Turn Negative on the Union and Sharpen Attack, says former SNP Leader

In his third critique of the Referendum Campaign, Gordon Wilson, Director of Options for Scotland and former SNP Leader and campaign strategist concentrates on what the Yes campaign should do to win the referendum on independence. There is no point in analysing the respective campaigns at this stage. That will come after September 19, when in any event attention will be focused on the aftermath, whatever the outcome.

So let's start from an agreed position. 100 days out, the No campaign leads with the Yes campaign within reach with doubtfuls converting to Yes on a 2 to 1 ratio. A no score draw would suit the No campaign. Yes needs to regain the initiative.

What can Yes do?

1. It should try to reinforce the emotional issue of Scottish national identity. Yes has not realised that the alternative default position to Scottish identity is British identity. It is late but there is still time. A vision of the Scottish independent future is desperately needed. It should also attack the corruption of the British establishment with its 850 strong non-elected parasitic House of Lords, continuing Westminster expenses scandals and refusal to publish a complete uncensored report on the illegal Iraq war

2. Yes should give up trading empty statistics with the Treasury as both sides have lost the attention of the public. It should be **sharper and more brutal** in its attacks.

Concentrate on What Will happen if Scotland Votes No

The North/South Divide

Most people are hostile to the greed and growing economic and political power of London and the south of England. It should be hammered home that voting No will leave Scotland completely at the mercy of the North/South divide.

Emigration: Staunch the Outward Flow

If that economic gap is not closed, Scotland will continue haemorrhaging its most qualified young people. British economic policy will still concentrate on its southern powerhouse base. No amount of increased devolution will give Scotland the opportunity to staunch the outward flow. Only independence will do so.

The Scottish people should be reminded bluntly that Westminster economic policy led to the loss of 2,000,000 Scots during the 20th century. For a country of 5,000,000 that was a tremendously damaging loss. Our young people must face the ongoing reality – if you vote No, be prepared to emigrate. And for the remaining tax payers in Scotland, don't expect a transfer fee payable by the London Government to cover their education costs!

The Public Expenditure Cuts Road Roller

Most Scots are oblivious to the huge UK public expenditure cuts of £25billion menacing Scotland's devolved parliament after the UK General Election in 2015. Scotland's share will be around £2.1billion. On top of that, there is the abolition of the Barnett formula when Scotland's expenditure will be constrained into a tight English mould – a case of double jeopardy.

At risk from these British cuts will be the Scottish NHS as it has to adopt the English cost-cutting privatisation programme, free care for the elderly, freedom from student fees, prescription charges and travel passes. There will be a massive jump in Council Tax to prop up reduced local government funding. Other budgets will crumple under stress.

If Scotland votes No, the English public will demand equality on the basis that we are all British and equal. And Scotland will have no political defence.

Now that Labour is throwing its weight into the campaign, Yes must drive home that it's not just the nasty Tories who are forcing through these savage cuts. Labour in London agree with the Tories and will carry them out in the increasingly unlikely prospect of forming the UK Government.

Political

The Tories are now in prime position to beat Labour in the General Election, with or without the help of UKIP MPs. If Labour voters vote No, they will have another southern English dominated Tory government. It's crude but for Labour voters swithering on voting No, it will be effective!

Additional Devolved Powers

There is a simple scornful response. Even if the promises are kept - Scotland with 5 million people would have a fraction of the powers of the Isle of Man with around 75,000 people."

Whether this message was welcome or irritating, it had to be said, for once more the SNP Government seemed to have run out of steam with too few popular initiatives to counter the never ending bad news stories purveyed by Better Together, United with Labour and above all the UK Government. The Treasury had made a mess of calculation of the start-up costs of new Government agencies. However, the Scottish Government response was scarcely more effective. Through lack of counter-estimates, it was forced to supply them in an emergency press conference two hours later. The fact that the UK figures were repudiated by two of their experts and the Scottish Government numbers were later validated forced a stalemate. Far more positive would it have been if they had been first into the field with assessments of the economic benefit to Scotland of the transfer of civil service jobs whose costs the Scots paid in their taxes for the benefit of London.

Better Together was also getting its act together with the switch of slogan to one of No Thanks (borrowed from Canada's Quebec referendum launched with a marvellously well designed full page advert in clear cut, non-verbose terms saying No Thanks because 64% of Young Scots wanted to stay in the UK, most Scots wanted to keep the UK pound, most Scots wanted to keep an extra £1,400 (one of the disputed Treasury figures) for public services and most Scots pensioners wanted UK pension security – all with promises of more powers for the Parliament, getting the best of both worlds and at no risk! Just vote No was the message. Even on the Yes side, I had to drool over the simplicity of the message and design! Could not Yes drop the verbiage in its advertising?

Then London spoiled it all. On 23 June George Osborne announced a UK Government plan for an extension of high speed rail (HS2) as a boost for the North. The North for General Election purposes was the North of England. The Coalition's boundary for the North stopped at Leeds leaving Newcastle (and Scotland) out in the cold. Not surprisingly, there was anger that Scotland had been ignored. And Scottish tax payers would be paying for it, too. Rather interestingly, the North/South Divide, covered in an earlier Salmond speech promising a 'northern light' to counter London's 'dark star' which then dropped out of focus, had re-emerged with Osborne's comments.

> "So the powerhouse of London dominates more and more and that's not healthy for our economy; it's not good for our country. We need a northern powerhouse too. Not one city but a collection of Northern cities; sufficiently close to each other that combined they can take on the world."

And the Prime Minister rubbed it home the same day when he said that this exciting vision was an attempt to make the most of our great northern cities so we got growth right across our economy. No word about a collateral strategy for industrial growth in the Scottish economy or in Wales or in Northern Ireland! They had no place in this grand British plan. It was an open goal, yet seemingly received only casual comment from the Yes side. Above all, the London dominance should have been a key reason WHY Scotland needed independence. Oh well!!

In this David and Goliath Contest (the UK Government had just issued a booklet to all Scottish households at a cost of £750,000), the Scottish Government did its best with two positive announcements. The first was on economic policy when John Swinney as Finance Minister announced that Scotland would borrow billions of pounds in the first three years of independence in an effort to kick start the Scottish economy. Spending would rise by 3% a year compared with the UK Government projection of

1%. The main planks were increased productivity, a rise in employment and more immigration. Although not spelt out, it was assumed that much of the spending would be on major infra-structural projects. It was a bold challenge to austerity but left unanswered how far Keynesian economics could go when there was a large budgetary deficit inherited from the UK.

Away from economics, Nicola Sturgeon as Deputy First Minister outlined interim proposals for the Scottish state when she announced a draft paving measure, The Scottish Independence Bill setting out the rights and duties of citizens, making nuclear disarmament constitutionally obligatory and seeking to strengthen human rights generally. It proposed that there would be a Constitutional Convention to frame a permanent Constitution. It got little coverage. It would only become relevant if Scotland voted Yes.

The clash between the 700th anniversary of the Battle of Bannockburn that secured Scottish independence historically and the UK engineered hosting of the Armed Forces Day both in Stirling seen by some to have an influence on the referendum passed off as pleasant occasions with virtually no political impact either way. The only fly in the ointment came from David Cameron when he used Armed Forces Day to reinforce the Better Together message. But was that not why it had been redeployed from Portsmouth? Then Europe re-emerged. Taking advantage of David Cameron's isolated campaign to prevent the election of Jean-Claude Juncker as President of the European Commission, Alex Salmond wrote in support of M. Juncker, pledging to do business with him and was later rewarded by hints of accelerated access to the EU emerging from M. Juncker's private office.

The political season had not yet been submerged in the avalanche of sporting events. The Treasury which had long since taken over the masterminding of the UK Government No campaign published alarmist figures of the set-up cost to Scotland of the formation of new Government Ministries and Agencies. £2.7billion was their estimate only to find that Professor Patrick Dunleavy named as an expert source torpedoed their quotation of his work by labelling this figure as 'bizarrely inaccurate', giving instead an estimate of £200million plus with further IT costs for tax and benefit changes at £900million.

The Treasury figures on oil were condemned by Sir Donald MacKay, one of Scotland's most senior oil and gas economists who dismissed them as ill-informed and 'well wide of the mark.' (Sunday Times on line reported 6 July 2014) Using other official figures from the Department of Energy and Climate Change and Oil and Gas UK, Donald MacKay forecast revenues of

£31.8billion between 2017and 2019 almost double the Treasury estimates of £15.8billion. In a scathing comment he wrote – 'if Danny (Alexander, Treasury Chief Secretary) looked at this he might conclude there is no hole in the Scottish Government's oil predictions and there is a mountain of black gold missing from his'. His comments were echoed by the Financial Times' investors magazine which stated that Westminster was deliberately downplaying the potential for oil and gas returns from the North Sea ahead of the referendum.

Not that this was more than water off a duck's back to Danny Alexander who blithely ignored the conclusions and after previously accusing Alex Salmond of painting 'a fantastical picture' of a separate Scotland's public finances, returned to the attack, claiming that 'a separate Scotland is unlikely to be able to provide the same level of support and risks missing out on the economic potential the North Sea has to offer'.

In the 'twilight' world of politics, there is nothing wrong in following up threats with blatant bribes so Cameron came out with promises of hundreds of millions of pounds to Glasgow and its surrounding area. It sounded good but was to be spread over the next two years. Much of it was pre-announced and a supplement to the Government's Cities Project in England. Naturally, there was a challenge for the Scottish Government to match it. And of course, this munificence was an example of how Scotland got the 'best of both worlds'!

During this period there were academic reports covered misleadingly by the media. A case in point was that Scotland had imported power from England on 7% of the time between January 2011 and January 2014. There was no mention that Scotland had exported power to England of the order of 95%. The report itself was sensible in highlighting the need for more Scottish base load capacity to allow for closures of coal and nuclear stations in the future, yet the Herald banner headline on 12 July stated 'Energy crisis warning after power imported from England.'

UK television coverage took place on 7 July with two UK programmes on the same night. The Channel 4 Dispatches programme was - as was customary - a slick hatchet job. The SNP and YES Scotland sensibly did not take part. Later, on BBC 2, was an hour long programme, Scotland, For Richer or Poorer – the economic implications for Scotland. It was fairer but reminded me of the tale of an address to a jury by an American trial lawyer – 'these are the conclusions on which I shall base my evidence'! And yet one cannot to be too critical. When the Yes campaign had consistently failed to show the economic reasons why Scotland needed to get rid of the London Government, why should all the blame fall on the BBC?

It was not all serious. One newspaper letter writer noting that Lords Haughey and Reid of Celtic FC were opposing independence while the Orange Order had vowed to march to save the Union wished he were a 'fly on the wall' when they met to discuss their joint campaign strategy!

By middle July, just before the campaign shut down for the Glasgow Commonwealth Games, there was a renewed spring in the step for Yes activists as polls showed the gap narrowing. Particularly worrying for No was a TNS BMRB poll that indicated they were losing the battle in Labour heartlands. Relying as they were on support from the affluent, the elderly and Conservatives in rural areas, they could lose if the huge population of West Central Scotland swung behind Yes in hope for social justice that they could never expect from London. Then their game would be a bogey.

At last, the Yes campaign tumbled to the issue that could be game changing – the threat to Scotland's prized NHS from the ongoing privatisation of the English NHS, aggravated by London budget cuts and those arising under the Barnett formula. When this message was conveyed by retired Chief Medical Officer for Scotland Sir Harry Burns as well as by the launch of a Health Yes Group, the theme made an impact but needed constant repetition to sink in. Alex Salmond put it pithily in a speech in Liverpool. (Courier 17 July 2014)

> "Scotland is one of the wealthiest countries in the world, with strong public finances, but under the Westminster system, cuts to public spending in England automatically trigger cuts in Scotland. So if private money replaces public spending in England, our budget will also be slashed no matter what we want or need."

With all respect to Alex a more significant contribution from Liverpool – significant because it was independent – came the same day from Peter Kilfoyle, former Labour MP for Liverpool Walton and Labour Minister, when prefacing his remarks about how wealth and talent was being stripped out of Liverpool for the betterment of London and the South, he declared:

> "As an issue (independence) it is bigger than any political party. It is about the aspirations of a country, and that is what

is important to me. It will basically enable the Scots to make decisions for themselves away from London. The sooner that people realise that this centralised country we call the United Kingdom actually mitigates the interests of people in the regions of England as well as the countries of these British Isles, I think it will be to the benefit of all of us."

And then blissful relief to all, including those disinterested in sport, the Glasgow Commonwealth Games provided an interlude. To a frenzy of Saltire flags as the Scottish team performed well on the medals table, the referendum moved out of the spotlight. Behind the scenes, preparations were made for the resumption of hostilities on August 4, fortuitously the 100th anniversary of the start of the disaster of the Great War when the death rate of Scots troops at 26% was more than double that of the UK as a whole. Even during the Games, special permission was given for display of the Union Flag (when there was no GB team) and anything remotely politically Scottish was hunted down by the stewards with the aid of the police. The SNP Government must have been asleep or naively complaisant when the rules were drawn up! Even during the truce, adverse reports from finance and industry trickled out. At issue was whether the superb performance of the athletes and the success of the Games would encourage self-confidence or take attention off the realities of austerity, poverty and food banks in modern Scotland. Again time would tell. On review, the Games failed to stimulate the demand for independence.

So far as the campaign was concerned, the British state marshalled its forces and deployed them, sometimes with guile and sometimes with brutality. The Empire certainly was striking back! The campaign launched by the British Parliament and Government outlined earlier on 21 December 2011 (House of Commons Library – Appendix 1) did not stop there. An update from the Commons Library is set out also in Appendix 1 (emailed reports from the Library to Craig Melville, researcher to Stewart Hosie MP dated June and July 2014). The volume of the material should speak for itself. The two Houses of Parliament at Westminster and Government Departments - especially the Treasury and Scotland Office – provided major input to the No campaign. As the Prime Minister and the Foreign Office had made clear, the British Government was not neutral.

Then the Governments, both UK and Scottish, stepped in with glossy leaflets. In design, pages 2 and 3 of the Scottish leaflet were messy but otherwise both were good. The UK leaflet edged it with a succinct, simple message. An Electoral Commission guidance leaflet followed. Here again the UK message was better, having been personalised to a family voting No. Business for Scotland later circulated a leaflet that matched the ones from the UK Government and Better Together in quality.

The next big event on August 4, the centenary of the outbreak of the Great War failed to embarrass either cause as it emphasised the sacrifice made by so many soldiers mown down by machine guns, gas attacks and the ghastliness of trench warfare and was handled with sensitivity.

Everyone was waiting for the big STV debate on August 5 between Alex Salmond and Alistair Darling. The No campaign tried to spike Alex Salmond in advance with the UK parties promising more powers if the country voted No. Fiscal Affairs Scotland forecast a Scottish financial 'black hole' with independence likely to cost £946 to £1,396 per person while former RBS Chairman Sir George Matthewson insisted that independence was an opportunity, not a threat.

So the scene was set. Alistair Darling was reckoned to be the underdog battling the SNP's master debater Alex Salmond. Everybody expected Salmond to win easily. That's not the way it turned out. Salmond opened and closed strongly setting out his vision for an independent Scotland. Yet, in the cross examination of Darling, he waffled on about quotes from No representatives that Scotland could be invaded by aliens and other trivial matters before forcing Darling into a spot of incoherence as he wriggled to avoid agreeing with the Conservative Prime Minister David Cameron that Scotland could be a successful independent country. Before that, damage had been done when Darling, an experienced lawyer, had persistently interrogated him on what was Salmond's Plan B for the currency.

Even if Salmond had performed well, the danger was that a modest performance by Darling would have been hailed by the media as a reverse for the First Minister. Darling was aggressive, if at times over-excited, and concentrated his fire. Stewart Paterson, Political Correspondent of the Glasgow Evening Times summed the debate very fairly, giving a points decision to Darling.

> "Alex Salmond opened strongly with his reasons why independence was needed. However, he then focused on the Better Together campaign rather than the UK Government, missing an opportunity to really pressure Mr Darling on why the Union was damaging Scotland.

Mr Darling identified a weak point and stuck to it, demanding answers on the currency, and was more successful in proving his campaign's point that the Yes campaign had not provided solid answers. But he was grudging in accepting Scotland could be independent."

While the media gave the baton of honour to Darling, the spot poll confirming it threw up some comforting straws for Yes. The undecideds and women seemed to go for Salmond. The poll confirmed the verdict that Darling had won overall. Prof John Curtice declared there was no clear winner. An earlier Ipsos Mori poll had indicated that almost one third of votes were up for grabs. Then Survation showed a drop of 4% in Yes support to 37% with No at 50%.

Although there was all in play, three problems faced the Yes leadership. Firstly, still trailing, it needed forward momentum. The Debate Part 1 had pushed support backwards. Secondly, there was psychological damage to SNP supporters. Alex Salmond had been their talisman, bringing success without measure. All of a sudden at a critical time, he had been proven fallible. Some were openly disbelieving. Thirdly, and more importantly, the issue of the currency and Plan B had assumed fresh prominence. In the Scottish Parliament, the First Minister coined a new phrase that the pound sterling was Scotland's pound. At the same time, he broadened out the options on the table such as using the pound regardless and a new Scottish currency, rejecting only the Euro, while strongly sticking to his Government's policy that Scotland would be able to negotiate a deal once a Yes vote had been won. Unionist bluster had to adapt to the 'realpolitik' as unionist columnist David Torrance frankly acknowledged in a Herald article – if not accepting the initial premise that independence was desirable.

The broad consensus of Yes supporters outside the SNP was that Alex Salmond needed to provide a simple, persuasive case. The Herald in an editorial thought he had failed to express a future vision of independence. He had been too often on the defensive. I reckoned publicly that he ought to have given a stronger economic case, showing how Scotland had been held back under the Union and explaining how we could do better.

For the political anoraks inside and outside the SNP, there was surprise at the strategy adopted and even more at the composition of his advisers. Tom Gordon, Political Editor of the Sunday Herald, pointed out that the advisory team consisted of special advisors, Geoff Aberdein and Stuart Nicholson, former MSPs Andrew Wilson and Duncan Hamilton, and his lifestyle coach Claire Howell. It was surprising the effective Nicola Sturgeon, John Swinney and Angus Robertson, the Campaign Director were not mentioned when they should have been involved. If Alex Neil had been there, the Salmond approach would have been much more political and hard-hitting. Significantly, it was reported, after initial criticism had bubbled up, that SNP MSPs had been instructed not to speak to the Press. All in all, a dark moment! Inside observers began to see parallels with the ill-fated initiative 'A Penny for Scotland' that had dogged the 1999 election and the new 'Pound for Scotland' controversy. It put an entirely different contemporary interpretation to the old adage – 'in for a penny, in for a pound'.

For those not obsessed with the minutiae of politics, it seemed a different matter on the ground. Edith and I visited the Yes stall on the Saturday in Dundee's Murraygate and found it buzzing with activity with a ready market for window and car posters. Saltire flags were being snapped up by children. There was no sign of despondency there. Even hardened political activists were astounded by the influx of volunteers who had no earlier involvement in campaigning. There was evidence also of the inroads being made into working class communities long alienated from conventional politics.

More signs became evident that it was not as gloomy as it had first appeared. In the immediate aftermath of the Salmond/Darling debate, there was a TNS poll published in both the Scotsman and Herald on 13 August. True, it disclosed a 4% growth in the No vote but was ameliorated by an indication that among the 71% of voters determined to vote, backing for Yes rose a point to 38%, its highest level since September 2013. The changes were at the expense of those who had been undecided. On the face of it, this was not wildly exciting for the Yes campaign but other issues were in play. On television Angus Robertson and Alex Salmond dealt more convincingly with the issue by widening the options on the currency.

Alex Salmond took a strong stance in the Scottish Parliament when he accused the main pro-UK parties of deliberately attempting to create instability in the financial markets as part of a plan to thwart the drive for independence. These remarks were made after Bank of England Governor Mark Carney revealed that he was putting contingency plans in place to protect the economy amid fears that uncertainty over an independent Scotland's currency would cause a run on the banks.

And at last, there was renewed focus on what would happen to Scotland if the country voted No. Both the First Minister and Alex Neil, the Health Minister warned of the adverse effects of Scotland within a continuing Union of extensive privatisation of the NHS in England. The radical changes could impact on Scotland through reduced 'consequentials' under the Barnett formula affecting Scotland's block grant (the 'consequentials' being the funds given to Scotland by London as a proportion of expenditure in England covering areas devolved to Scotland). Any reduction or rise less than inflation would make the sustenance of a public health service more difficult. This was a very real fear amongst Scots. It also provoked a furious outcry from unionists. A Sunday Herald editorial on 17 August commented:

> "Tomorrow, the First Minister will also pledge to enshrine free healthcare 'forever' in the written constitution of an independent Scotland. The No camp's apoplectic response to this new tactic is understandable; bluntly it works. As the Panelbase poll we report on today shows, the future of the NHS has the potential to deliver a victory to the Yes campaign in a month's time.

> Crucially, it could secure majority support from women, who have so far been resistant to Yes. Unionists say that these NHS warnings are a flat lie, a cynical exercise in scaremongering."

Leaving aside whose scaremongering was better, the Panelbase survey showed that by 57% to 43%, people were more inclined to vote Yes if the NHS was an issue. The NHS was second only to the economy and jobs on the voters' list of priorities. Another ICM poll put Yes on 38%, up four on the previous month and No on 47%, up two with a corresponding drop in undecideds to 14%. Stripping out the undecideds put the gap at 55% to 45%, a narrowing of four points. Significantly, Prof. Curtice in the Scotsman drew attention to the oddity that while many thought the Scottish Government's currency plans were unconvincing, the No side's threat to refuse access to the pound was widely disbelieved. He pointed out that the No campaign needed to do much work to mine the seam if it is to prove rich on polling day.

With under four weeks to go, the Yes campaign's hopes rested on the impact of social media and the on-ground efforts. Stewart Kirkpatrick, Head of Digital at Yes Scotland, in an email to the author of 21 August 2014, explained how the digital campaign had operated:

"In the past two years, Yes Scotland's Facebook likes have grown from 5,000 to 225,000, Twitter followers from 5,000 to 61,000. YouTube views have grown from 25,000 to 500,000. (We have 4,000 YouTube subscribers.) Website traffic has quadrupled. The No campaign have 168,000 Facebook likes, 30,000 Twitter followers and 670 YouTube subscribers. These articles show the effectiveness of our work:

- Edinburgh University blog post by Strathclyde Academics: Independence Referendums Social Media Project update: https://www.aqmen.ac.uk/node/1062

- What Scotland Thinks: (Earlier piece by one of the above academics): http://blog.whatscotlandthinks. org/2013/11/referendum-campaigns-on-social-media/

- BBC report on Glasgow University study showing our tweeters are more numerous and active: http://www. bbc.co.uk/news/uk-scotland-scotland-politics-25642809

- Velocity Digital: Who's winning the social media battle (It finds we are by a mile): http://www.velocitydigital.co.uk/ whos-winning-the-indyref-social-media-battle/

- 'Yes Scotland has a larger social community than that of Better Together': http://fatbuzzblog.blogspot. co.uk/2014/04/a-social-referendum.html

A large reason for all of the above is the fact that we are a genuine grassroots campaign. Unlike the other lot, we genuinely have tens of thousands of people campaigning for us every day. These people are committed, enthused and well-informed. We send out regular guides on the issues to supporters - and also have well-established rules on how we expect our supporters to behave.

When I first got into online journalism in 2000, the name of the game was to get people to visit my employer's website (scotsman.com in my case). Now, however, we don't assume that people will visit the website at all (though many do). Instead we focus on pushing out bitesize, attractive, targeted messages to where Undecideds are spending their time on social media. That's why we focus so much on short videos and punchy infographics. Our aim is that these will grab the attention of Undecideds, or at the very least that they are seized on by our supporters, who can then 'share' them on their social media profiles for their friends and families to see.

However, it is not just through the official campaign that the strength of the Yes movement comes out. We are blessed in having creative allies online who continually produce fascinating content and brilliant ideas."

The strength of digital campaigns had proved itself in the first Obama Presidential campaign. One veteran SNP MSP told me the referendum would have been hopeless without the existence of the sponsoring Scottish Government and given the hostility of the print media, the presence of the new means of communication through the technology of the social media in their various manifestations. As the polls closed, YES Scotland had 106,000 followers on Twitter while the No side had 42,500. The pattern was repeated across all the other social networking platforms. In this referendum, the acid test of effectiveness would be September 18!

As the final four weeks approached, the pendulum was beginning to swing back to Yes although almost imperceptibly. There was a substantial set-back when the much respected Sir Ian Wood who had built up a worldwide oil supply and engineering business on the back of the first oil boom publicly questioned the amount of oil remaining to be   extracted. From his remarks there was little doubt that he was not a Yes voter; nevertheless within days academic and industry sources validated the SNP 24billion barrels figure as a realistic top range estimate. If Sir Ian were right, there would be less long term benefit to Scotland and thus a reason for people to vote No.

Having followed the oil issue since I had launched the SNP's 'It's Scotland's Oil' campaign in the seventies (incidentally on a very conservative assessment of oil prices and reserves), I considered the oil revenues secondary to using the industry to build up Scottish engineering. I was also staggered by the ignorance. All the talk was of the North Sea whereas the future lay in the eastern Atlantic. No one seemed to be aware that the UK was in negotiations with Ireland, Iceland and the Faeroes (through the agency of Denmark) to set Scotland's boundaries for ocean bed mineral exploration in the Atlantic. In any event, the extent of Scotland's extractable reserves depended on the price of oil which was predicted by international agencies to rise substantially over a thirty year period.

Surveys said that twice as many people believed that YES Scotland's campaign was more effective than that of Better Together although half of all undecided voters did not know which campaign was best. There is no doubt that the positive message of YES Scotland had impacted better compared to the negativism of their opponents. Yet the gap remained and it was going to need herculean efforts from the Yes movement to overtake No and dash past them to the winning post.

Chapter 17:

COUNTDOWN TO DESTINY

Alex Salmond did it again. Retrieving his reputation as one of the best debaters in the UK, the First Minister put on a commanding display in the second television Debate with Alistair Darling on the BBC on August 25. The timing was good as postal ballots were in process of issue. The Debate, shown throughout the UK and relayed worldwide, marked the commencement of the final stages of the campaign. What would follow in the course of the next three weeks would be a titanic contest of an intensity never seen in recent UK or Scottish General Elections.

Salmond tackled the currency issue head on. Casually conceding there were three sets of Plan B, he took the initiative by seeking a mandate for a currency zone and challenging Darling to join the fight if Yes won on September 18. Having extracted from Darling that Scotland could use the pound, he followed on by concentrating on the NHS and Britain's treatment of children in poverty and the disabled under the social security changes being implemented from London. Darling visibly crumbled on a taunt that he was in bed with the Tories. A spot poll immediately after the Debate registered that Salmond had won by a margin of 71% to 29%. The strategic message from the First Minister was that this referendum gave Scotland the opportunity to take control of its own democracy and to choose the government it wished to solve the country's economic and social priorities. Who better to do this, asked Mr Salmond, than the people who lived and worked in Scotland?

In the first STV Debate won by Darling, there was some evidence that undecided voters' judgments could be swayed by the demeanour of the protagonists rather than by the force of their arguments. There was a widespread opinion that the combative nature of the format requiring each participant to cross examine the other was not conducive to either side being able to make a calm, cogent case. That being so, a win was essential to inspire the tens of thousands of workers to redouble their efforts. Even then sticking in mind reluctantly was that the failure of both campaigns to shift support substantially signified a lesser opportunity for movement to Yes. This was not positive thinking!

After three weeks of gloom and defeatism following the first debate, there was a new spring in the step of the activists engaged on the ground. The gloom transferred to the No campaign whose week did not improve when their first referendum broadcast was slated by both Yes and No campaigners because it depicted a dithering housewife drifting towards a decision to vote No. Patronising and sexist was a general opinion. As one commentator for No put it on TV, so far as attitudes were concerned, the broadcast could easily have been shown in the sixties or seventies. A Yes panellist felt it sounded like 'manspeak', that is scripted by a man for delivery by a woman.

Even one of Better Together's blockbusters from 130 business leaders writing to the Scotsman warning of the dangers to business of Yes was trumped immediately by a riposte from 200 business people backing the opportunities from independence. It asked Scotland to look outwards and claimed that the real problem for Scotland's economy was the threat from London to leave the European Union. One signatory, Prof Nathu Puri, founder of a business in the Midlands and a former Labour donor, commented on the implications of Scottish independence for the rest of the UK:

> "The London-centricity of Britain's economy is unsustainable. We must reindustrialise the nations and regions outside of South East England. We must rebalance the British economy by sector and geography to ensure sustainable economic growth. Scottish independence will be a major step forward towards that goal in the interests of not just Scots, but business and jobs in Wales, Northern Ireland, the Midlands and the north of England."

The battle raged at town hall and street meetings. With cries of protest from Labour MP, Jim Murphy that his series of meetings in 100 towns in 100 days had been sabotaged by 'mobs' of Yes supporters, there was some bad publicity for Yes. True, he had been hit by an egg (an egg too far!), but before politics had been depersonalised and tamed by television, election candidates frequently encountered hecklers and had to deal with them by dexterity of reply or retreat! Humour was a great weapon. In fact, experienced hustings hands preferred opposition as it attracted an audience that may otherwise have sauntered by with disinterest. In Dundee City Square in the seventies and eighties, outdoor meetings were always 'interesting' when the pubs scaled mid afternoon!

Meanwhile, activists and the media awaited anxiously for polls to show if there were any permanent changes as a result of the BBC Debate. On 30 August came the first real indication of forward momentum by the Yes campaign. Support for independence rose 4.4% in a Survation survey to 47% with No Thanks at 53%. No might be still ahead but the gap had closed to 6 points with 17 days to go. The next poll from YouGov hit the headlines. YouGov in its polling outturns normally gave Yes lower than the average. For that reason alone, the results posted on 1 September (with field work running from 28 August) had to be taken seriously, especially as there now seemed to be a trend in evidence.

YouGov demonstrated a 4% rise in headline support (excluding undecideds) in Yes support from 43% in August to 47%. With No support falling from 57% to 53%, the gap was only 6%. A swing of 3% could lead to a Yes victory. Given that there had been a drop of 1% in the number of undecided voters, there had been a 3% transfer from No to Yes. In the detail, there were surprising revelations. Yes support was ahead in all age groups save 60+ where admittedly the differential of 69% No to 31% Yes had obviously impacted on the outcome. It demonstrated that there was much work to be done. A large minority of those born outside the UK (40%) favoured Yes. Much less support was displayed by those born in the UK.

The atmosphere changed dramatically as the news sank in that a win was possible. Repositioning was in the air. Already, even before YouGov, Secretary of State Alistair Carmichael had signalled that in the event of a Yes vote he would resign from the Coalition Government and join the Scottish Government Team Scotland to negotiate the terms of independence. In the UK, there was a rude awakening with a wobble in the value of sterling. Although nobody wished to say it in public, it had been surmised that failure to negotiate a common sterling zone could lead to a run on the pound. This was early proof. Despite all the fuss over currency, there was little doubt, said Nobel-laureate economist Joseph Stiglitz during the Edinburgh Festival, that the UK would cave in on a joint currency union.

Worse was still to come for the No campaign. Still rattled from the super-fast closing of the gap, losing the argument over the NHS being deprived of funds from privatisation in England and haemorrhaging support amongst Labour voters, its back was to the wall. Shortly the Unionist roof was due to fall in.

A further YouGov poll published by the Sunday Times put Yes ahead for the first time in this prolonged campaign. The poll assessed support for Yes at 51% and unionists at 49% - overturning a 22 point lead in the space of a month. YES Scotland issued its own Panelbase survey placing No ahead at 52% to 48%, a razor thin majority. Both polls showed that the gender gap had closed. There was growth in support for Yes from women voters. This had lagged significantly behind during the whole campaign. The upward movement reflected fresh flows to Yes from Labour voters. It was also evident that some No voters were switching to Yes and that the battle was no longer confined to gleaning the undecideds.

This time the shock was felt in Westminster and the London media which had taken a No vote for granted. All the English Sundays and UK media reacted sharply. The break up of the UK had at last replaced discussion on UKIP. Anyone watching the television coverage could not wonder at the ignorance of journalists in the London 'bubble' struggling to understand what was happening in Scotland. A series of ignoramuses appeared on the press reviews and were completely at sea. They still did not get it. And of course it was initially the English papers which were reviewed. Only very rarely did they condescend to have a journalist from Scotland who knew the issues, reasons and trends.

The Sunday Times with prior knowledge of their survey was able to mount its usually impressive assessments including a warning from its Economics Editor, David Smith that falling oil revenues and lack of currency plans would wreck the nationalists' economic plans for voting Yes. He forecast that even with oil, Scotland would run a bigger budget deficit than the rest of the UK and ignored the impact on the former UK itself.

Even the Governor of the Bank of England re-iterated that given the reactions of the UK political parties, a monetary arrangement would not be possible without infringing upon rUK sovereignty. His careful wording left open the possibility that a UK financial crisis could force a change of minds for the UK parties. Then to calm markets and save the UK monetary system, an Anglo-Scottish deal would be devised by the Governor.

The political ramifications followed. Better Together was rubbished by its own supporters. Douglas Alexander was given the blame and largely sidelined from leading the campaign. UK pundits assessed the need of Prime Minister Cameron and Opposition Leader Miliband to resign if they lost Scotland. Constitutional experts puzzled over what would happen after the 2015 General Election if Labour were elected on the strength of Scottish MPs who would then be disqualified ten months later. What moral or legal authority would Scottish MPs have to vote on English and UK matters during the interregnum?

There was general panic in London. The Sunday Times ran a story that the Queen was a unionist and seriously worried about the future of her kingdom only for the story to be rebutted in an unprecedented statement from Buckingham Palace rebuking the attempt to drag her into the debate:

> "The sovereign's constitutional impartiality is an established principle of our democracy and one which the Queen has demonstrated throughout her reign. As such the monarch is above politics and those in political office have a duty to ensure this remains the case.
>
> Any suggestion that the Queen would wish to influence the outcome of the current referendum campaign is categorically wrong. Her Majesty is simply of the view this is a matter for the people of Scotland."

This rebuke stopped the publicity at a stroke. Was it genuine? Some of us remembered the Silver Jubilee in 1977 when she declared that she could not forget she had been crowned Queen of the United Kingdom (see Wilson, SNP: The Turbulent Years). She took sides then. The vow of silence did not last as she made an informal aside on the last Sunday before the poll that the Scots should think very carefully before casting their vote. The controversy revived. Later Prime Minister Cameron was overheard saying that that on receiving confirmation of the result she 'purred' down the line. The Queen would not be amused!

Meanwhile the jitters were increased when a TNS poll with nine days to go and showing a large figure of undecideds at 23% gave No 39% down from 45% a month before and Yes up from 32% to 38%. There appeared no doubt. The trend lay towards Yes and the momentum was with them.

Something had to be done. On Sunday 7 September, Chancellor George Osborne ignoring the rule that Government Ministers should make no announcements during the official period of the campaign told a mildly astonished Andrew Marr that substantial new powers for the Scottish Parliament would shortly be announced. The Government had previously blocked a third question on devo.max appearing in the ballot paper as an alternative to independence and the *status quo*. Sure enough former Prime Minister Gordon Brown who had years before claimed to have saved the world from the financial crisis (the UK part of which he had caused through slack regulation of the UK banks) now rode like St George to the rescue of the Union and to slay the nationalist dragon.

So on Monday 8 September, speaking to an invited audience of Labour supporters with the media present (a reluctance to open his meetings to the general public seemed to form his meeting pattern), Gordon Brown announced a package to save the Union involving discussions amongst the UK parties to reach agreement on whatever powers would be on offer. There was no definition of what, if any, new powers would be granted in the event of Scotland voting No. Instead there would be an accelerated programme to deliver this uncertain package – assuming English MPs agreed! It was not so much a 'pig in a poke' that was on offer than a 'poke with no pig'.

Some suspension of belief had to take place. No longer a Prime Minister and a regular absentee from the Commons, Gordon Brown did have an ego. With some justification, he could claim the emergency required the assumption of consular powers and like Cincinnatus leaving his farm to come to the rescue of the Roman Republic, he was ready. He expected those with real authority like the Prime Minister, the Leader of the Opposition and the three Scottish party leaders to fall into line. Bereft of ideas to deal with this impending catastrophe they readily did so. As the campaign drew to a close, continuing nervousness in London led to the offer of more powers for the Scottish parliament. There was no mention of 'economic' proposals and of course silence as to whether any guarantees would be worthless in a House of Commons dominated by resentful English MPs. This was what happened in respect of the 1979 devolution referendum when an all party backbench rebellion imposed an impossible 40% threshold of the total electorate) for a Yes vote and sabotaged the outcome (where Yes obtained just over 50% of the votes cast). Scotland may propose but England disposes! There are some rules in British political life that never change. Nevertheless the offers were on the table. Would they lead to a hardening of the No vote as was intended or would they be discounted as too little or too late?

This was not the first time this sucker-punch of 'vote No now and get a better offer later' had been used. There had been many times when Westminster had made short term promises to deflect pressure. For example, immediately before the 1979 devolution referendum, Sir Alec Douglas Home, a former Conservative Prime Minister, had invited the Scots to vote No so that they could get a better Assembly from the Conservatives. It never materialised. Incoming Prime Minister, Margaret Thatcher dismissed it and it was only after 18 years of industrial dereliction and a change of Government that a new offer of a Scottish Parliament appeared on the agenda. Few would remember this and the Yes campaign would need to stir memories as there was a danger that some Yes supporters might be swayed by a soft option, however spurious it might be. A full page newspaper Vote Yes advertisement depicting Cameron and Miliband bore the message: 'If they really wanted to give Scotland more powers they'd have done it before now.'

The intensity of the battle was huge. The broadcasting networks moved their news presentations and principal political correspondents north. Day by day the alternate cases were brought forth, dissected and replaced by new stories. For the ordinary citizen the 'white noise' must have been difficult to absorb and by this time, many might have ducked for cover – except for the excitement. Scotland and the UK had never seen anything like it. The country was on the move. Regiments of volunteers on both sides manned every major centre. The topic of independence was discussed in the pubs, at places of work, amongst friends and within families. There was much debate. The population was split down the middle. For some there was emotional intensity – to keep the Union or to win freedom. For most there was a discussion on the question of how to make Scotland a more prosperous, fair and equal society – within the Union or with independence and it was good natured on the whole.

Many of the exchanges were in the social media. The printed press had less influence – just as well since with one exception, the Sunday Herald, it was predisposed in tone to No or outright hostile to Yes. Denying that there was panic in London the three UK Party leaders sallied into Scotland from their redoubts in London. There was much merriment with cartoonists and journalists having a field day caricaturing 'the three amigos of the apocalypse' or 'the three stooges' as they abandoned the civilised exchanges of Prime Ministers Questions for a barbaric ungrateful Scotland.

The last full campaigning week saw a resumption of the negative campaigning. As the polling narrowly strengthened in favour of Yes, bringing the gap down to a two point lead for No, Prime Minister Cameron called in leading retailers and businessmen to give support to the Union by claiming that independence would lead to higher food prices. ASDA, John Lewis and M & S answered the appeal. Morrisons, Aldi and Lidl kept silent. Apart from the politics, the threat of higher food prices to poor pensioners and those reliant on the ever growing number of food banks was cruel. It was intended to influence the vote regardless of human cost to the defenceless poor and may well have done so. Just when the attacks slackened out came a report from Deutsche Bank that Scottish independence could lead to the Great Depression as in the thirties. It was news to us all that Scotland, ignored on the world stage for centuries, was so important. There were hints from antagonists that Scotland could be another German Weimar Republic, associated with the rise of the Nazis.

On top of this, RBS, Lloyds and Clydesdale reported that they would move their registered offices and as with Standard Life and Aegon, would have suitable English subsidiaries to deal with the savings of their English customers. These were bound to have an impact despite a little publicised statement from the Bank of England that savings up to the usual £85,000 limit would be guaranteed during the 18 month negotiating position. Project Fear was alive and well. In the case of RBS, the Treasury jumped the gun by making the announcement to the BBC before a final decision was ready for release, leading to share dealings overnight against the City Code. Alex Salmond demanded an investigation. A statement by RBS that there would be no changes in jobs and operations in Scotland got subdued coverage. Meanwhile Whips were contacting MPs for a possible recall of Parliament in the event of a Yes vote. Chancellor of the Exchequer, George Osborne and Governor Carney postponed attendance at a G20 Finance Ministers meeting in Australia to be in attendance on the Friday.

With its limited firepower the SNP could only describe these orchestrated London campaigns as more scaremongering and assert that Scotland would not be bullied. It held a photo opportunity for prominent entrepreneurs. The Chairman of pub group Wetherspoons responded by saying that there was a lot of nonsense talked, particularly by businessmen and politicians, to say that it was impossible for Scotland to survive as successfully as by itself.

Odd comments were made. Prime Minister Cameron matched Gordon Brown with emotion, being close to tears as he appealed to Scots at a hastily arranged meeting in Edinburgh not to use the referendum just to kick the 'effing Tories' and a few days later in Aberdeen to assure Scots that neither he as Prime Minister nor his Government would be there for ever – a politically risky admission for a politician in the run up to a General Election!

Watching the campaign from the sidelines, I noticed a change in the attitude of the London broadcasting coverage. It is easy of course in any tight campaign for each side to complain of bias. From the start, the BBC was editorially hostile. Any calamity facing Scotland was given splash coverage; the other side was ignored. Spokespersons for No always seemed to have the last word. To portray the hallowed BBC as other than unbiased is close to sacrilege. Yet, the BBC is a UK institution. It is run by metropolitans whose knowledge of and interest in Scotland is vestigial. During the Second World War, the BBC was an instrument of propaganda. Now Britain was fighting for its survival against an outlandish move to break up the Union. From a London perspective, the whole idea was ridiculous and had to be resisted in the national interest!

Many years before at a time when the SNP obtained no UK coverage, I received a letter from a Director General explaining how they had held seminars for London news producers to inform them that there was a separate Scottish dimension. The letter honestly admitted that metropolitan attitudes were difficult to shift. Even with the BBC's move to Salford, staff there complained they were looked down upon by those still based in London. I thought Alex Salmond put it very neatly when asked if the BBC's reporting was biased, he replied:

> "Yes, absolutely, of course it is ..... but they don't realise they're biased. It's the unconscious bias, which is the most extraordinary thing of all."

An incomplete report by BBC Political Editor, Nick Robinson led to up to 2,000 demonstrators outside BBC Scotland's Pacific Quay and a 16,000 strong on-line petition calling for his dismissal. When introduced to BBC Director General Tony Hall prior to the results programme, I mentioned that Nick Robinson could now be accredited as a war correspondent, pointing out that the Roman historian, Tacitus was the first reporter to have trouble with the Caledonians!

On its BBC 24 channel, the BBC featured in its review of the papers a journalist from Inverness given a token three minutes before being dismissed, with the second contributor, an American professor, allowed an uncontested ten minutes to spout anti-independence bile. Labour MPs accused the BBC of bias against Better Together. The NUJ claimed intimidation. The BBC claimed to be rigorously impartial. Allan Little was particularly measured, knowledgeable and fair. As for the BBC and STV big Debates, these were fair although the formats, particularly of mutual cross-examination, gave rise to more heat than light. The other debates were both watchable and fair.

ITV UK News commenced by being much more balanced, yet as polls narrowed, they, to, turned prejudicial. As for Channel 4 News, it was its usual irreverent self at the beginning but redeemed itself with a serious report from the east end of Glasgow in the final week. Scottish Television was reasonably fair with its Scotland Tonight programme grabbing the laurels. As for Sky, it had been generally balanced apart from a few lapses. One of the Yes strategists commented that its main weakness, as with the BBC, was to have ill-informed and hostile Westminster based journalists on, from left and right, who agreed with each other. To be fair, Sky sought to fix it latterly in the campaign.

I formed the impression that some of the journalists on safari in Scotland did not like to be marooned in the outback. Seeing them in their rain coats in teeming rain and mirk, they had my sympathy! Yet it also has to be acknowledged that there were many first class pieces, measured and reflective and a credit to journalism. And has Scotland ever received such attention within the UK or from abroad? Meantime, the international media gathered.

In a last throw of the unionist dice, the three UK party leaders signed up to a solemn 'Vow' to deliver more powers, to enable the Scottish Parliament to protect the NHS and to guarantee continuation of the Barnett formula saving mainline Scottish funding – all to the disgruntlement of Southern Tory MPs and Wales. There were three last minute opinion polls bringing out a four point lead for better Together. These were followed on the Thursday of the referendum by one from Ipsos Mori showing Yes losing by only two points. The pollsters gave a health warning that these results could be invalidated by an exceptionally high turnout. Too close to call was the universal assessment. Final rallies took place. The guns fell silent. Referendum day had arrived.

Thursday broke gray with misty drizzle in the East. This did not deter the voters. They came out in droves with some queues formed early on. Booked to appear on the BBC and STV results programmes, I turned up in Glasgow with high hopes and few expectations. Hard experience and the prevailing opinion polls had led me to the view that victory was unlikely and that a sound result on the night was the best to be hoped for. The first few returns confirmed my assessment. Beginning with Clackmannan where there was an 8% differential in favour of No, the pattern was set. Council region after region cast No vote after No vote. Even SNP areas of strength such as Aberdeenshire, Angus, Moray and Perth & Kinross turned their backs on independence. It was not until late in the morning that Dundee, Glasgow, North Lanarkshire and West Dunbartonshire produced affirmations of Yes. In all, 2,001,926 (55.3%) Scots voted No and 1,617,989 (44.7%) Yes. The council results are given in Appendix 2. Throughout the country, tens of thousands of Yes volunteers could not understand the result. Many were in tears. Their dreams had been shattered.

The poll from Lord Ashcroft pointed up some of the issues. For gender, the Yes gap had closed at 47% for men and 44% for women, both very near the overall breakdown. The clearest disparities came with age. In the 16-17 age group, there had occurred a dramatic change where 71% now chose independence. Opposition was greatest amongst the over 65s at 73% No to 27% Yes. As this was a numerically large sector of dependable voters, it is arguable that it tipped the overall result to the negative. The issue here was demonstrably pensions with 37% so motivated, yet this age group undoubtedly responded to the message of security, 'betterness' together and loyalty to the United Kingdom.

So what can we make of this? Firstly, the unspoken issue of identity that Yes was nervous about clearly mattered. Choice of identity is not possible to turn round short term. From 1960 onwards Scotland had moved progressively in identity from British to British/Scottish and currently to Scottish/British. For this referendum, the process of moving to a clear-cut Scottish identity was not complete. In time, with the passing of the generations, the demographics will improve. Still, very little effort by Yes was put into assurances on pensions and quality for life for the elderly. Too late was played the powerful link between grandparents and grandchildren. If the principle had been promoted early enough that grandparents owed a duty to future generations rather than to themselves, more support could have been won.

More important was the finding that only 10% of people voting Yes considered no more Conservative Governments as important, yet Yes majored on this at every opportunity. Only 20% said they had voted Yes on the basis that Scotland's future as an independent country looked brighter, a poor return for a case based on Scotland's wealth and resources. The proposition that all decisions about Scotland should be taken in Scotland attracted a massive 70%. It was obvious that this democratic message had hit home to dramatic effect. YouGov had a different analysis showing that 51% of 16 and 17 year olds voted No as did all other age groups apart from those aged 25 – 39. A total of 74% of those voters who were born elsewhere in the UK voted No. Some 51% of Scots born voters supported independence.

Looking at important considerations for No voters, the Ashcroft survey accorded 25% to extra powers within the security of the UK, 27% to attachment to the UK and a substantial 47% to risks over the currency, EU entry, the economy, jobs and prices. This validates the argument in earlier chapters that there should have been a stronger negative campaign by Yes to show that with the mismanagement of the Scottish economy, there was greater risk to prosperity from remaining within the UK.

It came as a surprise to the SNP when it received a majority of MSPs in 2011 and had to deliver a referendum. There was no escape through a third question on devo.max. Was the referendum a disaster waiting to happen? It could have been. Yet a miracle occurred. As with the 2011 election, no one saw it coming. The campaign caught fire spontaneously. Yes Groups were formed throughout the nation – around 300 autonomous groups. Operating almost independently of the YES Scotland and mobilised through Face Book, Twitter and other social media, they recruited enthusiastic volunteers who over long, arduous months worked hard to reach voters. Canvassing, holding street stalls and delivering leaflets, they transformed Scottish politics. As the campaign progressed, the general public caught the excitement and attended packed town hall meetings in a manner not seen for two generations. By the time the referendum was held, Yes supporters were in a state of democratic ecstasy while on No there was anxiety. For the declaration of the result, there were around 1,200 media from all round the world. No one seeing the gatherings of Yes supporters bearing their Saltire flags could be other than impressed by this democratic revolution.

Out of this contest, Scotland emerged a changed and better nation. In the eyes of the world, it had experienced a serious peaceful debate. It confronted itself and its identity without rancour or violence, something rare in this estranged, alienated world. It proved that politics could still reach the people, something evidenced by the extraordinary turnout of 84.6%, a record in all ways and confirmation of how engaged the Scottish people had been. In an article in the Sunday Herald, Alyn Smith summed up the achievement:

> "...... it was an energising, spirited and overwhelmingly good natured debate about who makes decisions for us in our interconnected world, and who they should be accountable to. Scotland walks taller today; this debate has changed us, and we now have a duty to make sure it changes politics, too."

Yes volunteers felt bereaved by the result. They had expected victory and their hopes were dashed. There were bitter tears. In their inexperience, they did not realise what an achievement the 45% Yes vote was. Nevertheless all this vision and energy could run into the dust as had happened in major reverses to the SNP in 1970 and 1979. Instead as the unionist parties, having promised 'major powers' to the Scottish Parliament with no delay, began reneging, the disappointment of defeat was replaced by anger. The commitment was made. In seven days, the SNP enrolled around 45,000 new members almost tripling its previous tally of 25,000 (latest count (82,000), making it the third largest party in the UK ahead of Liberal Democrats. The Scottish Greens tripled its membership, with rises also going to the Scottish Socialists. The fight was not over.

On the Friday 19 September, the architect of it all, Alex Salmond announced his intention to resign as SNP Leader and as First Minister to the shock of all and the dismay of most. In the period from 1990, he had come to personify the SNP and become the finest politician of his generation. He took responsibility for the outcome of the referendum and foresaw the need for fresh leadership in a political situation 'redolent' with opportunity. In doing so, he opened the door to fresh strategies for winning independence and paved the way for a new era.

This book opened with quotations from an earlier SNP leader, Jimmy Halliday. It is fitting that it closes with one from Alex Salmond:

> "The real guardians of progress are not the politicians at Westminster, or even at Holyrood, but the energised activism of tens of thousands of people who I predict will refuse meekly to go back into the political shadow."

Alex Salmond, Friday, 19 September 2014

APPENDIX 1:

SCOTTISH INDEPENDENCE

Reports from House of Commons Library on Committees, Debates and Government Papers

1. Letter from the Library to Craig Melville for Stewart Hosie MP, 21 December 2012

    You asked for information on the number of Committees that have been examining Scotland's case for independence. You also wanted a list of debates in the Commons and Lords which have examined the subject.

    For the current Session the following Committees are currently or have looked into the issue. I have provided a link to the Committee pages, on which you can access any reports they have published, and any evidence they have taken.

Committees

House of Lords Select Committee on the Constitution
The Agreement on a referendum on independence for Scotland Report, 7th Report of Session 2012-13, HL Paper 62

House of Lords Select Committee on Economic Affairs
Economic Implications for the United Kingdom of Scottish Independence

Defence Committee
Defence Implications of Possible Scottish Independence

Energy and Climate Change Committee
The impact of potential Scottish independence on energy and climate change

Foreign Affairs Committee
The Foreign Policy Implications of and for a separate Scotland

Scottish Affairs Committee
The Referendum on Separation for Scotland

I have searched for debates over the last two Sessions.

Debates

Scotland and the Union
HC Deb 29 Nov 2012 vol 554 cc405-440

UK Constituent Parts (EU)
HC Deb 21 Nov 2012 vol 553 cc141-167WH

Scottish Separation (BBC)
HC Deb 16 Oct 2012 vol 551 cc22-31WH

Referendum (Scotland)
HC Deb 15 Oct 2012 vol 551 cc63-80

Scotland: Referendum
HL Deb 15 Oct 2012 vol 739 cc1310-1321

Constitutional Settlement
HL Deb 11 Oct 2012 vol 739 cc1168-1203

Scottish Separation
HC Deb 10 Jul 2012 vol 548 cc24-49WH

Constitutional Status (Scotland)
HC Deb 25 Oct 2011 vol 534 c288-94

You might also find the Standard Note on the Referendum on independence for Scotland (SN06478) very useful. The author of this note, Paul Bowers, can be contacted on extension 3441 if you have any further questions on the subject.

2. Letters from the Library to Craig Melville for Stewart Hosie MP, 21 June and 28 July 2014

> The following list contains material that explicitly mentions the referendum and Scottish independence but there may be other Committee and reports that touch on the subject but are not included here.

Committees

Business, Innovation and Skills Select Committee
The Implication of Scottish Independence - Report in preparation

Scottish Affairs Select Committee
The Referendum on Separation for Scotland – 11 Reports published:

• Eleventh Report of the inquiry - The Referendum On Separation For Scotland: The Impact On Higher Education, Research And Tuition Fees

• Tenth Report of the inquiry - The Referendum on Separation for Scotland: A Defence Force for Scotland – A Conspiracy of Optimism?

• Ninth Report of the inquiry - The Referendum on Separation for Scotland: The Need for Truth

• Eighth Report of the inquiry - The Referendum on Separation for Scotland: How would Separation affect jobs in the Scottish defence industry?

• Seventh Report of the inquiry - The Referendum on Separation for Scotland: Separation shuts shipyards

• Government Response to Seventh Report of the inquiry

• Sixth Report of the inquiry - The Referendum on Separation for Scotland: The proposed section 30 Order - Can a player also be the referee?

• Fifth Report of the inquiry - The Referendum on Separation for Scotland: Terminating Trident—Days or Decades?

• Fourth Report of the inquiry - The Referendum on Separation for Scotland: a multi-option question?

• Third Report of the inquiry - The Referendum on Separation for Scotland: making the process legal

- Second Report of the inquiry - The Referendum on Separation for Scotland: Do you agree this is a biased question?

- First Report of the inquiry - The Referendum on Separation for Scotland: Unanswered Questions

House of Lords Select Committee on the Constitution
Scottish independence: constitutional implication of the referendum - 8th Report published 16 May 2014, HL Paper 188

Debates

The Economic Implications for the United Kingdom of Scottish Independence
Lords Debate 26 June 2013 HL 746 cc761-800

Scotland: Independence
Lords question for short debate on what is their response to the Scottish Government's declaration that, if the people of Scotland vote for independence, Scottish independence day will be 24 March 2016.
HL Deb 05 Dec 2013, vol 750 cc392-413

Scotland: Independence Referendum
Lords motion to take note of the implications for the United Kingdom of the forthcoming Scottish independence referendum. Agreed to on question.
HC Deb 30 Jan 2014, vol 751 cc1360-1449

Motion for leave to bring in a Bill on Scotland (Independence) (Westminster Representation)
Agreed to on question. Presentation and first reading (Bill 196).
HC Deb 02 Apr 2014, vol 578 cc887-891

Motion for leave to bring in a Bill on Representation of the People (Scotland)
Motion opposed. Negatived on division (16 to 226).
HC Deb 25 Mar 2014, vol 578 c156-9

Adjournment debate on Defence in Scotland after 2014 Agreed to on question.
HC Deb 18 Mar 2014, vol 577 cc746-760

Westminster Hall Adjournment debate on Scotland and North-east England Post-2014
HC Deb 04 Mar 2014, vol 576 cc213-239WH

Westminster Hall Adjournment debate on Currency in Scotland after 2014
HC Deb 12 Feb 2014, vol 575 cc291-318WH

Backbench debate on Scotland's Place in the UK
HC Deb 06 Feb 2014, vol 575 cc457-506

Lords question for short debate on Scotland: Independence
HL Deb 05 Dec 2013, vol 750 cc392-413

Government reports

The Government's webpage on the independence referendum[1] has links to documents produced in connection with the referendum debate; the link below its section on publications called 'see all publications'[2] generates an up-to-date list of documents on the subject, listed below, which produced 24 results as at 10 June 2014.

1. Scottish independence referendum: personal finance
    2 June 2014
    Scotland Office
    Research and analysis
    Part of a collection: Referendum factsheets

2. Scotland analysis: Fiscal policy and sustainability
    28 May 2014
    HMT, OAG and Scotland Office
    Research and analysis
    Part of a collection: Scotland analysis

3. Scottish independence referendum: Scotland in the UK
    7 May 2014
    Scotland Office
    Policy paper

---

[1] https://www.gov.uk/government/topical-events/scottish-independence-referendum

[2] https://www.gov.uk/government/publications?publication_filter_option=all&topics%5B%5D=scottish-independence-referendum

4. Letter from the Chief Secretary to John Swinney on the Scottish government white paper
    7 May 2014
    HMT and Scotland Office
    Correspondence

5. Work and pensions - summary leaflet
    1 May 2014
    Scotland Office
    Research and analysis
    Part of a collection: Scotland analysis papers: summary leaflets

6. Scottish independence referendum: Our place in the world
    28 April 2014
    Scotland Office
    Research and analysis
    Part of a collection: Referendum factsheets

7. Scotland analysis: work and pensions
    24 April 2014
    DWP and Scotland Office
    Research and analysis
    Part of a collection: Scotland analysis

8. Energy - summary leaflet
    10 April 2014
    Scotland Office
    Research and analysis
    Part of a collection: Scotland analysis papers: summary leaflets

9. Scottish independence referendum: money and the economy
    26 March 2014
    Scotland Office
    Research and analysis
    Part of a collection: Referendum factsheets

10. Borders and citizenship - summary leaflet
    13 March 2014
    Scotland Office
    Research and analysis
    Part of a collection: Scotland analysis papers: summary leaflets

11. Business and microeconomic framework - summary leaflet
     13 March 2014
     Scotland Office
     Research and analysis
     Part of a collection: Scotland analysis papers: summary leaflets

12. Defence - summary leaflet
     13 March 2014
     Scotland Office
     Research and analysis
     Part of a collection: Scotland analysis papers: summary leaflets

13. Europe and international - summary leaflet
     13 March 2014
     Scotland Office
     Research and analysis
     Part of a collection: Scotland analysis papers: summary leaflets

14. Security - summary leaflet
     13 March 2014
     Scotland Office
     Research and analysis
     Part of a collection: Scotland analysis papers: summary leaflets

15. Science and research - summary leaflet
     13 March 2014
     Scotland Office
     Research and analysis
     Part of a collection: Scotland analysis papers: summary leaflets

16. Financial services and banking
     13 March 2014
     Scotland Office
     Research and analysis
     Part of a collection: Scotland analysis papers: summary leaflets

17. Macroeconomic and fiscal performance - summary leaflet
     13 March 2014
     Scotland Office
     Research and analysis
     Part of a collection: Scotland analysis papers: summary leaflets

18. Devolution and the legal implications of Scottish independence - summary leaflet
    13 March 2014
    Scotland Office
    Research and analysis
    Part of a collection: Scotland analysis papers: summary leaflets

19. Currency - summary leaflet
    13 March 2014
    Scotland Office
    Research and analysis
    Part of a collection: Scotland analysis papers: summary leaflets

20. Further HM Treasury analysis on Scotland: forecasts for the Scottish deficit in 2016-17
    11 March 2014
    HMT and Scotland Office
    Research and analysis
    Part of a collection: Scotland analysis

21. Scotland analysis: Defence
    28 February 2014
    CO, MOD and Scotland Office
    Research and analysis
    Part of a collection: Scotland analysis

22. White paper unravelling
    27 January 2014
    Scotland Office
    Policy paper

23. Scotland analysis: borders and citizenship
    23 January 2014
    Home Office
    Research and analysis
    Part of a collection: Scotland analysis

24. Scottish independence referendum: what you need to know
    20 January 2014
    Scotland Office
    Research and analysis
    Part of a collection: Referendum factsheets

APPENDIX 2:

REFERENDUM POLL RESULTS
18 September 2014

Should Scotland be an independent country?

		VOTES	PERCENTAGE
NO		2,001,926	55.3%
YES		1,617,989	44.7%
Turnout	84.6%	Rejected ballots	3,430

Breakdown by Council Areas

Council	Yes Vote	%	No Vote	%	Diff.%	Turnout	Yes / No
Aberdeen City	59,390	41	84,094	59	17	82%	No
Aberdeenshire	71,337	40	108,606	60	21	87%	No
Angus	35,044	44	45,192	56	13	86%	No
Argyll & Bute	26,324	42	37,143	59	17	88%	No
Clackmannanshire	16,350	46	19,036	54	8	89%	No
Dumfries & Galloway	36,614	34	70,039	66	31	87%	No
Dundee City	53,620	57	39,880	43	15	79%	Yes
East Ayrshire	39,762	47	44,442	53	6	85%	No
East Dunbartonshire	30,624	39	48,314	61	22	91%	No
East Lothian	27,467	38	44,283	62	23	88%	No
East Renfrewshire	24,287	37	41,690	63	26	90%	No

Edinburgh	123,927	39	194,638	61	22	84%	No
Na h-Eileanan an Iar	9,195	47	10,544	53	7	86%	No
Falkirk	50,489	47	58,030	53	7	89%	No
Fife	114,148	45	139,788	55	10	84%	No
Glasgow	194,779	53	169,347	47	7	75%	Yes
Highland	78,069	47	87,739	53	6	87%	No
Inverclyde	27,243	50	27,329	50	0	87%	No
Midlothian	26,370	44	33,972	56	13	87%	No
Moray	27,232	42	36,935	58	15	85%	No
North Ayrshire	47,072	49	49,016	51	2	84%	No
North Lanarkshire	115,783	51	110,922	49	2	84%	Yes
Orkney	4,883	33	10,004	67	34	84%	No
Perth & Kinross	41,475	40	62,714	60	20	87%	No
Renfrewshire	55,466	47	62,067	53	6	87%	No
Scottish Borders	27,906	33	55,553	67	33	87%	No
Shetland	5,669	36	9,951	64	27	84%	No
South Ayrshire	34,402	42	47,247	58	16	86%	No
South Lanarkshire	100,990	45	121,800	55	9	85%	No
Stirling	25,010	40	37,153	60	20	90%	No
West Dunbartonshire	33,720	54	28,776	46	8	88%	Yes
West Lothian	53,342	45	65,682	55	10	86%	No

Abbreviations

Annual National & Special
Conferences (Autumn & Spring)   Conference, ANC & SC

General Business Committee   GBC

National Assembly   Assembly

National Council   Council, NC

National Executive Committee   Executive, NEC

Senior Officebearers Committee   SOBs

Standing Orders & Agenda
Committee   SOAC

Bibliography

Douglas, Dick (1995) *At the Helm: The Life & Times of Dr Robert McIntyre*, NP Publications

Ewing, Winnie (2004) *Stop the World* Ed. Michael Russell, Birlinn Ltd

Finlay, Richard J (1995) *Independent and Free: Scottish Politics and the Progress of The Scottish National Party, 1918-1945*, John Donald Publications Ltd

Halliday, James (2011) Y*ours for Scotland*, Scots Independent (Newspapers) Ltd

Jones, Bill (1979) *British Politics Today*, ed. Bill Jones & Dennis Kavanagh, Manchester University Press

Kemp, Arnold (1993) *The Hollow Drum*, Mainstream Publishing Company (Edinburgh) Ltd

Lynch, Peter (2002) *SNP The History of the Scottish National Party*, Welsh Academic Press (First Edition)

Mackinnon, Mary Stewart, (1994) *A Scot at Westminster*, The Catelone Press, Canada

Maxwell, Stephen (2012) *Arguing for Independence*, Luath Press Ltd

Pittock, Murray (2008) *The Road to Independence Scotland Since the Sixties*, Reaktion Books Ltd

Sillars, Jim (2014) *In Place of Fear II*, Vagabond Voices

Torrance, David (2010) *SALMOND Against the Odds*, Birlinn Ltd

Torrance, David (2013) *The Battle for Britain, Scotland and the Independence Referendum*, Biteback publishing Ltd

Wilson. Gordon (2009) *SNP: The Turbulent Years1960-1990*, Scots Independent (Newspapers) Ltd

Wilson, Gordon (2011) *Pirates of the Air The Story of Radio Free Scotland*, Scots Independent (Newspapers) Ltd

Wolfe, Billy (1993) *Scotland Lives*, Reprographia

Records

SNP Conference Agendas and Outcomes of Conference Proceedings

SNP National Council, National Executive Committee, National

Assembly, & Sub-Committees, Agendas, Minutes, Reports & Memoranda

SNP Pamphlets & Leaflets

SNP Collections, National Library of Scotland

Official Reports, The Scottish Parliament

House of Commons Library Research Department

Correspondence, Emails & Oral Conversations

INDEX